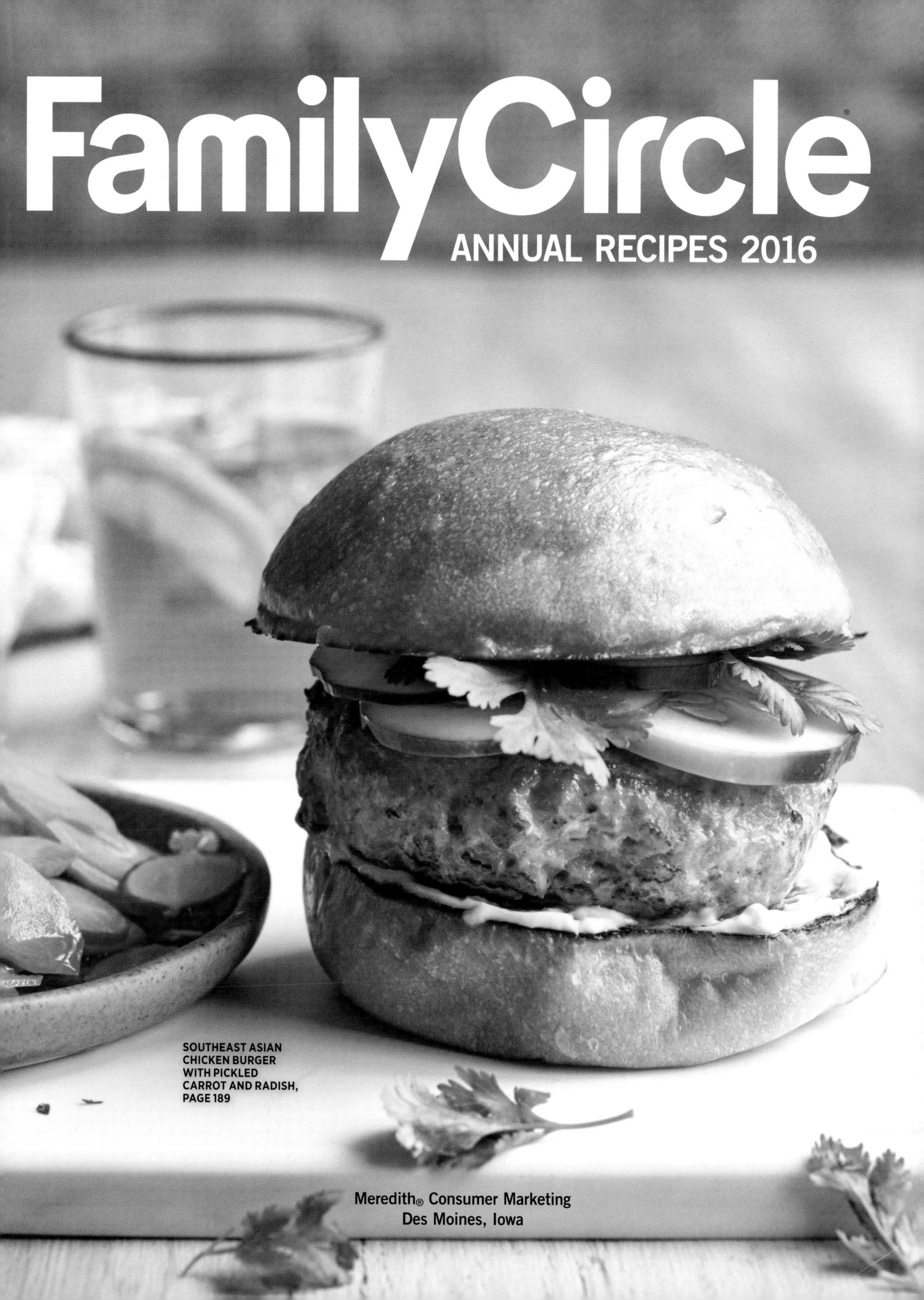

FamilyCircle®

ANNUAL RECIPES 2016

SOUTHEAST ASIAN
CHICKEN BURGER
WITH PICKLED
CARROT AND RADISH,
PAGE 189

Meredith® Consumer Marketing
Des Moines, Iowa

**BLING OUT YOUR
BROWNIES, PAGE 49**

WELCOME TO WHAT'S FRESH AND NEW IN FOOD—AND TO MORE OF IT!

In the last few years there has been a trend back to cooking at home and eating real, wholesome food. Helping you feed your family—and feeding our own families—nutritious, delicious food is something we feel pretty strongly about at *Family Circle*. But we also know that life is busy and schedules don't allow for a lot of time to shop for, prepare and clean up after an elaborate meal every night of the week. So we carefully consider the recipes we include in our magazine. There are recipes to suit every need and situation—quick weeknight meals to get you out the door and onto the next thing—and spectacular, celebratory recipes for special occasions. We're happy to say there are more of both kinds of recipes—and everything in between—in this year's magazines, so your choices are better and broader than ever. This book, a bound collection of every recipe that appeared in the 2016 issues, is organized by month so you can easily find just the kind of recipe you're looking for.

For a winter bake sale, whip up a batch of brownies in your favorite flavor (Bacon-Pecan [page 49] or Vietnamese Coffee [page 50], anyone?). In summer, gather friends for a celebration of Latin flavors at a backyard barbecue featuring Cuban-Style Pork Loin (page 139), Yuca Fries (page 136) and Jicama Slaw (page 139). When the weather turns cool, warm up with a selection of slow cooker chilies, including Fiery Green Chili (page 250), Chicken Chili with Cilantro Pesto (page 251)—and classic Texas-Style Chili (page 250). November and December bring the holidays and a selection of 25 of our favorite cookies—and 50 of our best side dishes for celebrating!

Everything we do at *Family Circle* has an eye on emerging food trends so that preparing meals for your family stays fresh, fun and something you look forward to. Happy cooking!

Linda

Linda Fears, Editor in Chief
Family Circle Magazine

Family Circle Annual Recipes 2016

Meredith Consumer Marketing
Consumer Marketing Product Director: Heather Sorensen
Consumer Marketing Product Manager: Wendy Merical
Consumer Marketing Billing/Renewal Manager: Tami Beachem
Business Director: Ron Clingman
Senior Production Manager: Al Rodruck

Waterbury Publications, Inc.
Editorial Director: Lisa Kingsley
Associate Editor: Tricia Bergman
Associate Editor/Food Stylist: Annie Peterson
Creative Director: Ken Carlson
Associate Design Director: Doug Samuelson
Graphic Designer: Mindy Samuelson
Contributing Copy Editors: Terri Fredrickson, Gretchen Kauffman
Contributing Indexer: Mary Williams

***Family Circle* Magazine**
Editor in Chief: Linda Fears
Design Director: Lisa Kelsey
Food Director: Regina Ragone, M.S., R.D.
Executive Food Editor: Julie Miltenberger
Associate Food Editor: Michael Tyrrell
Associate Food Editor: Melissa Knific

Meredith National Media Group
President: Tom Harty

Meredith Corporation
Chairman and Chief Executive Officer: Stephen M. Lacy

In Memoriam: E.T. Meredith III (1933–2003)

LET'S EAT! Coming together around the family table at the end of the day to enjoy a home-cooked meal soothes away the day's stresses and satisfies on so many levels. This collection of recipes from the 2016 issues of *Family Circle* magazine makes it easier than ever to serve tasty food you cook yourself—whether it's a 30-minute dinner, a holiday celebration or a special evening with friends. Recipes are organized by month to take advantage of what's in season and to make it easy to find the perfect recipe for any occasion.

Skillet Apple-Plum Cobbler (page 207) is part of the "Apple Abundance" story that appeared in the September issue. Other sweet treats featuring apples from that issue include Apple Cupcakes with Salted Caramel Frosting, Apple-Cardamom Coffee Cake and The Best Apple Pie Ever.

CORNMEAL
BISCUITS,
PAGE 35

LONE STAR
BEEF CHILI,
PAGE 35

CONTENTS

CHICKEN SCHNITZEL WITH
FENNEL-GRAPEFRUIT
SALAD, PAGE 17

JANUARY

11

22

29

CHICKEN REDUX

Try these eight ways to reinvent a dinnertime favorite.

COCONUT-CASHEW
CHICKEN CURRY

Coconut-Cashew Chicken Curry

MAKES 6 servings **PREP** 15 minutes
COOK 23 minutes

- 1½ **cups dry jasmine or basmati rice**
- 1½ **lb skinless boneless chicken thighs or breasts, cut into 1½-inch pieces**
- 2 **tsp sweet Indian curry powder (such as Madras)**
- ¾ **tsp salt**
- 2 **tbsp vegetable oil**
- 1 **cup diced yellow onions**
- 3 **cloves chopped garlic**
- 1 **tbsp grated, peeled ginger**
- 1 **can (13.5 oz) coconut milk**
- 1 **cup unsalted chicken broth**
- ⅔ **cup raw unsalted cashews, toasted**
- **Sliced scallions, cilantro and chopped cashews, for garnish (optional)**

■ Cook rice following package directions. Meanwhile, toss chicken in a bowl with 1 tsp of the curry powder and ½ tsp of the salt. In a straight-sided skillet, heat oil over medium-high. Brown chicken 4 minutes, turning once. Remove to a plate with a slotted spoon.

■ Reduce heat to medium. Add onions to skillet; cook 3 minutes. Stir in remaining 1 tsp curry powder, the garlic and ginger; cook 1 minute. Add coconut milk, broth and cashews. Bring to a simmer; cook 5 minutes.

■ Transfer half the sauce to a blender and puree until smooth. Whisk blended sauce into rest of sauce in pan. Stir in chicken. Return to a simmer. Cook 10 minutes. Season with remaining ¼ tsp salt.

■ Serve chicken and sauce over rice. Garnish with scallions, cilantro and chopped cashews, if using.

PER SERVING 600 **CAL**; 34 g **FAT**; 29 g **PRO**; 46 g **CARB**; 1 g **FIBER**

ROASTED CHICKEN WITH SALSA VERDE

Roasted Chicken with Salsa Verde

MAKES 6 servings **PREP** 20 minutes **ROAST** at 450° for 45 minutes

- 1 **whole chicken (4 lb)**
- ¾ **tsp plus ⅛ tsp kosher salt**
- ⅓ **cup plus 1 tbsp extra-virgin olive oil**
- ¼ **tsp plus ⅛ tsp black pepper**
- ½ **cup packed fresh basil**
- ½ **cup packed fresh parsley**
- ¼ **cup pitted green olives**
- 1 **clove garlic**
- 1 **tbsp fresh lemon juice plus 1 tsp grated lemon zest**

■ Heat oven to 450°. Place chicken on a cutting board. Remove giblets and discard. Pat entire chicken dry and place breast side down. Using kitchen shears, cut on either side of backbone to remove it; discard. Flip over chicken and, using your palms, flatten it (this technique is called spatchcock). Place on a rimmed sheet pan fitted with a rack. Season under skin with ¼ tsp of the salt. Rub skin with 1 tbsp of the oil and season with ½ tsp more of the salt and ¼ tsp of the pepper. Roast at 450° for 45 minutes, or until internal temperature registers 165°.

■ While chicken roasts, make salsa verde. In a food processor, combine basil, parsley, olives, garlic, lemon juice and zest and remaining ⅛ tsp each salt and pepper. Pulse until roughly chopped. Pour in remaining ⅓ cup oil while machine is running.

■ Let chicken rest 10 minutes; carve and serve with salsa verde.

PER SERVING 300 **CAL**; 22 g **FAT**; 29 g **PRO**; 1 g **CARB**; 0 g **FIBER**

CREAMY CHORIZO
CHICKEN CUTLETS

Chicken Tinga Tacos

MAKES 4 servings PREP 15 minutes
COOK 45 minutes

- 4 skinless bone-in chicken thighs (about 1½ lb)
- ½ tsp chipotle chile powder
- ½ tsp ground cumin
- ½ tsp salt
- ½ tsp dried oregano
- 2 tbsp vegetable oil
- 1 cup thinly sliced yellow onion
- 3 cloves garlic, sliced
- 2 chipotles in adobo, seeded and diced; 1 tsp adobo reserved
- 1 can (14.5 oz) diced fire-roasted tomatoes
- ½ cup unsalted chicken broth
- 12 small corn tortillas, warmed
     Sliced avocado and Cotija or feta cheese (optional)

■ Season chicken on both sides with chipotle powder, cumin, salt and oregano. In a large, lidded, straight-sided skillet or Dutch oven, heat oil over medium-high. Brown 3 minutes on each side. Remove to a plate.

■ Reduce heat to medium. Add onion; cook 3 minutes. Stir in garlic and chipotles; cook 1 minute. Add adobo, tomatoes, broth and chicken. Bring to a simmer, then reduce heat to medium-low. Cover and simmer 35 minutes, until meat easily falls off the bone.

■ Remove chicken from skillet to a cutting board. Shred, discarding bones. Stir meat back into sauce. Serve on corn tortillas (3 per person) with sliced avocado and cheese, if using.

PER SERVING 410 CAL; 17 g FAT; 29 g PRO; 34 g CARB; 6 g FIBER

Creamy Chorizo Chicken Cutlets

MAKES 4 servings PREP 15 minutes COOK 10 minutes

- 1 tbsp olive oil
- 3 oz Spanish-style cured chorizo, casing removed, quartered and sliced
- 4 chicken cutlets (about 1¼ lb)
- 1 tsp sweet paprika
- ½ tsp plus ⅛ tsp salt
- ¼ tsp black pepper
- ¼ cup finely diced shallots
- 3 cloves garlic, sliced
- ½ tsp smoked paprika
- 1 cup unsalted chicken broth
- ½ cup cream cheese
- ¼ cup parsley, chopped, for garnish
     Mashed potatoes (optional)

■ In a large pan, heat oil over medium. Add chorizo and cook 3 minutes. Remove to a plate with a slotted spoon.

■ Season chicken on both sides with ½ tsp of the sweet paprika, ½ tsp of the salt and the pepper. Increase heat to medium-high. Brown chicken 2 minutes per side. Remove to a plate with chorizo.

■ Stir in shallots, garlic, remaining ½ tsp sweet paprika and the smoked paprika. Cook 2 minutes. Pour in chicken broth and remaining ⅛ tsp salt, scraping bottom of pan. Bring to a simmer. Whisk in cream cheese until melted; return chorizo and chicken; cook 1 more minute. Garnish with parsley. Serve over mashed potatoes, if desired.

PER SERVING 370 CAL; 20 g FAT; 42 g PRO; 4 g CARB; 1 g FIBER

CHICKEN
TINGA
TACOS

CHICKEN SCHNITZEL
WITH FENNEL-
GRAPEFRUIT SALAD

This recipe takes the classic Austrian dish schnitzel—which is usually made with veal and served with buttered noodles—and lightens it by swapping the noodles for a refreshing salad.

Chicken Schnitzel with Fennel-Grapefruit Salad

MAKES 4 servings **PREP** 15 minutes **COOK** 8 minutes

- 4 **tbsp olive oil**
- 2 **tbsp white wine vinegar**
- 2 **tsp honey**
- 1 **tsp plus ⅛ tsp salt**
- ½ **tsp black pepper**
- 2 **medium grapefruit, peeled, sliced crosswise**
- 1 **small fennel bulb, cored and very thinly sliced, fronds chopped**
- ¼ **cup all-purpose flour**
- 2 **eggs**
- ¾ **cup plain bread crumbs**
- 4 **chicken cutlets (about 1¼ lb), pounded to ⅛-inch thickness**
- 2 **tbsp unsalted butter**
- 4 **packed cups arugula**

■ In a bowl, whisk 2 tbsp of the olive oil, the vinegar, honey, ¼ tsp plus ⅛ tsp of the salt and ¼ tsp of the pepper. Gently toss with grapefruit and fennel; cover and refrigerate.

■ In a shallow dish (we like pie plates!), combine flour with ½ tsp of the salt and remaining ¼ tsp pepper. Beat eggs in a separate dish. In a third dish, combine bread crumbs with remaining ¼ tsp salt. Coat chicken cutlets in flour, then dip into egg, allowing excess to drip off. Finally, coat cutlets in bread crumbs.

■ In a skillet, heat 1 tbsp of the oil and 1 tbsp of the butter over medium-high. Add 2 cutlets. Cook 2 minutes; flip and cook another 2 minutes, until chicken is golden brown. Repeat with remaining 1 tbsp oil, 1 tbsp butter and 2 cutlets.

■ Toss arugula into salad and serve on top of cutlets.

PER SERVING 370 **CAL**; 19 g **FAT**; 9 g **PRO**; 43 g **CARB**; 9 g **FIBER**

HEALTHY FAMILY DINNERS

Everything is better with pasta! Noodle around with these six recipes.

RIGATONI PIE

Rigatoni Pie

MAKES 8 servings **PREP** 20 minutes
COOK 21 minutes **BAKE** at 400° for 30 minutes

- 1 lb rigatoni
- 2 tsp canola oil
- ½ medium onion, grated
- 1 can (28 oz) crushed traditional or fire-roasted tomatoes
- 1 tsp sugar
- ½ tsp garlic salt
- ½ tsp dried oregano
- 1¼ lb lean ground beef (93%)
- 1 large egg, lightly beaten
- 8 oz (2 cups) shredded Italian cheese blend or part-skim mozzarella
- 2 tbsp grated Parmesan
  Chopped parsley (optional)

■ Heat oven to 400°. Bring a large pot of lightly salted water to a boil. Add rigatoni and cook 12 to 13 minutes, until al dente. Drain and rinse in cold water.

■ While pasta cooks, heat oil in a large nonstick skillet over medium. Add onion and cook 3 minutes. Stir in crushed tomatoes, sugar, garlic salt and oregano. Bring to a simmer; cook 3 minutes. Crumble in ground beef and simmer, uncovered, 15 minutes, breaking meat into small pieces with a spoon and stirring occasionally.

■ Place cooled pasta in a large bowl and toss with egg and ½ cup of the shredded cheese. Coat a 9-inch springform pan with nonstick cooking spray. Prop up pan on its side and begin stacking noodles in pan (so they are standing on end). Return pan to upright position and gently move noodles around until they are all level.

■ Spoon tomato sauce onto noodles, pressing some of the sauce into centers of noodles. Place pan on a sheet of foil and bake at 400° for 15 minutes. Sprinkle remaining 1½ cups shredded cheese and the grated Parmesan over pie. Bake 15 minutes more. Cool 10 minutes. Garnish with parsley, if using.

PER SERVING 421 **CAL**; 10 g **FAT**; 31 g **PRO**; 52 g **CARB**; 4 g **FIBER**

PHILLY CHEESESTEAK PENNE

Philly Cheesesteak Penne

MAKES 6 servings **PREP** 20 minutes **FREEZE** 15 minutes **COOK** 7 minutes

- 8 oz flank steak
- 1 cup skim milk
- 2 tbsp all-purpose flour
- ¾ tsp salt
- 1 tbsp Worcestershire sauce
- 1 box (16 oz) penne
- 2 tbsp canola oil
- 1 large green sweet pepper, seeded and sliced
- 1 medium onion, sliced into half-moons
- 1 piece (6 oz) provolone, shredded (1½ cups)
- ¼ tsp black pepper

■ Freeze steak 15 minutes (this will help you make paper-thin slices). Meanwhile, bring a large pot of lightly salted water to a boil.

■ In a small saucepan, whisk milk, flour and ¼ tsp of the salt. Remove steak from freezer and cut it into the thinnest strips possible. Toss steak in a bowl with Worcestershire and ¼ tsp of the remaining salt.

■ Cook penne following package directions. Drain pasta, reserving ½ cup pasta water.

■ Heat milk mixture over medium, whisking occasionally, until it begins to bubble. Simmer 2 minutes. Meanwhile, heat 1 tbsp of the oil in a large stainless-steel skillet over medium-high. Add beef and cook 2 to 3 minutes. Remove to a plate and reduce heat to medium. Add remaining 1 tbsp oil, the pepper slices and onion to skillet; season with remaining ¼ tsp salt. Cook 4 minutes.

■ Toss pasta with veggies, steak and any drippings. Whisk ¾ cup of the shredded provolone into milk mixture. Stir cheese sauce into pasta mixture, thinning if needed with some of the reserved pasta water. Toss pasta with remaining ¾ cup shredded cheese and the black pepper.

PER SERVING 501 **CAL**; 16 g **FAT**; 26 g **PRO**; 61 g **CARB**; 3 g **FIBER**

GREEK SALMON AND ORZO

Ziti with Mini Meatballs

MAKES 8 servings PREP 30 minutes
COOK 12 minutes

- **1 lb ground sirloin**
- **8 oz mushrooms, trimmed, cleaned and grated**
- **½ cup grated Parmesan, plus more for serving (optional)**
- **⅓ cup Italian-seasoned dry bread crumbs**
- **1 large egg**
- **½ tsp salt**
- **½ tsp black pepper**
- **2 tbsp canola oil**
- **1 box (16 oz) ziti**
- **1 pkg (5 oz) baby kale, chopped**
- **3 cloves garlic, sliced**
- **½ tsp crushed red pepper flakes**
- **½ cup low-sodium chicken broth**

■ In a large bowl, combine ground sirloin, grated mushrooms, ¼ cup of the Parmesan, the bread crumbs, egg and ¼ tsp each of the salt and pepper. With wet hands, roll into ¾- to 1-inch meatballs (about 54). In a 12-inch nonstick skillet, heat 1 tbsp of the oil over medium-high heat.

■ Meanwhile, bring a large pot of lightly salted water to a boil. Add ziti and cook 10 minutes. Drain, reserving ½ cup pasta water.

■ Once oil is hot, add half the meatballs. Cook 4 minutes, turning until browned all over. Transfer to a plate and add remaining 1 tbsp oil to skillet. Cook remaining meatballs and remove to plate.

■ Reduce heat in skillet to medium and add kale, garlic and red pepper flakes. Cook 2 minutes. Stir in chicken broth, reserved pasta water and remaining ¼ tsp each salt and pepper. Cook 2 more minutes. Stir ziti into skillet.

■ In a large bowl, combine meatballs and pasta mixture with remaining ¼ cup Parmesan. Gently toss to combine. Serve with additional grated Parmesan, if using.

PER SERVING 497 **CAL**; 12 g **FAT**; 31 g **PRO**; 66 g **CARB**; 4 g **FIBER**

Greek Salmon and Orzo

MAKES 4 servings PREP 15 minutes COOK 9 minutes

- **1 cup dry orzo (about 6½ oz)**
- **12 oz fresh salmon**
- **½ tsp salt**
- **½ tsp black pepper**
- **⅛ tsp ground coriander**
- **2 tbsp fresh lemon juice**
- **2 tsp sugar**
- **1 tsp Dijon mustard**
- **3 tbsp olive oil**
- **½ cup crumbled feta cheese**
- **⅓ cup finely diced red onion**
- **3 tbsp chopped fresh dill**

■ Heat broiler to high. Bring a medium pot of lightly salted water to a boil. Add orzo and cook 9 minutes. Drain.

■ Meanwhile, place salmon on a foil-lined baking sheet. Season with ¼ tsp each of the salt and pepper and the coriander. Broil salmon, 4 inches from heat, 8 minutes.

■ While salmon and pasta cook, whisk lemon juice, sugar, mustard and remaining ¼ tsp each salt and pepper. While whisking, add oil in a thin stream.

■ Remove salmon from foil, leaving skin stuck to foil. Break apart with a fork and place in a medium serving bowl. Add orzo, dressing, feta, red onion and dill. Gently toss to combine. Serve warm or at room temperature.

PER SERVING 437 **CAL**; 20 g **FAT**; 27 g **PRO**; 34 g **CARB**; 2 g **FIBER**

ZITI WITH MINI
MEATBALLS

SESAME PORK
NOODLES

Sesame Pork Noodles

MAKES 6 servings **PREP** 35 minutes
COOK 11 minutes

- 1¼ **lb boneless center-cut pork chops, trimmed**
- ½ **tsp plus ⅛ tsp salt**
- ½ **tsp black pepper**
- 2 **tbsp canola oil**
- 12 **oz linguine or rice noodles**
- ½ **cup low-sodium chicken broth**
- 3 **tbsp low-sodium soy sauce**
- 3 **tbsp rice vinegar**
- 2 **tbsp sugar**
- 1 **tbsp toasted sesame oil**
- 1 **piece (2 inches) ginger, peeled and grated (1 tbsp)**
- 2 **cloves garlic, minced**
- 2 **tsp cornstarch**
- 8 **oz snow peas, strings removed, halved lengthwise**
- 1 **sweet red pepper, cored and thinly sliced**
- ⅔ **cup shredded carrots**
- 2 **scallions, sliced**
- 2 **tbsp toasted sesame seeds**

■ Bring a large pot of lightly salted water to a boil. Season pork chops with ½ tsp of the salt and ¼ tsp of the black pepper. Heat canola oil in a large stainless-steel skillet over high. Add linguine to boiling water and cook 9 minutes. (If using rice noodles, cook 4 to 6 minutes. Drain, rinse under cold water and drain again.)

■ Meanwhile, add pork chops to oil in skillet and cook 4 to 6 minutes, depending on thickness, turning once.

■ While pork cooks, whisk broth, soy sauce, vinegar, sugar, sesame oil, ginger, garlic and cornstarch. Remove pork to a cutting board and reduce heat under skillet to medium-high. Add snow peas, sweet pepper and carrots to skillet. Cook 3 minutes. Add broth mixture; bring to a simmer and cook 2 minutes. Slice pork into strips. In a large bowl, toss noodles, pork, contents of skillet, scallions and sesame seeds and serve.

PER SERVING 468 **CAL**; 14 g **FAT**; 26 g **PRO**; 56 g **CARB**; 4 g **FIBER**

ONE-POT CAVATAPPI

One-Pot Cavatappi

MAKES 6 servings **PREP** 15 minutes **COOK** 16 minutes **LET STAND** 5 minutes

- 1 **tbsp olive oil**
- 12 **oz turkey sausage, casings removed**
- 1 **small onion, thinly sliced**
- 2 **cups low-sodium chicken broth**
- 1 **pkg (2 cups) grape tomatoes, halved**
- 12 **oz cavatappi or other corkscrew-shape pasta**
- ½ **tsp garlic salt**
- 1 **bag (5 oz) baby spinach**
- ¾ **cup ricotta**
- ½ **cup fresh basil leaves**

■ In a large stockpot or Dutch oven, heat oil over medium-high. Crumble in sausage and brown 5 minutes. Add onion and cook 2 minutes.

■ Stir in chicken broth, tomatoes, pasta and garlic salt. Bring to a boil and cook, stirring frequently, 9 minutes. Stir in spinach in batches. Remove from heat, cover and let stand 5 minutes. Uncover and fold in ricotta. Divide among bowls and garnish with fresh basil.

PER SERVING 403 **CAL**; 12 g **FAT**; 23 g **PRO**; 50 g **CARB**; 4 g **FIBER**

JUST SOUPER

Grab a spoon to enjoy these easy suppers from the slow cooker.

TEXAS STEAK AND POTATO SOUP

Texas Steak and Potato Soup

MAKES 8 servings **PREP** 15 minutes
COOK 5 minutes
SLOW COOK on HIGH for 4 hours

- 1 **tbsp canola oil**
- 1¼ **lb beef chuck, cut into 1-inch pieces**
- 1 **onion, sliced**
- 3 **cloves garlic, sliced**
- 1 **tbsp chili powder**
- ¼ **tsp salt**
- 2 **cans (14½ oz each) fire-roasted diced tomatoes**
- 1 **large beef bouillon cube (such as Knorr), dissolved in 2 cups hot water**
- ¾ **lb small (1-inch round) potatoes, quartered**
- 6 **oz green beans, trimmed and cut into 1-inch pieces**
  Shredded Tex-Mex blend cheese, for garnish (optional)
  Sliced scallion, for garnish (optional)

■ Coat slow cooker with nonstick cooking spray.

■ In a large nonstick skillet, heat oil over medium-high. Add beef, onion and garlic; cook 4 minutes, stirring occasionally. Season with chili powder and salt; cook 1 minute. Spoon mixture into slow cooker. Stir in tomatoes, bouillon cube, potatoes and green beans.

■ Cover and cook on HIGH for 4 hours.

■ Top each serving with cheese and scallion, if using.

PER SERVING 227 **CAL**; 11 g **FAT**; 16 g **PRO**; 16 g **CARB**; 3 g **FIBER**

WINTER VEGETABLE
MINESTRONE

Winter Vegetable Minestrone

MAKES 8 servings **PREP** 20 minutes
SLOW COOK on HIGH for 6 hours or LOW for 8 hours

- 6 **cups reduced-sodium vegetable broth**
- 1 **can (28 oz) plum tomatoes, broken apart**
- ½ **butternut squash, peeled, seeded and cut into 2-inch pieces**
- 1 **onion, sliced**
- 2 **carrots, sliced and cut into ¼-inch coins**
- 4 **cloves garlic, sliced**
- 1 **tsp dried oregano**
- 1 **tsp salt**
- ¼ **tsp black pepper**
- ½ **cup ditalini pasta**
- 8 **oz Swiss chard, tough stems removed and sliced**
- 1 **can (15½ oz) red kidney beans, drained and rinsed**
- ½ **tsp red pepper flakes**
- ½ **cup basil, torn into bite-size pieces**
- ⅓ **cup grated Parmesan**

■ Spray slow cooker with nonstick cooking spray.

■ Add vegetable broth, tomatoes, squash, onion, carrots, garlic, oregano, ½ tsp of the salt and the black pepper to slow cooker.

■ Cover and cook on HIGH for 6 hours or LOW for 8 hours.

■ During last 30 minutes of cooking stir in ditalini, Swiss chard, beans, red pepper flakes and remaining ½ tsp salt.

■ Add basil and sprinkle each serving with some grated Parmesan.

PER SERVING 216 **CAL**; 2 g **FAT**; 10 g **PRO**; 42 g **CARB**; 10 g **FIBER**

CARIBBEAN TURKEY AND SWEET POTATO SOUP

Caribbean Turkey and Sweet Potato Soup

MAKES 8 servings **PREP** 15 minutes **SLOW COOK** on LOW for 4½ hours

- 2 **tbsp chopped ginger**
- 1 **tbsp dried onion flakes**
- 1 **tsp ground allspice**
- 1 **tsp cumin**
- 1 **tsp salt**
- ¾ **tsp black pepper**
- ½ **tsp dried thyme**
- ½ **tsp garlic salt**
- 1½ **lb boneless turkey breast, cut into 1-inch pieces**
- 2 **cups reduced-sodium chicken broth**
- 1 **can (13.5 oz) light coconut milk**
- 2 **large sweet potatoes, peeled and cut into 2-inch pieces**
- 1 **can (15 oz) black beans, drained and rinsed**
- 2 **cups cooked white rice**
- 2 **tbsp lime juice**
- 3 **tbsp chopped cilantro**

■ Coat slow cooker with nonstick cooking spray.

■ In a bowl, combine ginger, onion flakes, allspice, cumin, ½ tsp each of the salt and pepper, the thyme and garlic salt. Place turkey in slow cooker and season with spice mixture.

■ Stir in chicken broth, coconut milk and sweet potatoes. Cover and cook on LOW for 4½ hours. During last 10 minutes of cooking, gently stir in beans, rice and remaining ½ tsp salt and ¼ tsp pepper.

■ Just before serving, add lime juice and cilantro.

PER SERVING 260 **CAL**; 5 g **FAT**; 25 g **PRO**; 28 g **CARB**; 3 g **FIBER**

FLORENTINE
WHITE BEAN SOUP

Chinese Chicken and Ramen

MAKES 8 servings **PREP** 15 minutes
SLOW COOK on HIGH for 4 hours or LOW for 6 hours

- 2 lb boneless, skinless chicken thighs
- ½ tsp salt
- ¼ tsp black pepper
- 6 cups reduced-sodium chicken broth
- 2 tbsp chopped ginger
- 4 cloves garlic, chopped
- 1 tbsp reduced-sodium soy sauce
- 6 cups coarsely chopped napa cabbage
- 2 pkg (3 oz each) uncooked ramen noodles
- 1 sweet red pepper, seeded and cut into matchsticks
- 2 tbsp mirin
- 3 scallions, sliced, for garnish
- ⅓ cup cilantro leaves, for garnish

■ Coat slow cooker with nonstick cooking spray.

■ Season chicken with salt and black pepper. Add to slow cooker with broth, ginger, garlic, soy sauce and cabbage. Cover and cook on HIGH for 4 hours or LOW for 6 hours. During last 10 minutes of cooking, stir in ramen noodles and sweet pepper.

■ Just before serving, stir in mirin and shred chicken. Garnish with scallions and cilantro.

PER SERVING 239 **CAL**; 7 g **FAT**; 25 g **PRO**; 17 g **CARB**; 1 g **FIBER**

Florentine White Bean Soup

MAKES 8 servings **PREP** 10 minutes **SOAK** overnight **COOK** 6 minutes
SLOW COOK on HIGH for 6 hours

- 1 lb dried cannellini beans
- 1 tbsp olive oil
- 4 oz chopped pancetta
- 2 medium onions, chopped
- 6 cloves garlic, sliced
- ¼ tsp red pepper flakes
- 4 cups reduced-sodium chicken broth
- 2 ribs celery, chopped
- 2 sprigs fresh rosemary
- 1 bag (8 oz) baby spinach
- 1 tsp salt
- ½ tsp black pepper
- ⅓ cup grated Parmesan
  Olive oil, for drizzling (optional)

■ Place beans in a bowl and cover with cold water. Soak overnight.

■ Coat slow cooker with nonstick cooking spray.

■ In a large skillet, heat oil over medium-high heat. Add pancetta, onions, garlic and red pepper flakes. Cook 6 minutes, stirring occasionally. Add to slow cooker. Stir in drained beans, chicken broth, celery, rosemary and 2 cups water.

■ Cover and cook on HIGH for 6 hours. During last 10 minutes of cooking, stir in spinach. Season with salt and black pepper.

■ Sprinkle some Parmesan over each serving and drizzle with olive oil, if using.

PER SERVING 280 **CAL**; 4 g **FAT**; 19 g **PRO**; 42 g **CARB**; 11 g **FIBER**

CHINESE CHICKEN
AND RAMEN

PUMPKIN SAGE
SCONES, PAGE 35

SAUSAGE, KALE
AND TORTELLINI
STEW, PAGE 35

FEBRUARY

39

41

55

IN A STEW

Take off the chill with dinners from your stovetop, slow cooker and pressure cooker.

CORNMEAL
BISCUITS

LONE STAR
BEEF CHILI

Stovetop: No special equipment is needed to make these recipes—just a nice big stockpot and a stove.

Lone Star Beef Chili

MAKES 6 servings **PREP** 20 minutes
COOK 1 hour 49 minutes

- 6 oz thick-cut bacon, diced
- 1½ lb beef chuck for stew
- ⅓ cup chili powder
- 1 tsp ground cumin
- ½ tsp salt
- ¼ tsp black pepper
- 1 large yellow onion, diced
- 1 green pepper, cored and diced
- 2 sweet red peppers, cored and diced
- 3 cloves garlic, chopped
- 1 can (28 oz) crushed tomatoes
- Sour cream
- Sliced scallions

■ Heat a large heavy stockpot or Dutch oven over medium-high. Add bacon and cook, stirring frequently, 8 minutes. Remove with a slotted spoon. Increase heat to high and add beef to pot. Brown 3 minutes. Turn over and brown 2 minutes more. Reduce heat to medium and stir in chili powder, cumin, salt and black pepper. Cook 1 minute. Return bacon to pot along with onion, peppers and garlic. Cook 5 minutes, stirring frequently. Add crushed tomatoes and 2 cups water. Bring to a simmer and reduce heat to medium-low. Partially cover pot and continue to cook for another 1½ hours, stirring occasionally and adjusting temperature as needed so chili doesn't burn.

■ Uncover and stir. Serve topped with sour cream and scallions.

PER SERVING 489 **CAL**; 25 g **FAT**; 50 g **PRO**; 18 g **CARB**; 5 g **FIBER**

Cornmeal Biscuits

MAKES 10 biscuits **PREP** 15 minutes
BAKE at 425° for 20 minutes

■ Heat oven to 425°. In a large bowl, blend 2 cups all-purpose flour, ¾ cup cornmeal, 2 tbsp sugar, 2½ tsp baking powder, 1 tsp salt and ¼ tsp baking soda. Pour 1 tbsp white vinegar into a measuring cup and add enough milk to equal 1 cup. With a pastry cutter, cut ⅔ cup shortening into flour mixture until the size of small peas. Add milk mixture and stir until dough comes together. Turn out onto counter dusted with cornmeal and pat to ½-inch thickness. Cut out with 2¾-inch biscuit cutter and place on a baking sheet. Reroll scraps and cut as many biscuits as possible. Bake at 425° for 18 to 20 minutes.

PER BISCUIT 275 **CAL**; 14 g **FAT**; 4 g **PRO**; 32 g **CARB**; 1 g **FIBER**

Sausage, Kale and Tortellini Stew

MAKES 8 servings **PREP** 15 minutes
COOK 30 minutes

- 2 tbsp olive oil
- 1 lb sausage, casing removed
- 1 medium onion, sliced
- 3 cloves garlic, sliced
- ¾ tsp Italian seasoning
- 8 cups packed chopped kale
- 4 cups reduced-sodium chicken broth
- 1 pkg (20 oz) refrigerated cheese tortellini
- ½ cup all-purpose flour
- 1 can (15 oz) small white beans or pink beans, drained and rinsed

■ In a very large stockpot, heat oil over medium-high to high. Crumble in sausage and cook, 6 to 7 minutes, until browned, stirring occasionally. Add onion, garlic and Italian seasoning; reduce heat to medium and cook 4 minutes.

■ Stir in kale and chicken broth. Cover and cook 8 minutes. Add 4 cups water, cover and bring to a boil over high, about 5 minutes. Add tortellini. Cook, covered, 3 minutes.

■ Meanwhile, whisk flour with ½ cup water. Add to pot and cook 3 minutes more, until slightly thickened. Stir in beans and heat through.

PER SERVING 453 **CAL**; 17 g **FAT**; 24 g **PRO**; 57 g **CARB**; 7 g **FIBER**

Pumpkin Sage Scones

MAKES 8 scones **PREP** 15 minutes
BAKE at 425° for 20 minutes

■ In a small bowl, blend 1¾ cups all-purpose flour, 1 tbsp baking powder, ½ tsp salt and ⅛ tsp cayenne. In a large bowl, blend ¾ cup solid-pack pumpkin, ¾ cup shredded Asiago cheese, ¼ cup melted butter, 1 large egg and 1 tbsp chopped fresh sage. Fold flour mixture into pumpkin mixture and turn out onto a well-floured piece of parchment paper. Pat into a 7- to 8-inch circle and, with a greased knife, cut into 8 wedges (leave wedges touching). Bake at 425° for 20 minutes, until dry to the touch.

PER SCONE 209 **CAL**; 10 g **FAT**; 6 g **PRO**; 23 g **CARB**; 2 g **FIBER**

RICOTTA ONION
MUFFINS

LENTIL-QUINOA
STEW

CURRIED ROOT VEGETABLE STEW

Slow Cooker: Stir everything together, then walk away—or out the door. Come home to a delicious dinner.

Lentil-Quinoa Stew

MAKES 6 servings **PREP** 15 minutes
SLOW COOK on HIGH for 3 hours or LOW for 5 hours

- 1½ lb boneless country-style pork ribs
- 1½ tsp garam masala spice blend
- 1 tsp salt
- 1 cup black beluga or French green lentils (see Tip)
- ¾ cup red quinoa
- 3 medium carrots, peeled and diced
- 2 ribs celery, diced
- ½ red onion, sliced
- 2 cloves garlic, chopped
- 2 cups chicken broth
- 2 cups boiling water
- ¼ cup chopped parsley
- ¼ cup chopped mint
  Plain Greek yogurt, for serving
  Lemon wedges, for serving

■ Rub pork with 1 tsp of the garam masala and ½ tsp of the salt and place in a slow cooker. Top with lentils, quinoa, carrots, celery, onion, garlic and remaining ½ tsp garam masala. Pour in broth and boiling water; cover and cook on HIGH for 3 hours or LOW for 5 hours.

■ Uncover stew and remove pork, using tongs. Shred or chop into bite-size pieces. Stir back into slow cooker, along with remaining ½ tsp salt, the parsley and mint. Scoop into bowls and serve with a spoonful of yogurt and a lemon wedge.

PER SERVING 435 **CAL**; 17 g **FAT**; 31 g **PRO**; 39 g **CARB**; 8 g **FIBER**

Tip: Look for black beluga or French green (le Puy) lentils at health food stores or order online. They maintain their shape when cooked, while the widely available brown and red varieties will melt or dissolve into the cooking liquid.

Ricotta Onion Muffins

MAKES 12 muffins **PREP** 10 minutes
BAKE at 375° for 20 minutes

■ Heat oven to 375°. In a medium bowl, whisk 2 cups all-purpose flour, 1 tbsp baking powder, 1 tsp salt and ½ tsp black pepper. In a medium skillet, melt ¼ cup unsalted butter over medium heat. Add 2 minced small shallots and cook 2 minutes. Remove from heat and scrape shallots and butter into a large bowl. Stir in 1 cup milk, ¾ cup ricotta, 1 large egg and 3 tbsp snipped fresh chives. Stir in flour mixture and spoon into 12 greased square or traditional standard-size muffin cups (¼ cup batter in each). Bake at 375° for 20 minutes.

PER MUFFIN 160 **CAL**; 7 g **FAT**; 5 g **PRO**; 19 g **CARB**; 1 g **FIBER**

Curried Root Vegetable Stew

MAKES 6 servings **PREP** 25 minutes
SOAK overnight **SLOW COOK** on HIGH for 4 hours or LOW for 7 hours

- 1 cup dried chickpeas
- 1 lb sweet potatoes, peeled and cut into 1½-inch pieces
- 1 lb purple Peruvian potatoes, cut into 1½-inch pieces (unpeeled)
- ¾ lb parsnips, peeled and diced
- ¾ lb carrots, peeled and diced
- 1 can (14.5 oz) vegetable broth
- 1 can (13.5 oz) coconut milk
- 3 tbsp Madras curry powder
- 1 tsp salt
- ¼ tsp black pepper
- ¼ cup cilantro leaves, chopped

■ Place chickpeas in a bowl and cover with cold water by 1 inch. Soak overnight.

■ Drain chickpeas and transfer to a slow cooker. Add sweet potatoes, purple potatoes, parsnips and carrots. In a medium bowl, whisk vegetable broth, coconut milk, curry powder, salt and pepper. Pour into slow cooker; submerge veggies, if possible. Cover and cook on HIGH for 4 hours or LOW for 7 hours.

■ Uncover and scoop out ¾ cup of the sweet potatoes and ½ cup of the cooking liquid. Mash potatoes with broth until smooth and gently stir back into slow cooker. Serve garnished with cilantro.

PER SERVING 413 **CAL**; 16 g **FAT**; 11 g **PRO**; 61 g **CARB**; 13 g **FIBER**

GERMAN CIDER
CHICKEN

Pressure Cooker: Preserve the color, flavor and nutrients of vegetables with this quick-cooking pot.

German Cider Chicken

MAKES 6 servings **PREP** 20 minutes
PRESSURE COOK 21 minutes

- 3   tbsp unsalted butter
- 1¾ lb boneless, skinless chicken breasts, diced
- 1   tsp salt
- 1   medium onion, sliced
- 3   tbsp all-purpose flour
- 1½ cups apple cider or juice
- ½   medium head green cabbage, diced
- 1   Granny Smith apple, cored and sliced into half-moons
- 1½ tsp caraway seeds
- ¼   tsp black pepper
- ½   cup heavy cream
- 1   tbsp Dijon mustard
- 1   bag (12 oz) wide egg noodles, cooked

■ In a pressure cooker, melt butter over medium-high. Season chicken with ½ tsp of the salt and brown 3 minutes. Remove with a slotted spoon and add onion. Cook 3 minutes and sprinkle with 2 tbsp of the flour. Add cider, cabbage, apple, caraway seeds, remaining ½ tsp salt and pepper. Seal cooker and bring up to pressure. Once pressure is reached, cook 10 minutes.

■ Carefully release pressure and stir chicken back into pot. In a small bowl, whisk heavy cream, mustard and remaining 1 tbsp flour. Add to pot and cook 5 minutes, until slightly thickened. Serve over noodles.

Classic Method: Follow through first step, switching to a large stockpot. Cover and simmer over medium

25 minutes, stirring occasionally, until cabbage is tender. Continue with second step.

PER SERVING 591 **CAL**; 19 g **FAT**; 39 g **PRO**; 62 g **CARB**; 6 g **FIBER**

Gumbo

MAKES 8 servings **PREP** 15 minutes
PRESSURE COOK 24 minutes

- 3   tbsp vegetable oil
- 1   pkg (12 oz) fully cooked andouille sausage, sliced into coins
- 1½ lb boneless, skinless chicken thighs, cut into 1-inch pieces
- 3   tbsp all-purpose flour
- 1   medium onion, diced
- 3   ribs celery, trimmed and sliced
- 4   cloves garlic, chopped
- 1   can (14 oz) Del Monte petite cut diced tomatoes with zesty jalapeños
- 2   cups chicken broth
- 1   cup uncooked white rice
- 8   oz (2 cups) frozen sliced okra, thawed
- ¼   tsp salt

■ In a pressure cooker, heat 2 tbsp of the oil over medium-high. Add sausage and cook 2 minutes. Remove to a bowl with a slotted spoon.

■ Add chicken to pot and cook 5 minutes, turning frequently. Remove to bowl with sausage. Add remaining 1 tbsp oil and reduce heat to medium. Sprinkle in flour and cook 4 minutes.

■ Stir in onion, celery and garlic and cook, stirring, 4 minutes. Add chicken, sausage, tomatoes, broth, 4 cups water, rice, okra and salt, scraping bottom of pot to release browned

bits. Seal cooker and bring up to pressure. Cook under pressure 6 minutes. Carefully release pressure and uncover. Return to heat and simmer 3 minutes.

Classic Method: Follow directions through second step, switching to a large stockpot. Follow third step, cooking onion, celery and garlic. Stir in tomatoes, broth, 4 cups water, rice, chicken and sausage; reserve okra. Cover, bring to a simmer and cook 15 to 20 minutes, until rice is tender. Uncover and stir in okra and salt. Simmer 5 minutes.

PER SERVING 380 **CAL**; 17 g **FAT**; 26 g **PRO**; 29 g **CARB**; 2 g **FIBER**

GUMBO

HEALTHY FAMILY DINNERS

Get hooked on these quick and easy seafood suppers.

SEARED SALMON WITH
CITRUS ROMAINE SALAD

Seared Salmon with Citrus Romaine Salad

MAKES 4 servings **PREP** 20 minutes
COOK 8 minutes

- 2 **oranges, peeled and sectioned**
- 2 **grapefruit, peeled and sectioned**
- 2 **tbsp orange juice**
- 2 **tbsp grapefruit juice**
- 2 **tbsp grapeseed oil**
- 2 **tsp honey**
- ½ **tsp salt**
- ⅛ **tsp plus ¼ tsp black pepper**
- 1 **lb salmon fillet, cut into 4 pieces**
- 2 **romaine lettuce hearts, cut into bite-size pieces**
- 1 **avocado, peeled and sliced**
- 2 **scallions, thinly sliced**
   Everything-flavored flatbreads (optional)

■ Refrigerate citrus sections until assembling salad. In a small bowl, whisk orange juice, grapefruit juice, grapeseed oil, honey and ⅛ tsp each of the salt and pepper. Set aside.

■ Heat a nonstick skillet over medium-high. Season salmon with ¼ tsp each of the salt and pepper. Place, skin sides down, in skillet and cook 3 to 4 minutes, until nicely seared. Turn fish and cook an additional 4 minutes or until cooked through. Remove to a plate.

■ In a large bowl, toss lettuce with 4 tbsp of the dressing. Add citrus sections, avocado slices and scallions. Toss gently.

■ Serve salmon over salad and drizzle with remaining dressing. Sprinkle remaining salt over salad. Serve with flatbreads, if desired.

PER SERVING 451 **CAL**; 22 g **FAT**; 30 g **PRO**; 35 g **CARB**; 15 g **FIBER**

CONNECTICUT-STYLE CLAM PIZZA

Connecticut-Style Clam Pizza

MAKES 6 servings **PREP** 10 minutes **COOK** 2 minutes **BAKE** at 450° for 15 minutes

- 2 **tbsp olive oil**
- 4 **cloves garlic, chopped**
- 2 **cans (6.5 oz each) chopped clams, drained and rinsed**
- ½ **tsp dried oregano**
- ¼ **tsp red pepper flakes**
- ¼ **cup chopped parsley**
- 1 **lb pizza dough (thawed, if frozen)**
- 2 **cups part-skim shredded mozzarella**

■ Heat oven to 450°. Coat a 16 x 12 x 1-inch baking pan with nonstick cooking spray.

■ Heat a large skillet over medium-high. Add olive oil and garlic; cook 1 minute or until lightly golden. Add clams, oregano and red pepper flakes. Cook 1 minute; stir in 3 tbsp of the parsley.

■ On a well-floured surface, roll out dough to a 16 x 12-inch rectangle. Roll up onto a well-floured rolling pin and unroll into prepared pan.

■ Sprinkle 1½ cups of the cheese over dough, leaving a ½-inch border on all sides. Evenly spoon clam mixture over cheese. Sprinkle with remaining ½ cup cheese. Bake at 450° for 15 minutes, until bottom of pizza is nicely browned.

■ Sprinkle remaining 1 tbsp parsley over pizza. Cut into 12 squares and serve.

PER SERVING 335 **CAL**; 14 g **FAT**; 19 g **PRO**; 35 g **CARB**; 1 g **FIBER**

Traditional souvlaki consists of small pieces of meat soaked in a lemony marinade, threaded on a skewer and grilled and then served in pita bread with tzatziki (cucumber-yogurt sauce). It is often served with fried potatoes. This lighter version of the Greek favorite features shrimp and oven fries.

Grilled Shrimp Souvlaki

MAKES 6 servings **PREP** 20 minutes **MARINATE** 15 minutes **GRILL OR BROIL** 4 minutes

MARINADE

- 2 **tbsp red wine vinegar**
- 1 **tsp Dijon mustard**
- ⅛ **tsp salt**
- ⅛ **tsp black pepper**
- 3 **tbsp olive oil**
- 2 **tbsp lemon juice**
- 1 **tbsp chopped dill**

SOUVLAKI

- 1 **lb large shrimp, peeled and deveined**
- 12 **mini pitas, warmed**
   Yogurt Sauce (recipe follows)
- 2 **cups shredded romaine lettuce**
- ½ **red onion, chopped**
- 1 **cup cherry tomatoes, quartered**
   Crispy Oven Fries (recipe follows; optional)

■ **Marinade.** In a small bowl, combine vinegar, mustard, salt and pepper. Gradually whisk in olive oil; stir in lemon juice and dill.

■ **Souvlaki.** Place shrimp in a resealable plastic bag with 3 tbsp of the marinade; shake to coat. Refrigerate 15 minutes.

■ Heat stovetop grill or broiler. Grill or broil shrimp 2 minutes per side.

■ On each pita, place about 2 tbsp Yogurt Sauce and a few shrimp. Add lettuce, onion and tomatoes. Drizzle remaining dressing over each souvlaki.

■ Serve with Crispy Oven Fries, if desired.

PER SERVING 324 **CAL**; 9 g **FAT**; 22 g **PRO**; 39 g **CARB**; 2 g **FIBER**

Yogurt Sauce

■ Combine 1½ cups fat-free plain Greek yogurt, ½ peeled, chopped cucumber, 2 tbsp chopped dill, 2 tsp lemon juice and ⅛ tsp salt.

Crispy Oven Fries

■ Heat oven to 450°. Cut 2 lb baking potatoes into 1-inch wedges. Toss with 2 tbsp olive oil and ¼ tsp each salt and black pepper. Bake at 450° for 15 to 20 minutes, until tender and browned, turning once. Broil 3 minutes.

GRILLED SHRIMP
SOUVLAKI

MEDITERRANEAN
SWORDFISH KABOBS

Fish benefits from shorter marinating times than poultry and meats do. The delicate flesh rapidly absorbs flavors and begins to break down and get mushy if it sits in the marinade too long.

Mediterranean Swordfish Kabobs

MAKES 4 servings **PREP** 30 minutes **MARINATE** 15 minutes **BAKE** at 450° for 15 minutes **BROIL** 3 minutes

12 bamboo skewers, soaked for 1 hour

MARINADE

3 tbsp olive oil

2 tbsp white balsamic vinegar

¼ cup chopped parsley

4 cloves garlic, chopped

2 tsp chopped fresh marjoram or oregano

½ tsp dried thyme

⅛ tsp salt

⅛ tsp black pepper

FISH AND VEGETABLES

1¼ lb swordfish, cut into 1½-inch cubes

2 medium summer squash, cut into ½-inch slices

10 oz button mushrooms, stems removed

1 sweet red pepper, seeded and cut into 1-inch dice

¾ tsp salt

¼ tsp black pepper

1 cup tricolor couscous

1¼ cups reduced-sodium vegetable broth

1 tsp chopped fresh marjoram or oregano

■ **Marinade.** In a small bowl, combine oil, vinegar, parsley, garlic, marjoram, thyme, salt and pepper.

■ **Fish.** Place fish and 3 tbsp of the marinade in a resealable plastic bag. Shake bag to coat fish. Refrigerate 15 minutes.

■ Heat oven to 450°. On each skewer, thread equal amounts of fish, squash, mushrooms and red pepper. Season with ½ tsp of the salt and the black pepper. Place on a large rimmed baking sheet and bake at 450° for 10 minutes. Turn, baste with marinade and bake an additional 5 minutes.

■ Prepare couscous following package directions, using broth and marjoram. Season with ⅛ tsp of the salt.

■ Sprinkle kabobs with remaining ⅛ tsp salt and serve with couscous.

PER SERVING 489 **CAL**; 19 g **FAT**; 34 g **PRO**; 45 g **CARB**; 5 g **FIBER**

TUNA AND GRAPE TOMATO SAUCE WITH OLIVE OIL WHIPPED POTATOES

Tuna and Grape Tomato Sauce with Olive Oil Whipped Potatoes

MAKES 4 servings **PREP** 15 minutes **MICROWAVE** 13 minutes **COOK** 15 minutes

1½ lb Yukon gold potatoes, peeled and quartered

2 tbsp unsalted butter, softened

¼ cup olive oil

1 tsp salt

⅛ tsp black pepper

2 cups grape tomatoes, halved

1 can (8 oz) reduced-sodium tomato sauce

3 cloves garlic, chopped

1 tbsp capers

½ tsp dried oregano

½ tsp red pepper flakes

4 tuna steaks, about 1 inch thick (5 oz each)

Lemon wedges, for squeezing

■ Place potatoes in a medium saucepan; cover with lightly salted cold water. Bring to a boil, reduce heat and simmer 15 minutes or until fork-tender. Drain. Add butter and gradually whip in olive oil with an electric mixer. Season with ½ tsp of the salt and the pepper.

■ Meanwhile, combine tomatoes, tomato sauce, garlic, capers, oregano, red pepper flakes and remaining ½ tsp salt in a 12 x 8 x 2-inch microwave-safe baking dish. Microwave, uncovered, 5 minutes.

■ Add tuna; turn to coat and spoon some sauce over the top. Cover with microwave-safe plastic wrap, venting slightly at one corner. Microwave on high 4 minutes.

■ Rotate pan. Uncover and flip fish over. Spoon some sauce on top of fish. Recover, vent and microwave on high 4 minutes. Let stand, covered, 10 minutes before serving.

PER SERVING 495 CAL; 20 g FAT; 40 g PRO; 39 g CARB; 4 g FIBER

Pesto-Baked Halibut

MAKES 4 servings **PREP** 25 minutes
BAKE at 425° for 23 minutes

½ lb small red-skinned potatoes, thinly sliced

½ tsp salt

¼ tsp black pepper

4 halibut fillets (about 6 oz each)

¼ cup prepared pesto

2 medium zucchini, cut into 2-inch matchsticks

2 medium carrots, cut into 2-inch matchsticks

2 shallots, thinly sliced

8 tsp olive oil

6 tsp vegetable broth

4 thyme sprigs

Lemon wedges, for squeezing

■ Heat oven to 425°. Place potatoes on a foil-lined baking sheet and season with ¼ tsp of the salt and ⅛ tsp of the pepper. Bake at 425° for 10 minutes, turning once.

■ Meanwhile, cut four 16 x 12-inch pieces of parchment paper. Fold in half crosswise. Draw a large half heart on each piece. Cut out and open.

■ Place a piece of fish near the fold of each heart and spread with 1 tbsp pesto. Top fillet with equal amounts of zucchini, carrots and shallots. Season with some of the remaining salt and pepper. Arrange potatoes over vegetables. Drizzle with 2 tsp oil and 1½ tsp broth and top with a thyme sprig. Repeat.

■ Starting at top of each heart, fold edges of parchment, sealing edges with narrow folds. Twist the ends to seal. Arrange packets on a large baking sheet and bake at 425° for 13 minutes.

■ Place packets on dinner plates; cut open.

PER SERVING 374 CAL; 18 g FAT; 35 g PRO; 16 g CARB; 4 g FIBER

**PESTO-BAKED
HALIBUT**

BLING OUT YOUR BROWNIES

It's a brownie bargain—2 recipes, 12 treats!

TRIPLE MINT

CHERRY-OAT

PUMPKIN CHEESECAKE SWIRL

LEMON TART

CHOCOLATE-COVERED STRAWBERRY

SALTED CARAMEL-PRETZEL

BACON-PECAN

VIETNAMESE COFFEE

S'MORES

CHOCOLATE-HAZELNUT

ALMOND-COCONUT

PEANUT BUTTER-BANANA

Brownies Basic Recipe

MAKES 16 servings **PREP** 10 minutes
BAKE at 350° for 25 minutes

- ¾ **cup all-purpose flour**
- ¾ **cup unsweetened cocoa powder**
- ¼ **tsp baking powder**
- ¼ **tsp salt**
- 1 **stick (½ cup) unsalted butter, softened**
- 1 **cup sugar**
- 2 **eggs**
- 1 **tsp vanilla extract**

■ Heat oven to 350°. Line an 8 x 8-inch pan with aluminum foil; coat with nonstick cooking spray.

■ In a large bowl, whisk flour, cocoa powder, baking powder and salt. In another large bowl, beat butter and sugar with a hand mixer until fluffy, about 2 minutes. Beat in eggs one at a time until well combined, then beat in vanilla.

■ Mix dry ingredients into wet ingredients on low speed until just combined.

■ Transfer to prepared pan and spread evenly. Bake at 350° for 22 to 25 minutes, until a toothpick inserted in center comes out clean. Cool 10 minutes, then lift out brownie in foil, place on a wire rack and cool completely.

Triple Mint

■ Fold 1¼ cups chopped mint Oreo cookies, ¼ tsp mint extract and all but 2 tbsp (from a 4.67-oz pkg) chopped Andes mints into batter. Scatter ¼ cup more chopped mint Oreo cookies on top. Bake as directed. Top with reserved 2 tbsp Andes mints.

PER BAR 230 **CAL**; 12 g **FAT**; 3 g **PRO**; 31 g **CARB**; 2 g **FIBER**

Pumpkin Cheesecake Swirl

■ To make cheesecake batter, beat 1 pkg (8 oz) softened cream cheese, ½ cup canned pumpkin puree, ¼ cup sugar, 1 egg, ¼ tsp pumpkin pie spice and ⅛ tsp salt until smooth. In a separate bowl, add ½ cup canned pumpkin puree, ½ cup milk and ½ tsp pumpkin pie spice to wet brownie ingredients. Alternate dollops of brownie and cheesecake batter in pan, then use a knife to make swirls. Add 10 to 15 minutes to baking time.

PER BAR 200 **CAL**; 13 g **FAT**; 4 g **PRO**; 19 g **CARB**; 2 g **FIBER**

Chocolate-Covered Strawberry

■ Reduce sugar to ⅔ cup; add ½ cup strawberry jam to wet ingredients. From a 1-oz bag of freeze-dried strawberries, chopped, set aside ¼ cup. Fold the rest into batter. To prepare frosting, beat 1½ cups confectioners' sugar, ¼ cup cocoa powder, 3 tbsp heavy cream and 2 tbsp strawberry jam with a hand mixer in a bowl. Frost, then scatter reserved ¼ cup chopped freeze-dried strawberries on top.

PER BAR 230 **CAL**; 8 g **FAT**; 3 g **PRO**; 36 g **CARB**; 2 g **FIBER**

Bacon-Pecan

■ In a skillet, cook 8 slices diced bacon over medium until crispy, about 5 minutes. With a slotted spoon, remove to a paper-towel-lined plate, reserving 2 tbsp of the bacon fat. Reduce butter to 6 tbsp and replace 2 tbsp of the butter with bacon fat. Fold cooked bacon and 1 cup pecan halves into batter. Place 16 pecan halves on top before baking.

PER BAR 250 **CAL**; 18 g **FAT**; 5 g **PRO**; 21 g **CARB**; 2 g **FIBER**

S'mores

■ Fold 1 cup mini marshmallows and 1½ cups roughly chopped graham crackers into batter. Scatter ¼ cup each mini marshmallows and chopped graham crackers on top before baking.

PER BAR 160 **CAL**; 7 g **FAT**; 2 g **PRO**; 24 g **CARB**; 2 g **FIBER**; 70 g **SODIUM**

Almond-Coconut

■ Mix ½ tsp almond extract into wet ingredients. Toast ¾ cup each shredded sweetened coconut and sliced almonds; fold into mixed batter. Scatter 2 tbsp each shredded sweetened coconut and sliced almonds (untoasted) on top.

PER BAR 190 **CAL**; 11 g **FAT**; 3 g **PRO**; 23 g **CARB**; 2 g **FIBER**

Blondies Basic Recipe

MAKES 16 servings **PREP** 10 minutes
BAKE at 350° for 30 minutes

- 1½   **cups all-purpose flour**
- ¼   **tsp salt**
- 1½   **sticks (¾ cup) unsalted butter, softened**
- 1   **cup packed light brown sugar**
- 1   **egg**
- 1   **tsp vanilla extract**

■ Heat oven to 350°. Line an 8 x 8-inch pan with aluminum foil; coat with nonstick cooking spray.

■ In a large bowl, whisk flour and salt. In another large bowl, beat butter and sugar with a hand mixer until fluffy, about 2 minutes. Beat in egg and vanilla until well combined.

■ Mix dry ingredients into wet ingredients on low speed until just combined.

■ Transfer to prepared pan and spread evenly. Bake at 350° for 25 to 30 minutes, until a toothpick inserted in center comes out clean. Cool 10 minutes, then use foil to lift blondie to a wire rack. Cool completely.

Cherry-Oat

■ Fold ⅔ cup each rolled oats and dried cherries into batter. Scatter 2 tbsp of each on top before baking.

PER BAR 220 **CAL**; 9 g **FAT**; 2 g **PRO**; 31 g **CARB**; 1 g **FIBER**

Lemon Tart

■ Mix ¼ cup milk and 2 tbsp lemon juice into wet ingredients. After adding batter to pan, dollop ¼ cup lemon curd on top, then use a knife to make swirls. Add 8 minutes to baking time. Refrigerate until firm.

PER BAR 200 **CAL**; 10 g **FAT**; 2 g **PRO**; 27 g **CARB**; 0 g **FIBER**; 50 g **SODIUM**

Salted Caramel-Pretzel

■ Replace ½ cup of the brown sugar with ½ cup caramel sauce and stir in ¼ tsp more salt. Fold 1½ cups roughly chopped small pretzels into batter. Scatter ½ cup chopped small pretzels on top before baking. Drizzle with 2 tbsp caramel sauce once cool.

PER BAR 230 **CAL**; 9 g **FAT** (6 g **SAT**); 3 g **PRO**; 35 g **CARB**; 1 g **FIBER**

Vietnamese Coffee

■ Add an extra ¼ cup all-purpose flour and 1 tbsp instant espresso powder to dry ingredients. In wet ingredients, replace brown sugar with 1 can (14 oz) sweetened condensed milk. Fold ½ cup chopped chocolate-covered espresso beans into batter. Top with 2 tbsp chopped espresso beans before baking.

PER BAR 240 **CAL**; 12 g **FAT**; 4 g **PRO**; 29 g **CARB**; 1 g **FIBER**

Chocolate-Hazelnut

■ Mix ½ tsp hazelnut extract into wet ingredients. Fold ¾ cup each chocolate chunks and chopped hazelnuts into batter. Scatter ¼ cup chocolate chunks and 2 tbsp chopped hazelnuts on top before baking.

PER BAR 290 **CAL**; 17 g **FAT**; 3 g **PRO**; 33 g **CARB**; 2 g **FIBER**

Peanut Butter-Banana

■ Beat ⅓ cup creamy peanut butter into wet ingredients. Fold 1 cup roughly chopped banana chips and ⅓ cup chopped peanuts into batter. To prepare frosting, in a bowl, combine 1½ cups confectioners' sugar, ¼ cup peanut butter and ¼ cup heavy cream with a hand mixer. Frost, then scatter another ¼ cup chopped banana chips and 2 tbsp chopped peanuts on top.

PER BAR 330 **CAL**; 18 g **FAT**; 5 g **PRO**; 38 g **CARB**; 2 g **FIBER**

BLENDING IN

Spice mixes are heating up grocery store aisles for a great reason: They're a simple, healthy way to boost flavor. Preparing your own saves money and lets you customize quantity and taste. Transform dinner in 1-2-3 with any of these combos.

Wok This Way

1 tbsp fennel + 1 tbsp mustard powder + 2 tsp ginger

Liven up chicken or fish with this Chinese-inspired blend. It also perks up veggies like broccoli and spinach.

Fired Up

1 tbsp smoked paprika + 2 tsp garlic powder + ½ tsp cayenne

Consider it the ultimate barbecue rub. In the off-season, try it on a roast—smoked paprika mimics the charred flavor you get from grilling.

Moroccan Medley

1 tbsp cinnamon + 1 tbsp cumin + 2 tsp dried parsley

This mix is ideal for beef or lamb and works particularly well as the flavor base for a stew or braised dish. Or swap out the parsley for coriander to create a Mexican-inspired meal.

WINGIN' IT

Score big with these Super Bowl MVPs.

GRILLED
CHIMICHURRI

BEER-BATTERED
THAI

Beer-Battered Thai

MAKES 30 wings **PREP** 25 minutes
FRY 45 minutes

- 8 cups vegetable oil
- ⅓ cup plus 1 cup cornstarch
- ½ tsp plus 1 tsp baking powder
- 1¼ tsp salt
- 1 cup all-purpose flour
- 1 tsp garlic powder
- ¾ tsp ginger powder
- ½ tsp plus ¼ tsp cayenne
- 1 bottle (12 oz) pilsner beer
- 3 lb drumettes and wings
- 6 tbsp lime juice
- ¼ cup fish sauce
- ¼ cup brown sugar
  Sliced scallions for garnish
  Lime zest for garnish

- In a large, heavy-bottomed pot, heat vegetable oil to 375°. In a bowl, mix ⅓ cup cornstarch and ½ tsp each baking powder and salt.

- In a separate bowl, whisk 1 cup each cornstarch and all-purpose flour, 1 tsp each baking powder and garlic powder, ¾ tsp each ginger powder and salt, and ½ tsp cayenne pepper. Pour in pilsner beer and whisk until smooth.

- Dredge drumettes and wings in dry mixture, then dip into batter, allowing excess to drip off. Fry wings in 2 to 3 batches 10 to 15 minutes each, until golden brown, making sure temperature stays close to 375°. (Keep first two batches warm in a 200° oven.)

- In a clean bowl, combine lime juice, fish sauce, brown sugar and ¼ tsp cayenne. Toss hot cooked wings with half the sauce; reserve other half to serve alongside. Garnish with sliced scallions and lime zest.

PER PIECE 120 **CAL**; 8 g **FAT**; 4 g **PRO**;
8 g **CARB**; 0 g **FIBER**

Grilled Chimichurri

MAKES 30 wings **PREP** 15 minutes
MARINATE 30 minutes **GRILL** 24 minutes

- ⅔ cup packed parsley
- ⅔ cup packed cilantro
- ¼ cup red wine vinegar
- 1 chopped garlic clove
- ¾ tsp salt
- ½ tsp red pepper flakes
- ½ cup vegetable oil
- 3 lb drumettes and wings

- Combine parsley and cilantro, red wine vinegar, garlic, salt and red pepper flakes in a food processor. While machine is running, slowly pour in vegetable oil.

- Pour half the chimichurri into a small bowl and remaining half into a resealable plastic bag with drumettes and wings. Marinate 30 minutes.

- Grill wings over medium heat 10 to 12 minutes per side (20 to 24 minutes total). Serve alongside bowl of chimichurri.

PER PIECE 50 **CAL**; 5 g **FAT**; 3 g **PRO**; 0 g **CARB**;
0 g **FIBER**

Smoky Maple

MAKES 30 wings **PREP** 10 minutes
COOK 3 minutes **BAKE** at 400° for 55 minutes

- 3 lb drumettes and wings
- 2 tbsp vegetable oil
- 2 tbsp melted unsalted butter plus 2 tbsp unsalted butter
- 1 tsp sweet paprika, plus more for sprinkling
- 1 tsp smoked paprika
- 1¼ tsp salt
- ¼ tsp black pepper
- ½ cup pure maple syrup

- Heat oven to 400°. Coat a large rimmed baking sheet with nonstick cooking spray. In a bowl, toss drumettes and wings with vegetable oil and 2 tbsp melted unsalted butter, 1 tsp sweet paprika, 1 tsp each smoked paprika and salt, and pepper. Spread wings in a single layer on prepared sheet.

- In a small skillet, combine pure maple syrup, 2 tbsp unsalted butter and ¼ tsp salt; simmer 3 minutes.

- Bake wings at 400° for 45 minutes, then toss with ⅓ cup of the syrup mixture and bake another 10 minutes. Drizzle with remaining syrup mixture. Sprinkle with more sweet paprika.

PER PIECE 50 **CAL**; 3 g **FAT**; 3 g **PRO**; 4 g **CARB**;
0 g **FIBER**

SMOKY MAPLE

CRUNCHY CHEDDAR

HONEY-HARISSA

Crunchy Cheddar

MAKES 30 wings **PREP** 25 minutes
COOK 4 minutes **BAKE** at 400° for 55 minutes

- ⅔ **cup plus 1 tbsp all-purpose flour**
- 1 **tsp plus ¼ tsp and ⅛ tsp salt**
- ½ **tsp black pepper**
- 3 **eggs**
- 4 **cups Cheez-It crackers**
- 3 **lb drumettes and wings**
- 1 **tbsp unsalted butter**
- ⅔ **cup milk**
- 3 **cups sharp cheddar, shredded**
- 1 **can (4 oz) diced mild green chiles**

■ Heat oven to 400°. In a bowl, combine ⅔ cup all-purpose flour, 1 tsp salt and black pepper. In a second bowl, beat eggs.

■ In a food processor, pulse Cheez-It crackers and ¼ tsp salt until it reaches the texture of bread crumbs; place in a third bowl.

■ Dredge drumettes and wings in flour mixture, followed by eggs, then cracker crumbs. Place on a baking sheet fitted with a wire rack and bake at 400° for 45 to 55 minutes.

■ Meanwhile, melt unsalted butter in a small saucepan. Stir in 1 tbsp all-purpose flour; cook 1 minute. Whisk in milk; bring to a simmer and cook 3 minutes, until thickened. Stir in shredded sharp cheddar until melted. Stir in diced mild green chiles and ⅛ tsp salt until combined. Serve alongside wings.

PER PIECE 140 **CAL**; 9 g **FAT**; 9 g **PRO**; 6g **CARB**; 0 g **FIBER**

Honey-Harissa

MAKES 30 wings **PREP** 15 minutes
FRY 45 minutes

- 8 **cups vegetable oil**
- ⅓ **cup all-purpose flour**
- ½ **tsp salt**
- 3 **lb drumettes and wings**
- 4 **tbsp unsalted butter**
- ⅓ **cup harissa**
- ⅓ **cup honey, plus more for drizzling**
- 1 **tbsp lemon juice**

■ In a large, heavy-bottomed pot, heat vegetable oil to 375°. In a bowl, combine all-purpose flour with ¼ tsp salt, then toss with drumettes and wings.

■ In a small pot, melt unsalted butter over medium. Stir in harissa, honey, lemon juice and remaining ¼ tsp salt. Stir until warm, cover and set aside.

■ Fry wings in 2 to 3 batches 10 to 15 minutes each, until golden brown, making sure temperature stays close to 375°. (Keep first two batches warm in a 200° oven.)

■ In a clean bowl, toss wings with sauce. Transfer to a platter and drizzle with more honey.

PER PIECE 100 **CAL**; 8 g **FAT**; 3 g **PRO**; 4 g **CARB**; 0 g **FIBER**

Crispy, succulent wings in a variety of flavors are a favorite form of sustenance for the sports-watching set. Serve them with lots of napkins and cold drinks!

TRIPLE PLAY

Chocolate lovers, rejoice: Three kinds of chocolate flavor these treats.

TRIPLE CHOCOLATE CHUNK COOKIES

Dutch-process cocoa is natural cocoa that has been treated with alkali, which mellows it and gives it a milder flavor than natural cocoa. It also gives it a slightly reddish hue. If you like the intense flavor of natural cocoa, you can certainly use it here instead.

Triple Chocolate Chunk Cookies

MAKES 2½ dozen **PREP** 20 minutes **MICROWAVE** 1 minute **BAKE** at 325° for 14 minutes per batch

- 1 **bar (4 oz) semisweet chocolate, chopped**
- 1¼ **cups all-purpose flour**
- ⅓ **cup Dutch-process cocoa powder**
- 1⅛ **tsp baking soda**
- ½ **tsp salt**
- 1 **stick (½ cup) unsalted butter, softened**
- ¾ **cup packed dark brown sugar**
- 1 **large egg**
- 2 **tsp vanilla extract**
- 2 **cups bittersweet chocolate chunks (Scharffen Berger) or large chocolate chips (Ghirardelli)**
- ⅓ **cup granulated sugar**

■ Heat oven to 325°. Line 3 large baking sheets with parchment paper.

■ Place chopped chocolate in a small glass bowl. Microwave 1 minute; stir until smooth and set aside to cool slightly.

■ In a medium bowl, whisk flour, cocoa powder, baking soda and salt.

■ In large bowl of a stand mixer, beat butter until smooth. Add brown sugar and beat on medium-high speed 5 minutes, occasionally scraping down sides of bowl. Add egg and beat 3 minutes more. Stir in vanilla and melted chocolate. On low speed, beat in flour mixture. Fold in chocolate chunks or chips.

■ Place granulated sugar in a small bowl. Scoop up 2 slightly heaping tbsp of dough and roll it into a ball between your hands. Roll ball in sugar to coat. Place cookie on prepared baking sheet and flatten slightly with your hand. Repeat with all the remaining dough and granulated sugar.

■ Bake cookies in batches at 325° for 14 minutes per batch or until cookies crack. Cool on pan a few minutes, then carefully transfer to a wire rack to cool completely.

SHEET PAN
CHICKEN,
PAGE 78

MARCH

59

64

78

30 UNDER 30

Dinners ready in less than half an hour, for when there's already a lot on your plate.

NOODLE BOWL

ROASTED VEGGIE QUINOA BOWL

We love these beautiful bowls—all-in-one meals of lean proteins, legumes, whole grains and lots of colorful and nutritious fresh vegetables.

Noodle Bowl

MAKES 6 servings **PREP** 20 minutes
COOK 13 minutes

- 12 oz rice stick noodles or thin vermicelli
- 2 scallions, trimmed and sliced
- 1 tbsp toasted sesame oil
- Toasted sesame seeds
- 2 boneless, skinless chicken breast cutlets (about ¾ lb)
- ¼ tsp salt
- ¼ tsp black pepper
- 2 tbsp vegetable oil
- 1 pkg (5 oz) shiitake mushrooms, sliced
- 4 oz sugar snap peas, strings removed
- 1 bunch watercress, tough stems trimmed
- 2 large carrots, peeled and shaved into thin strips
- 4 radishes, trimmed and sliced
- ½ cup dry-roasted peanuts, coarsely chopped
- ½ cup bottled peanut sauce, thinned with a few tbsp water
- Lime wedges

■ Bring a large pot of salted water to a boil. Add noodles and cook following package directions. Drain and rinse in cool water. Toss in a bowl with sliced scallions, sesame oil and sesame seeds. Set aside.

■ Season chicken with salt and pepper. Heat oil in a large stainless-steel skillet over medium-high. Add chicken and cook 4 minutes, until nicely browned; turn and cook an additional 4 minutes, until internal temperature reaches 165°. Remove to cutting board; cut into cubes. Reserve skillet.

■ Return skillet to medium. Add mushrooms and sauté 4 minutes, adding a pinch of salt. Remove to a plate and add snap peas and a few tbsp of water to skillet. Cook 1 minute, until peas are bright green.

■ Divide noodles among 6 bowls and add chicken, mushrooms, snap peas, watercress, carrots, radishes and peanuts. Drizzle with peanut sauce and garnish with lime wedges.

PER SERVING 496 **CAL**; 18 g **FAT**; 19 g **PRO**; 64 g **CARB**; 3 g **FIBER**

Roasted Veggie Quinoa Bowl

MAKES 6 servings **PREP** 10 minutes
ROAST at 450° for 25 minutes
COOK 15 minutes

VEGGIES

- 4 cups ½-inch cubes butternut squash
- 3 tbsp olive oil
- 2 tsp curry powder
- ¼ tsp salt
- Pinch of black pepper
- 1 can (15.5 oz) chickpeas, drained and rinsed
- 3 cups low-sodium chicken broth
- 1½ cups tricolor quinoa
- 1 pkg (11 oz) fresh baby spinach
- 1 medium red onion, sliced
- Chopped parsley
- ¾ cup crumbled feta cheese

DRESSING

- ¼ cup fresh lemon juice
- 2 tbsp mayonnaise
- ½ tsp curry powder
- 1 tsp sugar
- ½ tsp salt
- ¼ tsp black pepper
- 3 tbsp olive oil

■ **Veggies.** Heat oven to 450°. Toss squash with 1½ tbsp of the oil and ¾ tsp of the curry powder. Spread on a large rimmed baking sheet and season with salt and pepper. Toss chickpeas with ½ tbsp of the oil and ½ tsp of the curry powder. Spread onto a small baking sheet. Roast squash and chickpeas at 450° for 25 minutes, stirring halfway through.

■ While squash roasts, combine chicken broth, quinoa and remaining ¾ tsp curry powder in a medium saucepan. Bring to a boil; cover and reduce heat to medium-low. Cook 15 minutes or until broth is absorbed.

■ Meanwhile, heat remaining 1 tbsp oil in a large nonstick skillet over medium to medium-high. Add spinach and cook until wilted, 2 minutes. Remove to a plate. Reduce heat to medium; add onion to the skillet and cook 5 minutes.

■ **Dressing.** In a medium bowl, whisk lemon juice, mayonnaise, curry powder, sugar, salt and pepper. While whisking, add olive oil in a thin stream.

■ Stir parsley into cooked quinoa and toss with a few tbsp of the dressing. Divide among 6 bowls. Top with roasted squash and chickpeas, spinach, onion and feta. Drizzle with dressing.

PER SERVING 473 **CAL**; 24 g **FAT**; 13 g **PRO**; 54 g **CARB**; 9 g **FIBER**

BIBIMBAP
SALAD BOWL

Vietnamese Rice Bowl

MAKES 4 servings **PREP** 15 minutes
COOK 8 minutes

- **2 tbsp packed light brown sugar**
- **2 tbsp fresh lime juice, plus wedges for garnish**
- **5 tsp fish sauce**
- **2 tbsp vegetable oil**
- **1 lb boneless pork chops, diced into ½-inch pieces**
- **2 tbsp chopped ginger**
- **1 tbsp roasted red chili paste (such as Thai Kitchen)**
- **2 cloves garlic, chopped**
- **1 lb Chinese cabbage, sliced**
- **1 can (8 oz) sliced bamboo shoots, drained**
- **4 scallions, sliced**
- **⅓ cup chopped mint, plus more for serving**
- **4 cups cooked white rice**

■ In a small bowl, whisk brown sugar, lime juice, fish sauce, and 3 tbsp water. Heat oil in a large skillet over medium-high. Add pork, ginger, chili paste and garlic. Sauté 2 minutes and remove to a plate with a slotted spoon. Stir in cabbage and cook 3 to 5 minutes, until tender and wilted. Stir in bamboo shoots and scallions; cook 1 minute. Return pork mixture to skillet. Pour in sauce and bring to a simmer. Stir in mint.

■ Serve over rice. Top with additional mint and serve with lime wedges.

PER SERVING 470 **CAL**; 15 g **FAT**; 26 g **PRO**; 57 g **CARB**; 3 g **FIBER**

Bibimbap Salad Bowl

MAKES 4 servings **PREP** 15 minutes **COOK** 8 minutes

- **1 large shallot, sliced (about ½ cup)**
- **½ cup rice vinegar**
- **3 tbsp low-sodium soy sauce**
- **2 tbsp vegetable oil**
- **2 tsp sugar**
- **1 lb ground sirloin or ground chicken**
- **2 cloves garlic, minced**
- **⅛ tsp salt**
- **4 large eggs**
- **2 scallions, sliced**
- **1 tsp chili garlic sauce**
- **1 pkg (5 oz) mixed greens**
- **1½ cups shredded carrots**
- **3 cups cooked brown rice**

■ Place sliced shallot in a medium bowl and toss with ¼ cup of the vinegar. Set aside.

■ Make dressing: In a small bowl, whisk remaining ¼ cup vinegar, 1 tbsp of the soy sauce, the oil and sugar.

■ Heat a large nonstick skillet over medium-high. Crumble in beef and sauté 4 minutes, breaking apart with a wooden spoon. Add minced garlic and salt; cook 1 minute. Remove to a bowl with a slotted spoon and lower to medium. Crack eggs into skillet and fry 3 minutes or to desired doneness.

■ Stir remaining 2 tbsp soy sauce, the scallions and chili garlic sauce into beef. In a large bowl, toss greens with shredded carrots, marinated shallot and dressing. Divide among 4 plates and spoon rice and beef mixture over salad. Top each serving with a fried egg.

PER SERVING 436 **CAL**; 20 g **FAT**; 35 g **PRO**; 27 g **CARB**; 3 g **FIBER**

VIETNAMESE RICE BOWL

Cook a big batch of rice on the weekend and store it in the fridge. It will be good for the week; use it in Bibimbap, Kung Pao Shrimp or Vietnamese Rice Bowl.

*Ground turkey has 3 to 6 grams less
fat per serving than lamb or beef.*

SHEPHERD'S PIE

Shepherd's Pie

MAKES 6 servings **PREP** 5 minutes
MICROWAVE 10 minutes **COOK** 10 minutes
BAKE at 450° for 15 minutes

- 2½ **lb russet baking potatoes, unpeeled**
- 3 **tbsp unsalted butter**
- 1 **pkg (20.9 oz) ground turkey**
- 2 **medium carrots, peeled and sliced into ¼-inch pieces**
- 2 **small shallots, minced**
- 3 **cloves garlic, chopped**
- ¾ **tsp plus ⅛ tsp salt**
- 5 **oz (4 packed cups) baby spinach**
- 1 **cup frozen peas, thawed**
- 1 **can (14.5 oz) reduced-sodium chicken broth plus ¼ cup water**
- 3 **tbsp all-purpose flour**
- 6 **tbsp chopped fresh dill**
- 1 **cup skim milk**
- ½ **cup crumbled feta cheese**

■ Heat oven to 450°. Pierce potatoes all over and place in microwave on paper towels. Microwave 9 to 10 minutes or until soft when pressed. Let cool slightly.

■ Meanwhile, melt 1 tbsp of the butter in a large cast-iron skillet over medium-high. Crumble in turkey and cook, breaking apart with a spoon, 3 minutes. Stir in carrots, shallots and garlic; season with ½ tsp of the salt. Cook 5 minutes. Stir in spinach and peas and cook 2 minutes.

■ Whisk broth, water, flour and 3 tbsp of the dill. Add to skillet and stir to completely coat mixture. Remove from heat.

■ Cut up potatoes and mash with milk, remaining 2 tbsp butter, remaining ¼ tsp plus ⅛ tsp salt, 3 tbsp dill and crumbled feta. Spoon onto turkey mixture and spread to pan edges. Bake at 450° for 15 minutes, until bubbly and lightly browned.

PER SERVING 499 **CAL**; 21 g **FAT**; 29 g **PRO**; 52 g **CARB**; 7 g **FIBER**

STEAK SALAD

Steak Salad

MAKES 6 servings **PREP** 5 minutes **COOK** 15 minutes **LET REST** 5 minutes

- 1 **cup quick-cook wheat berries (such as Nature's Earthly Choice)**
- 1¼ **tsp salt**
- 1½ **lb boneless sirloin steak**
- ¼ **tsp black pepper**
- 3 **tbsp olive oil**
- 1 **cup grape tomatoes, halved**
- ¼ **cup cider vinegar**
- 1 **tsp grainy mustard**
- 1 **pkg (10 oz) baby spinach**
- 1 **Gala apple, cored and sliced**

■ Cook wheat berries following package directions (15 minutes) with ½ tsp of the salt. Drain.

■ Meanwhile, season steak with ¼ tsp of the salt and the pepper. Heat 2 tbsp of the oil in a large stainless-steel skillet over medium-high. Add steak; cook 5 minutes. Flip; cook 6 more minutes or to desired doneness. Let rest 5 minutes.

■ Reduce heat to medium. Add tomatoes and cook 3 minutes. Whisk in vinegar, remaining 1 tbsp oil, mustard and ¼ tsp salt. Remove from heat.

■ In a very large bowl, toss spinach, wheat berries, apple, dressing from pan and remaining ¼ tsp salt. Slice steak and serve over salad.

PER SERVING 413 **CAL**; 19 g **FAT**; 26 g **PRO**; 36 g **CARB**; 8 g **FIBER**

ITALIAN FRITTATA

Italian Frittata

MAKES 4 servings **PREP** 5 minutes **COOK** 10 minutes **BAKE** at 400° for 15 minutes
BROIL 3 minutes (optional)

- ¾ **lb all-purpose potatoes, shredded**
- 7 **large eggs**
- 5 **large egg whites**
- ⅓ **cup skim or low-fat milk**
- 2 **tsp Dijon mustard**
- ¾ **tsp salt**
- ¼ **tsp freshly ground black pepper**
- 1 **tbsp olive oil**
- 2 **plum tomatoes, seeded and diced**
- ½ **cup fresh basil, sliced**
- 6 **oz fresh mozzarella, cubed (about ¾ cup)**
- 2 **tbsp grated Parmesan**
   Green salad, for serving

■ Heat oven to 400°. Place shredded potatoes in a colander and rinse with cool water. Drain and press dry with paper towels. In a large bowl, whisk eggs, egg whites, skim milk, mustard, ½ tsp of the salt and the pepper.

■ Heat oil in a 10-inch nonstick oven-safe skillet over medium-high. Add drained potatoes and cook, stirring frequently, 5 minutes. Sprinkle with remaining ¼ tsp salt.

■ Fold in diced tomatoes and half the basil. Pour in egg mixture; reduce heat to medium. Scatter in mozzarella.

■ Cook 5 minutes, occasionally running a spatula between egg mixture and edge of pan. Sprinkle with Parmesan and transfer to oven. Bake at 400° for 15 minutes or until 160° and set in center. Broil on high 3 minutes (if desired) to brown. Top with remaining ¼ cup basil and serve with a green salad alongside.

PER SERVING 395 **CAL**; 22 g **FAT**; 27 g **PRO**; 20 g **CARB**; 2 g **FIBER**

Moroccan Beef Stir-Fry

MAKES 6 servings **PREP** 10 minutes
COOK 14 minutes

- 1 **cup couscous**
- 2 **tbsp plus 1 tsp extra-virgin olive oil**
- 1 **lb thinly sliced sirloin**
- 1 **tbsp all-purpose flour**
- ½ **tsp ground cumin**
- ½ **tsp ground ginger**
- ¼ **tsp ground cinnamon**
- ½ **tsp salt**
- ⅛ **tsp ground cayenne**
- 1 **cup diced yellow onion**
- 1 **can (8 oz) tomato sauce**
- 1 **cup beef broth**
- 1 **can (15.5 oz) chickpeas, drained and rinsed**
- 1 **cup dried apricots**
- 1 **cup pitted dates, halved**
- ½ **cup parsley, chopped**
- ¼ **cup toasted sliced almonds**

■ Combine couscous, 1¼ cups water and 1 tsp of the oil in a small pot and bring to a boil. Cover, remove from heat and set aside.

■ In a bowl, toss beef with flour, cumin, ginger, cinnamon, ¼ tsp of the salt and the cayenne. In a large skillet, heat 1 tbsp of the oil over medium-high. Sauté beef 2 minutes and remove to a plate with a slotted spoon. Pour remaining 1 tbsp oil into skillet and add onion; sauté 2 minutes. Stir in tomato sauce, broth, chickpeas, apricots and dates. Bring to a simmer. Reduce heat to medium-low and cook 10 minutes. Stir in cooked beef, parsley and remaining ¼ tsp salt. Serve over fluffed couscous and garnish with almonds.

PER SERVING 580 **CAL**; 17 g **FAT**; 27 g **PRO**; 83 g **CARB**; 11 g **FIBER**

MOROCCAN BEEF
STIR-FRY

ZUCCHINI AND CARROT RIBBONS

PECORINO-CRUSTED SALMON

Kung Pao Shrimp

MAKES 4 servings   PREP 20 minutes   COOK 12 minutes

- **3 tbsp reduced-sodium soy sauce**
- **2 tbsp rice vinegar**
- **2 tsp cornstarch**
- **1 tsp sriracha**
- **1 tsp sugar**
- **2 tbsp canola oil**
- **12 oz shelled and deveined medium shrimp**
- **1 cup chopped onion**
- **2 sweet red peppers, seeded and cut into 1-inch chunks**
- **1   cup sliced celery**
- **6 oz brown mushrooms, stems removed, quartered**
- **½ cup sliced water chestnuts, quartered**
- **½ cup cashews**
- **3 cups cooked white rice**
- **4 scallions, sliced**

■ In a small bowl, combine soy sauce, vinegar, cornstarch, sriracha and sugar.

■ Heat 1 tbsp of the oil in a large nonstick skillet over medium-high. Add shrimp and stir-fry 3 minutes; remove to a plate. Add remaining 1 tbsp oil. Stir in onion; cook 2 minutes. Add red peppers, celery and mushrooms. Stir-fry 5 minutes.

■ Add soy sauce mixture and simmer 1 minute, until thickened. Stir in shrimp, water chestnuts and cashews; cook 1 minute. Serve with rice and top with scallions.

PER SERVING 449 CAL; 16 g FAT; 19 g PRO; 60 g CARB; 4 g FIBER

Pecorino-Crusted Salmon

MAKES 4 servings   PREP 10 minutes   COOK 20 minutes   BAKE at 450° for 12 minutes

- **¾ cup jasmine rice**
- **½ tsp ground turmeric**
- **½ tsp salt**
- **½ tsp black pepper**
- **¾ cup frozen peas, thawed**
- **2 tbsp chopped parsley**
- **1 large egg white**
- **1 tbsp Dijon mustard**
- **½ cup panko bread crumbs**
- **½ cup grated Pecorino Romano cheese**
- **1½ lb salmon fillet, cut in 4 pieces**
- **Zucchini and Carrot Ribbons (recipe follows)**

■ Heat oven to 450°. Combine rice, 1½ cups water, turmeric and ¼ tsp each salt and pepper in a saucepan. Bring to a boil then reduce heat to medium-low. Cover; cook 20 minutes. Stir in peas and 1 tbsp of the parsley.

■ Meanwhile, line a baking sheet with aluminum foil. In a small bowl, whisk egg white and mustard. In a shallow dish, combine panko, Pecorino Romano, and remaining 1 tbsp parsley and ¼ tsp each salt and pepper. Brush egg-mustard mixture onto salmon pieces, then dip salmon, top down, into crumb mixture and place on foil-lined baking sheet. Spoon remaining crumb mixture onto salmon. Bake at 450° for 12 minutes, until golden. Serve with yellow rice and Zucchini and Carrot Ribbons.

PER SERVING 532 CAL; 16 g FAT (4 g SAT); 49 g PRO; 43 g CARB; 2 g FIBER

Zucchini and Carrot Ribbons

MAKES 4 servings   PREP 10 minutes   COOK 3 minutes

■ Trim 2 medium zucchini. Using a peeler, shave zucchini into long strips. Peel 2 carrots and shave into thin strips. Heat 1 tbsp olive oil in a large nonstick skillet over medium-high. Add zucchini and carrot ribbons; sauté 3 minutes. Toss with 1 tbsp fresh lemon juice, 1 tbsp snipped fresh chives, ½ tsp salt and ⅛ tsp black pepper.

PER SERVING 70 CAL; 4 g FAT; 3 g PRO; 7 g CARB; 2 g FIBER

KUNG PAO
SHRIMP

*Angel hair cooks
quickly; check halfway
through cooking time
if you like your pasta
al dente.*

Garlicky Shrimp and Green Beans

MAKES 6 servings **PREP** 10 minutes **COOK** 6 minutes

1	**lb angel hair pasta**
12	**oz fresh green beans, sliced on the bias into 1-inch pieces**
⅓	**cup extra-virgin olive oil**
⅓	**cup sliced shallots**
4	**cloves garlic, sliced**
¼	**tsp red pepper flakes**
1¼	**lb peeled and deveined small shrimp**
¼	**cup chopped parsley**
½	**tsp salt**

■ Bring a pot of salted water to a boil. Add pasta, return to a boil and cook 6 minutes. During last 3 minutes, add green beans. Drain, reserving ½ cup of the pasta water.

■ Meanwhile, heat oil in large skillet over medium-high. Add shallots, garlic and red pepper flakes; cook 1 minute. Add shrimp. Cook 1 minute, flip and cook 1 minute more. Stir in parsley.

■ Transfer to a large bowl. Toss with pasta, reserved pasta water and salt.

PER SERVING 480 **CAL**; 14 g **FAT**; 24 g **PRO**; 63 g **CARB**; 5 g **FIBER**

GARLICKY
SHRIMP AND
GREEN BEANS

RAINBOW SLAW,
RECIPE PAGE 77

BACON
CHEESEBURGER
SOUP

Pappardelle with Mushroom and Turkey Ragu

MAKES 6 servings **PREP** 10 minutes
COOK 23 minutes

- 2 **tbsp olive oil**
- 1 **onion, chopped**
- 1 **lb ground turkey**
- 4 **cloves garlic, chopped**
- 1 **can (28 oz) fire-roasted crushed tomatoes**
- 6 **oz cremini mushrooms, stems removed, sliced**
- 1 **tsp dried oregano**
- 1 **tsp salt**
- ¼ **tsp red pepper flakes**
- 1 **lb dried pappardelle pasta**
- 1 **cup part-skim ricotta**
- ½ **cup basil, cut into ribbons**
- 2 **tbsp grated Parmesan**

■ Heat oil in a large nonstick skillet over medium-high; add chopped onion and cook 3 minutes. Crumble in turkey and add garlic; cook 5 minutes, stirring occasionally. Stir in tomatoes, mushrooms, oregano, salt and red pepper flakes. Simmer 15 minutes, uncovered, stirring occasionally.

■ Meanwhile, cook pasta following package directions. Drain, reserving ½ cup of the pasta water.

■ Toss pasta with sauce and reserved pasta water. Spoon into a large serving bowl. Add ricotta and basil. Gently stir. Sprinkle with Parmesan and serve immediately.

PER SERVING 513 **CAL**; 12 g **FAT**; 36 g **PRO**; 64 g **CARB**; 4 g **FIBER**

Bacon Cheeseburger Soup

MAKES 6 servings **PREP** 7 minutes **COOK** 23 minutes

- 3 **slices bacon**
- 1 **lb ground sirloin**
- ½ **tsp black pepper**
- ¼ **tsp salt**
- ¾ **cup diced onion**
- ¼ **cup all-purpose flour**
- 4 **cups skim milk**
- 1 **can (14.5 oz) unsalted beef broth**
- ¼ **cup ketchup**
- 2 **tbsp yellow mustard**
- 1 **lb russet potatoes, peeled and diced**
- 8 **oz pkg shredded extra-sharp cheddar**
- 1 **medium ripe tomato, diced**
- 2 **scallions, sliced**

■ In a large stockpot, cook bacon over medium to medium-high until crisp, 5 minutes, turning occasionally. Remove to paper towels.

■ Crumble ground sirloin into pot and season with ¼ tsp of the pepper and ⅛ tsp of the salt. Brown 4 minutes, breaking apart with a wooden spoon. Remove to a bowl with a slotted spoon.

■ Reduce heat to medium. Add onion and cook 3 minutes. Sprinkle with flour and cook, stirring, 1 minute. Whisk in milk and broth. Increase heat to medium-high and whisk in ketchup, mustard and remaining ¼ tsp pepper and ⅛ tsp salt. Stir in diced potatoes and bring to a simmer. Cook 10 minutes.

■ Remove pot from heat and stir in cheese. Add ground sirloin back to pot. Divide soup among 6 bowls. Crumble bacon. Top each serving with tomato, scallions and crumbled bacon. Serve with Rainbow Slaw (recipe, page 77).

PER SERVING 497 **CAL**; 22 g **FAT**; 32 g **PRO**; 31 g **CARB**; 2 g **FIBER**

PAPPARDELLE WITH MUSHROOM AND TURKEY RAGU

Cajun Flounder with Red Beans and Rice

MAKES 4 servings **PREP** 10 minutes **COOK** 20 minutes

- **1 cup brown rice**
- **1 tbsp plus 1 tsp extra-virgin olive oil**
- **¼ cup finely diced red onion**
- **2 cloves minced garlic**
- **¾ tsp salt**
- **¼ tsp black pepper**
- **1 can (15.5 oz) small red beans, drained and rinsed**
- **4 flounder fillets (4 oz each)**
- **1 tbsp salt-free Cajun spice blend**

■ Combine rice, 2 cups water, 1 tsp of the oil, the onion, garlic, ½ tsp of the salt and the pepper in a small pot. Bring to a boil. Reduce heat to medium-low, cover and cook 20 minutes, until water is absorbed. Stir red beans into pot and set aside.

■ Meanwhile, season flounder with remaining ¼ tsp salt and the Cajun spice blend. Heat remaining 1 tbsp oil in a nonstick skillet over medium-high. Cook flounder 2 minutes; flip and cook another 1 to 2 minutes. Serve over red beans and rice with Collard Greens and Pecans.

PER SERVING 310 **CAL**; 6 g **FAT**; 10 g **PRO**; 53 g **CARB**; 9 g **FIBER**

Collard Greens and Pecans

MAKES 4 servings **PREP** 10 minutes **COOK** 7 minutes

■ Heat 1 tbsp extra-virgin olive oil in a skillet over medium-high. Add ¼ cup thinly sliced red onion; sauté 2 minutes. Stir in 1 bag (16 oz) frozen chopped collard greens, thawed, and ⅓ cup water. Cook 5 minutes, stirring frequently. Stir in ⅓ cup chopped pecans, 2 tsp cider vinegar, ½ tsp salt and ¼ tsp freshly cracked black pepper.

PER SERVING 140 **CAL**; 10 g **FAT**; 3 g **PRO**; 6 g **CARB**; 4 g **FIBER**

COLLARD GREENS AND PECANS

CAJUN FLOUNDER WITH RED BEANS AND RICE

SOUTHWESTERN
VEGGIE BOWL

TEX-MEX
SAUSAGE
AND PEPPERS
WITH FUSILLI

Southwestern Veggie Bowl

MAKES 6 servings **PREP** 10 minutes **COOK** 20 minutes **MICROWAVE** 2 minutes **LET STAND** 5 minutes

- 1 cup white rice
- 5 tbsp plus 2 tsp olive oil
- 2½ tsp chili powder
- 2 cans (15.5 oz each) black beans, drained and rinsed
- 1 tsp salt
- ½ tsp freshly ground black pepper
- 2 poblano peppers, seeded and thinly sliced
- 1½ cups frozen roasted corn, thawed
- ⅓ cup lime juice
- 2 tbsp chopped cilantro
- 2 tsp honey
- 2 pkg (8 oz each) cherry tomatoes, halved
- 1 avocado, peeled, pitted and sliced

■ Combine rice, 2 cups water, 2 tsp of the oil and 2 tsp of the chili powder in a medium saucepan. Bring to a boil, then cover and reduce heat to medium-low. Simmer 20 minutes.

Uncover and stir in beans, ½ tsp of the salt and ⅛ tsp of the pepper. Cover and let stand 5 minutes.

■ Meanwhile, heat 1 tbsp of the oil in a medium nonstick skillet over medium-high. Add poblano peppers and cook, stirring, 4 minutes. Season with ⅛ tsp salt. Microwave corn 1 to 2 minutes; season with ⅛ tsp each salt and black pepper.

■ Make dressing: In a medium bowl, whisk lime juice, cilantro, honey and remaining ½ tsp chili powder, ¼ tsp salt and ⅛ tsp black pepper. While whisking, add remaining 4 tbsp oil. Toss a few tbsp of dressing with tomatoes.

■ Spoon rice and beans into 6 bowls. Top with peppers, corn, tomatoes and avocado, dividing equally. Drizzle with dressing and serve.

PER SERVING 533 **CAL**; 19 g **FAT**; 15 g **PRO**; 79 g **CARB**; 16 g **FIBER**

Tex-Mex Sausage and Peppers with Fusilli

MAKES 6 servings **PREP** 10 minutes
COOK 15 minutes **BROIL** 2 minutes

- 1 can (14½ oz) diced tomatoes with jalapeños
- 1 pkg (12 oz) Southwest-seasoned chicken sausage, sliced into ¼-inch coins
- 1 can (15 oz) pigeon peas, drained
- 1 large sweet red pepper, seeded and sliced
- ¾ lb fusilli pasta
- 1½ cups shredded Mexican cheese blend

■ Heat broiler to high. In a large ovenproof skillet, combine tomatoes, sausage, pigeon peas and pepper. Bring to a simmer over medium-high and simmer 15 minutes, stirring occasionally.

■ Meanwhile, cook pasta following package directions. Drain, reserving ½ cup of the pasta water. Add to skillet.

■ Stir cooked fusilli and 1 cup of the cheese into skillet. Sprinkle remaining ½ cup cheese over pasta. Broil 2 minutes. Serve immediately.

PER SERVING 489 **CAL**; 17 g **FAT**; 24 g **PRO**; 58 g **CARB**; 6 g **FIBER**

VEGETARIAN FRIED RICE

Teriyaki Tofu and Soba Bowl

MAKES 6 servings **PREP** 10 minutes
COOK 12 minutes

- 1 pkg (12.8 oz) soba noodles (such as Roland)
- ¼ cup low-sodium soy sauce
- 3 tbsp rice vinegar
- 2 tbsp sugar
- 2 tsp cornstarch
- 2 tbsp vegetable oil
- 2 pkg (5.5 oz each) teriyaki baked tofu, cubed
- 3 cloves garlic, sliced
- 1 lb baby bok choy, chopped
- 1 sweet yellow pepper, thinly sliced
- 1½ cups bean sprouts
- 1½ cups edamame

■ Bring a large pot of salted water to a boil. Add soba and cook 3 minutes. Drain and rinse immediately under cold water until cool. Set aside.

■ Whisk soy sauce, vinegar, sugar, cornstarch and ¾ cup water. Heat oil in a large skillet over medium-high. Add tofu and sauté 4 minutes, turning every minute to brown. Add garlic, bok choy and pepper. Cook 3 minutes. Pour in sauce and bring to a simmer; cook 2 minutes. Using tongs, toss with sprouts, edamame and cooked soba until heated through.

PER SERVING 400 **CAL**; 7 g **FAT**; 24 g **PRO**; 61 g **CARB**; 6 g **FIBER**

Vegetarian Fried Rice

MAKES 6 servings **PREP** 10 minutes **COOK** 20 minutes

- 1½ cups brown rice
- 1 lb extra-firm tofu, cut into 1-inch cubes
- 2 tbsp cornstarch
- ¼ tsp salt
- ¼ cup vegetable oil
- 3 eggs, beaten
- 2 red or orange sweet peppers, diced
- 1 medium onion, diced
- 3 garlic cloves, sliced
- 1 pkg (5 oz) baby spinach
- ⅓ cup low-sodium soy sauce
  Sriracha and sliced scallions (optional)

■ Add brown rice and 3 cups water to a medium pot and bring to a boil. Reduce heat to medium-low, cover and cook 20 minutes, until water is absorbed. Set aside.

■ Meanwhile, toss tofu cubes with cornstarch and salt. Heat 1 tbsp of the oil in a large skillet over medium-high. Add eggs and scramble 1 minute. Remove to a plate with a slotted spoon. Pour in 2 tbsp of the remaining oil. Add tofu and cook 4 minutes, carefully stirring every minute. Remove to plate with eggs. Pour in remaining 1 tbsp oil and stir in peppers, onion and garlic. Sauté 5 minutes. Stir in spinach until wilted, 1 minute.

■ Add rice to pan. Sauté 1 minute. Stir in soy sauce, then carefully fold in eggs and tofu.

■ Serve with sriracha, scallions and more soy sauce, if desired.

PER SERVING 430 **CAL**; 18 g **FAT**; 18 g **PRO**; 49 g **CARB**; 6 g **FIBER**

TERIYAKI TOFU AND SOBA BOWL

SHEET PAN
CHICKEN

Sheet Pan Chicken

MAKES 4 servings **PREP** 10 minutes
BAKE at 450° for 30 minutes

- 4   small chicken thighs (about 1¼ lbs)
- 4   small drumsticks (about 1 lb)
- 1½ lb tricolor small new potatoes
- 2   sweet peppers, seeded and cut into large dice
- 1   onion, peeled and cut into 8 wedges
- 4   cloves garlic, peeled and smashed
- 2   tbsp olive oil
- 1   tsp salt
- 1   tsp dried Italian seasoning
- ¼   tsp black pepper
- ½   cup basil, cut into ribbons
     Lemon wedges, for squeezing

■ Heat oven to 450°. Coat a large rimmed baking sheet with nonstick cooking spray.

■ Place chicken pieces, potatoes, peppers, onion and garlic on prepared pan. Drizzle with olive oil and season with salt, Italian seasoning and black pepper.

■ Bake at 450° for 30 minutes (stir vegetables after 20 minutes) or until chicken reaches internal temperature of 165° and vegetables are tender.

■ To serve, sprinkle basil on top and squeeze with lemon wedges.

PER SERVING 500 **CAL**; 16 g **FAT**; 52 g **PRO**; 35 g **CARB**; 6 g **FIBER**

Balsamic-Glazed Pork Tenderloin

MAKES 4 servings **PREP** 7 minutes **COOK** 10 minutes **ROAST** at 425° for 15 minutes
BROIL 2 minutes **LET REST** 5 minutes

- 2   lb sweet potatoes, peeled and cut into 2-inch chunks
- ½   cup milk
- ½   cup grated Parmesan
- 1   tbsp unsalted butter
- ¾   tsp salt
- ½   cup balsamic vinegar
- 1   lb pork tenderloin
- ¼   tsp black pepper
- ¼   cup toasted chopped walnuts
     Broccoli Rabe with Prosciutto (recipe follows; optional)

■ Heat oven to 425°. In a large pot, cover sweet potatoes with 1 inch water and bring to a boil. Reduce heat to a simmer; cook 10 minutes. Drain sweet potatoes and return to pot. Mash with milk, Parmesan, butter and ¼ tsp of the salt.

■ Meanwhile, pour vinegar into a very small skillet. Bring to a boil and simmer 5 minutes or until just thickened. (Don't over-reduce or vinegar will become sticky and burn.)

■ Place pork on a foil-lined baking sheet. Season with remaining ½ tsp salt and the pepper. Roast at 425° for 15 minutes. Carefully remove from oven and increase heat to broil. Brush balsamic glaze on pork and broil 2 minutes. Let rest 5 minutes.

■ Slice pork and serve over sweet potatoes. Scatter walnuts on top and drizzle with remaining balsamic glaze. Serve with Broccoli Rabe with Prosciutto.

PER SERVING 420 **CAL**; 14 g **FAT**; 32 g **PRO**; 40 g **CARB**; 5 g **FIBER**

Broccoli Rabe with Prosciutto

MAKES 4 servings **PREP** 10 minutes
COOK 6 minutes

■ Chop 1 bunch (12 oz) broccoli rabe into 1-inch pieces, separating leaves from stems. Heat 2 tbsp extra-virgin olive oil in a large sauté pan over medium. Stir in 2 oz diced prosciutto; cook 2 minutes. Add broccoli rabe stems; sauté 2 minutes. Mix in chopped leaves; cook 2 minutes more. Stir in ⅛ tsp each salt and freshly cracked black pepper.

PER SERVING 420 **CAL**; 14 g **FAT**; 32 g **PRO**; 40 g **CARB**; 5 g **FIBER**

BALSAMIC-GLAZED PORK TENDERLOIN

BROCCOLI RABE WITH PROSCIUTTO

CURRIED CHICKEN
WITH MANGO SALSA,
PAGE 87

84

93

100

HEAVY METAL

Cooking in cast iron will rock your world.

**PORK CHOPS WITH
ROSEMARY LEMON
POTATOES**

Pork Chops with Rosemary Lemon Potatoes

MAKES 4 servings **PREP** 20 minutes
COOK 18 minutes **BAKE** at 400° for 10 minutes

- 1 **tbsp plus 2 tsp rosemary, chopped**
- 1 **tbsp lemon juice**
- 2 **cloves garlic, minced**
- 2 **tsp grated lemon zest**
- 1⅛ **tsp salt**
- ¼ **tsp black pepper**
- 4 **bone-in pork chops (about 1¾ lbs)**
- 4 **tbsp canola oil**
- 1½ **lb Yukon gold potatoes, thinly sliced**
- ¾ **lb green beans**

■ Heat oven to 400°.

■ In a small bowl, combine 1 tbsp rosemary, the lemon juice, garlic, 1 tsp lemon zest, ½ tsp salt and the pepper. Rub half the mixture onto pork chops. Heat 2 tbsp oil in a 12-inch cast-iron skillet over high. Add 2 chops and brown 2 minutes, turning once. Transfer to a plate. Repeat with remaining 2 chops.

■ Reduce heat to medium-high. Toss potatoes with remaining herb mixture and ½ tsp salt. Fan slices into pan and drizzle with 1 tbsp oil. Cook, covered with foil, 5 minutes, without stirring. If you can, flip potatoes onto a plate or flip in pan with a spatula. Pour remaining oil into pan around edges of potatoes. Cook 5 more minutes, covered.

■ Return chops to pan; carefully transfer to oven. Bake at 400° for 8 to 10 minutes.

■ Meanwhile, bring a medium saucepan of water to a boil. Add green beans and cook 4 minutes. Drain and toss with 2 tsp rosemary, 1 tsp lemon zest and ⅛ tsp salt.

PER SERVING 468 **CAL**; 22 g **FAT**; 33 g **PRO**; 38 g **CARB**; 6 g **FIBER**

BEEF POT PIE

Beef Pot Pie

MAKES 6 servings **PREP** 20 minutes **COOK** 13 minutes **BAKE** at 425° for 13 minutes

- 2 **tbsp olive oil**
- 1½ **lb sirloin, cubed**
- 1 **tbsp Worcestershire sauce**
- ¾ **tsp salt**
- ¼ **tsp black pepper**
- 1½ **lb potatoes, peeled and diced**
- 2 **large carrots, peeled and cut into ¼-inch half-moons**
- 2 **medium parsnips, peeled, cut into ¼-inch half-moons**
- 1 **small red onion, chopped**
- 3 **cloves garlic, chopped**
- 1 **can (14.5 oz) low-sodium beef broth**
- 2 **tbsp cornstarch blended with ½ cup water**
- 1 **cup frozen peas, thawed**
- 1 **refrigerated pastry crust (from a 15-oz pkg)**
- 1 **egg, beaten with 2 tbsp water**

■ Heat oven to 425°.

■ Add oil to a 3-inch-deep 10-inch or 12-inch cast-iron skillet over high. Toss sirloin with Worcestershire, ½ tsp salt and the pepper. Add to pan and brown, stirring, 2 to 3 minutes. Remove with a slotted spoon and reduce heat to medium.

■ Stir next 5 ingredients plus ¼ tsp salt into pan. Cook 5 minutes, then stir in broth. Bring to a boil and simmer 5 minutes until crisp-tender. Add cornstarch mixture, followed by beef and peas.

■ Remove from heat and top with pastry, tucking edges into pan. Brush with egg wash, cut a few vent holes in crust and bake at 425° for 13 minutes, until browned on top and bubbly.

PER SERVING 528 **CAL**; 22 g **FAT**; 28 g **PRO**; 58 g **CARB**; 6 g **FIBER**

SALMON AND VEGGIES

Hash is a versatile dish. For a classic take, stir in diced ham or corned beef to boost both protein and flavor. Or go Italian: Swap in crumbled sausage and peppers for the asparagus and zucchini.

Veggie Hash and Eggs

MAKES 4 servings **PREP** 20 minutes **COOK** 29 minutes

- 3 **tbsp olive oil**
- 1 **small onion, diced**
- 1 **lb red potatoes, rinsed and cut into ½-inch cubes**
- ¾ **tsp salt**
- 1 **bunch asparagus (1 lb), trimmed and cut into ½-inch pieces**
- 1 **lb zucchini, trimmed and cut into ½-inch pieces**
- ¼ **tsp black pepper**
- 1 **cup frozen peas, thawed**
- 2 **tsp fresh thyme or chives**
- 8 **large eggs**

■ Heat 1 tbsp oil in a 12-inch cast-iron skillet. Add onion and cook 3 minutes. Stir in potatoes, ¼ cup water and ¼ tsp salt. Cook, stirring, 10 minutes, adding ¼ cup more water halfway through.

■ Stir in asparagus, zucchini, 1 tbsp oil, ½ tsp salt and the pepper. Cook 5 minutes. Stir in peas and thyme and cook 3 minutes.

■ Meanwhile, poach eggs in simmering water (in 2 batches) 4 minutes or until desired doneness. Alternately, heat ½ tbsp oil in a large nonstick skillet. Fry 4 eggs to desired doneness and repeat. Spoon eggs over hash.

PER SERVING 398 **CAL**; 21 g **FAT**; 23 g **PRO**; 34 g **CARB**; 8 g **FIBER**

Salmon and Veggies

MAKES 4 servings **PREP** 10 minutes **COOK** 15 minutes

- 1 **cup tricolor quinoa**
- 1 **tbsp olive oil**
- 1 **lb skinless salmon fillets, thawed if frozen**
- ¾ **tsp salt**
- ½ **tsp black pepper**
- 2 **sweet yellow peppers, cored and sliced**
- 1½ **cups thinly sliced carrots**
- 3 **leeks, cleaned and sliced**
- 4 **cups packed baby spinach**
- 1 **tbsp salted butter**
- 1 **tsp lemon zest**
- 2 **tbsp fresh lemon juice (optional)**

■ Place quinoa and 2 cups water in a medium saucepan. Bring to a boil, cover and reduce heat to medium-low. Cook 15 minutes.

■ Meanwhile, heat oil in a 12-inch cast-iron skillet over high. Season salmon on both sides with ¼ tsp each salt and pepper. Add to skillet and cook 4 minutes, turning once. Remove to a plate and reduce heat under pan to medium.

■ Stir next 3 ingredients into skillet. Cook, stirring frequently, 5 minutes. Gradually add spinach, ½ tsp salt, ¼ tsp pepper, butter and lemon zest. Cook 3 minutes, until spinach is wilted. Place salmon over veggies, cover with foil and cook 2 minutes. Drizzle with lemon juice, if desired, and serve with quinoa.

PER SERVING 512 **CAL**; 18 g **FAT**; 34 g **PRO**; 55 g **CARB**; 7 g **FIBER**

VEGGIE HASH
AND EGGS

WHITE VEGGIE
LASAGNA

White Veggie Lasagna

MAKES 6 servings **PREP** 15 minutes
COOK 10 minutes **BAKE** at 375° for 45 minutes

- 1 **bunch broccoli rabe, tough stems trimmed, cut into 1-inch pieces**
- 1 **tbsp olive oil**
- 1 **pkg (10 oz) white mushrooms, sliced**
- 1 **yellow squash, grated**
- ¾ **tsp plus ⅛ tsp salt**
- ½ **tsp black pepper**
- 2 **cups 2% milk**
- 3 **tbsp all-purpose flour**
- 2 **tbsp dried parsley**
- **Pinch ground nutmeg**
- 9 **oven-ready lasagna noodles**
- 1 **container (15 oz) part-skim ricotta**
- 1 **pkg (8 oz) shredded part-skim mozzarella**
- 2 **tbsp grated Parmesan**

■ Heat oven to 375°.

■ In a 12-inch cast-iron skillet, bring 1 inch of water to a boil. Add broccoli rabe and cook 2 minutes. Drain.

■ Add olive oil to skillet and heat over medium-high. Add mushrooms and squash and season with ¼ tsp each salt and pepper. Cook 3 minutes, then add broccoli rabe and ¼ tsp salt. Cook 2 more minutes. Remove vegetables to a bowl and set skillet aside.

■ In a medium saucepan, whisk milk, flour, parsley, ¼ tsp plus ⅛ tsp salt, ¼ tsp pepper and the nutmeg. Bring to a boil over high; simmer 3 minutes, until thick.

■ Spoon ½ cup white sauce into bottom of cast-iron skillet. Top with 3 noodles, half the ricotta (about 1 cup), half the vegetables, ½ cup white sauce and 1 cup mozzarella.

Repeat with 3 noodles, remaining ricotta and vegetables, and ½ cup white sauce. Top with 3 noodles, remaining white sauce and mozzarella, and the Parmesan. Cover with foil and bake at 375° for 20 minutes. Uncover and bake 20 to 25 minutes or until knife-tender. Cool 5 minutes before serving.

PER SERVING 431 **CAL**; 19 g **FAT**; 29 g **PRO**; 39 g **CARB**; 4 g **FIBER**

Curried Chicken with Mango Salsa

MAKES 4 servings **PREP** 20 minutes
COOK 42 minutes

CHICKEN

- 2 **tsp curry powder**
- ½ **tsp salt**
- ¼ **tsp black pepper**
- 4 **small boneless, skinless chicken breast cutlets (about 1¼ lb)**
- 2 **tbsp olive oil**

RICE

- 1 **cup black japonica rice, rinsed and drained, or brown rice (see Note)**
- ¼ **tsp curry powder**
- 2 **cups reduced-sodium chicken broth**

SALSA

- 1 **cup diced mango**
- 1 **avocado, peeled, pitted and diced**
- 1 **jalapeño, seeded and minced**
- 4 **scallions, sliced**
- 1 **tbsp lime or lemon juice**
- ⅛ **tsp salt**
- ¼ **tsp black pepper**

■ **Chicken.** Combine curry powder, salt and pepper in a bowl. Rub on chicken.

■ Heat oil in a 10-inch cast-iron skillet over high. Add chicken and cook (in batches, if needed) 3 minutes. Flip over; cook 1 minute. Remove to a plate and lower heat to medium.

■ **Rice.** Carefully add rice and curry powder to pan. Pour in broth and bring to a boil. Reduce heat to medium-low and cover tightly with foil (you can top this with a sheet pan for a tighter seal, if desired). Cook 28 minutes.

■ **Salsa.** While rice cooks, gently stir mango, avocado and jalapeño in a bowl. Add half the sliced scallions, the lime juice, salt and pepper.

■ Uncover rice and sprinkle with remaining scallions. Return chicken to pan. Cover and cook 10 minutes. Spoon salsa over chicken before serving.

Note: If using brown rice, increase broth to 2½ cups and cook 10 to 15 minutes more before returning chicken to pan.

PER SERVING 506 **CAL**; 19 g **FAT**; 41 g **PRO**; 51 g **CARB**; 8 g **FIBER**

Skip the super-acidic ingredients—such as tomato sauce—when cooking in cast iron; they impart a dark color and off-flavor to your food.

CURRIED CHICKEN WITH MANGO SALSA

HAM (OR LAMB!)

Mix-and-match dishes for an easy Easter feast.

GLAZED HAM

Whether you go for a sweet glaze on a salty ham or for a savory rub on a tender leg of lamb, either dish is the essence of a spring feast.

Glazed Ham

MAKES 16 servings **PREP** 10 minutes
LET STAND 45 minutes
BAKE at 325° for 2 hours, then at 425° for 15 minutes

- 1 spiral-cut ham (about 8 lb)
- 1 recipe glaze (recipes follow)

■ Remove ham from packaging and place in a roasting pan fitted with a rack. Let stand at room temperature 45 minutes.

■ Heat oven to 325°. Pour 2 cups water in bottom of roasting pan. Cover ham tightly with foil. Bake at 325° for 2 hours.

■ Meanwhile, prepare one of the glazes.

■ Carefully remove roasting pan from oven and discard foil. Increase heat to 425°. Brush half of glaze on ham and save the rest to serve alongside. Return ham to oven and bake at 425° for 15 minutes, until glaze darkens.

Note: Spiral ham takes about 15 minutes per lb to heat.

Apricot-Mustard Glaze

- ¾ cup apricot jam
- ¼ cup Dijon mustard
- 2 tbsp apricot juice, apple juice or water

■ In a pot over medium-high, combine ingredients. Bring to a simmer; cook 2 minutes. Cover and remove from heat.

PER SERVING 270 **CAL**; 11 g **FAT**; 36 g **PRO**; 4 g **CARB**; 0 g **FIBER**

Spicy Honey Glaze

- 1 cup honey
- 2 tbsp unsalted butter
- ¾ tsp red pepper flakes

■ In a pot over medium-high, combine ingredients and 2 tbsp water. Bring to a simmer; cook 2 minutes. Cover and remove from heat.

PER SERVING 330 **CAL**; 13 g **FAT**; 36 g **PRO**; 18 g **CARB**; 0 g **FIBER**

Maple-Bourbon Glaze

- ¾ cup pure maple syrup
- ⅓ cup bourbon
- ½ tsp black pepper
- ¼ tsp salt
- 2 tbsp unsalted butter

■ In a pot over medium-high, combine ingredients. Bring to a simmer; cook 2 minutes. Cover and remove from heat.

PER SERVING 310 **CAL**; 13 g **FAT**; 36 g **PRO**; 10 g **CARB**; 0 g **FIBER**

Ras el hanout is a Moroccan spice blend containing up to 50 ingredients, including ginger, black pepper, cumin, cinnamon, cloves, cayenne and allspice.

Roasted Lamb

MAKES 8 servings **PREP** 15 minutes
LET STAND 45 minutes
ROAST at 400° for 1 hour 30 minutes
LET REST 10 minutes

- 1 **butterflied leg of lamb (about 3 lb)**
- 1 **recipe rub (recipes follow)**
- 1 **tbsp extra-virgin olive oil**

■ Pat dry lamb. Let stand at room temperature for 45 minutes.

■ Heat oven to 400°.

■ Choose one of the rubs to season lamb. Roll lamb tightly and secure with butcher's twine. Place on a baking sheet fitted with a wire rack. Brush outside of lamb with olive oil. Continue seasoning as directed in each rub recipe.

■ Roast at 400° for 1 hour 15 minutes to 1 hour 30 minutes, until temperature reaches 130° with an instant-read thermometer. Let rest 10 minutes (temperature will increase to 135°, medium-rare). Slice and serve.

Paprika–Brown Sugar Rub

- 2 **tbsp packed brown sugar**
- 1½ **tsp kosher salt**
- 1 **tsp smoked paprika**
- 1 **tsp sweet paprika**
- 1 **tsp onion powder**
- 1 **tsp garlic powder**
- ¼ **tsp cayenne pepper**

■ Rub 1 tbsp brown sugar on inside of lamb (butterflied side). In a bowl, combine 1 tbsp brown sugar with the other ingredients. Rub half on inside of lamb and half on outside.

PER SERVING 230 **CAL**; 9 g **FAT**; 30 g **PRO**; 4 g **CARB**; 0 g **FIBER**

Ras el Hanout Rub

- 4 **tsp ras el hanout (such as Frontier)**
- 1½ **tsp kosher salt**
- 1 **tsp lemon zest**

■ Combine all ingredients in a bowl. Rub half on inside of lamb (butterflied side) and half on outside.

PER SERVING 220 **CAL**; 10 g **FAT**; 16 g **PRO**; 0 g **CARB**; 0 g **FIBER**

Rosemary-Garlic Rub

- 1½ **tsp kosher salt**
- ½ **tsp black pepper**
- 3 **large cloves garlic, minced**
- 1 **tbsp chopped rosemary**

■ Season inside of lamb (butterflied side) with ½ tsp salt and ¼ tsp pepper. Sprinkle on garlic and rosemary. Season outside of lamb with 1 tsp salt and ¼ tsp pepper.

PER SERVING 210 **CAL**; 9 g **FAT**; 30 g **PRO**; 0 g **CARB**; 0 g **FIBER**

ROASTED
LAMB

ROASTED POTATOES
AND ARTICHOKES

WILD MUSHROOMS
AND SHALLOTS

Roasted Potatoes and Artichokes

MAKES 8 side-dish servings
PREP 10 minutes
ROAST at 400° for 20 minutes
COOK 8 minutes

- 1½ **lb fingerling potatoes, cut crosswise into 2-inch pieces**
- 3 **tbsp extra-virgin olive oil**
- 1 **tsp salt**
- ½ **tsp black pepper**
- 1 **small yellow onion, diced**
- 2 **boxes (10 oz each) frozen artichoke hearts, thawed**
- ½ **tsp lemon zest**
- 1 **tsp lemon juice**

■ Heat oven to 400°. On a rimmed baking sheet, toss potatoes with 1 tbsp oil, ½ tsp salt and ¼ tsp pepper. Roast at 400° for 20 minutes; turn once.

■ Meanwhile, heat 1 tbsp oil in a large skillet over medium. Add onion and cook 3 minutes. Increase heat to medium-high and stir in 1 tbsp oil and the artichokes. Cook 5 minutes, stirring a few times, until browned. Mix in lemon zest and juice, ½ tsp salt and ¼ tsp pepper. Toss artichokes with potatoes in a serving bowl.

PER SERVING 140 **CAL**; 5 g **FAT**; 3 g **PRO**; 21 g **CARB**; 5 g **FIBER**

Wild Mushrooms and Shallots

MAKES 8 side-dish servings
PREP 15 minutes **COOK** 21 minutes

- 3 **tbsp extra-virgin olive oil**
- ½ **cup sliced shallots**
- 4 **cloves garlic, sliced**
- 2 **tbsp unsalted butter**
- 1½ **lb mixed wild mushrooms, sliced**
- 1 **tsp chopped fresh thyme**
- 2 **tbsp brandy or dry sherry**
- ¾ **tsp salt**
- ¼ **tsp black pepper**

■ Heat 1 tbsp oil in a large skillet over medium heat. Stir in shallots and garlic; cook 3 minutes. Remove to a bowl.

ASPARAGUS-WHITE CHEDDAR TART

■ Increase heat to medium-high. Add butter and 2 tbsp oil. Stir in mushrooms. Cook 15 to 18 minutes, stirring occasionally, until mushrooms are browned.

■ Return shallots and garlic to pan. Add thyme. Pour in brandy, scraping bottom of pan to release any brown bits. Season with salt and pepper.

PER SERVING 60 **CAL**; 5 g **FAT**; 0 g **PRO**; 1 g **CARB**; 0 g **FIBER**

Asparagus-White Cheddar Tart

MAKES 8 servings **PREP** 10 minutes
COOK 3 minutes **BAKE** at 400° for 20 minutes

- 1 **lb asparagus, ends trimmed**
- 1 **sheet puff pastry (from a 17.3-oz box), thawed**
- 1 **egg**
- 1 **tsp Dijon mustard**
- 8 **oz shredded sharp white cheddar (2 cups)**
- 1 **tbsp extra-virgin olive oil**
  Freshly ground black pepper (optional)

■ Heat oven to 400°. Bring a pot of salted water to a boil. Add asparagus and cook 3 minutes. Drain and rinse under cold water.

■ Roll out puff pastry on a lightly floured surface to 10 x 16 inches. Place on a baking sheet. Beat egg with mustard. Brush on pastry. Bake at 400° for 12 minutes.

■ Carefully remove pastry from oven and sprinkle with 1¾ cups cheese. Top with asparagus, followed by ¼ cup cheese. Return to oven and bake 8 minutes, until pastry is browned and cheese is melted.

■ Drizzle tart with oil and, if desired, season with pepper.

PER SERVING 270 **CAL**; 20 g **FAT**; 11 g **PRO**; 13 g **CARB**; 1 g **FIBER**;

CHEESY BAKED ORZO
WITH BACON AND PEAS

Kale Soufflé

MAKES 8 servings PREP 15 minutes
COOK 2 minutes BAKE at 375° for 40 minutes

4	tbsp unsalted butter
¾	cup grated Parmesan
3	tbsp all-purpose flour
1	cup milk
10	oz frozen chopped kale, thawed, squeezed dry
½	tsp plus ⅛ tsp salt
¼	tsp nutmeg
¼	tsp black pepper
5	large eggs, separated, plus 1 large egg white
⅛	tsp cream of tartar

■ Heat oven to 400°. Spread 1 tbsp butter on bottom and sides of a 6-cup soufflé dish. Sprinkle in ¼ cup Parmesan, turning to coat completely.

■ Melt 3 tbsp butter in a small pot over medium heat. Stir in flour; cook 1 minute. Whisk in milk and bring to a simmer; cook 1 minute, until thickened. Stir in kale, ½ tsp salt, nutmeg and pepper.

■ Whisk egg yolks in a large bowl. Slowly stir in ⅓ of warm kale mixture into yolks. (Mixing too quickly could cause eggs to scramble.) Stir in remaining mixture and ½ cup Parmesan.

■ In a separate bowl, beat egg whites, cream of tartar and ⅛ tsp salt on low speed for 1 minute. Increase speed to high and beat 1 to 2 minutes, until stiff peaks form.

■ Gently fold egg whites into yolk mixture. Don't overmix or the soufflé won't rise properly.

■ Transfer to prepared dish. Place in oven and reduce heat to 375°. Bake 35 to 40 minutes, until soufflé has risen and is browned. Quickly insert an instant-read thermometer into center of soufflé; temperature should register at least 140°. Serve immediately.

PER SERVING 170 CAL; 12 g FAT; 10 g PRO; 6 g CARB; 1 g FIBER

Cheesy Baked Orzo with Bacon and Peas

MAKES 12 servings PREP 10 minutes COOK 15 minutes BAKE at 400° for 20 minutes

8	oz bacon, diced
2	cloves garlic, chopped
2	tbsp all-purpose flour
2½	cups milk
8	oz shredded Gruyère cheese
½	tsp salt
¼	tsp black pepper
1	lb orzo
1½	cups frozen peas, thawed
¼	cup grated Parmesan

■ Heat oven to 400°. Heat a large skillet over medium. Add bacon; cook 8 minutes, until crispy. Remove to a plate with a slotted spoon. Pour off all but 3 tbsp of the bacon fat. Stir in garlic; cook 1 minute. Whisk in flour; cook 1 minute. Whisk in milk, bring to a simmer and cook 5 minutes. Stir in Gruyère, salt and pepper until smooth. Set aside.

■ Meanwhile, bring a large pot of salted water to a boil. Add orzo; cook 2 minutes less than package directions. Drain. Stir into sauce with peas and cooked bacon.

■ Transfer orzo to a 2-quart baking dish. Top with Parmesan. Bake at 400° for 20 minutes, until bubbling and lightly browned.

PER SERVING 290 CAL; 9 g FAT; 17 g PRO; 34 g CARB; 2 g FIBER

KALE SOUFFLÉ

SPICE UP YOUR SEDER

Celebrate with these three kosher-for-Passover dishes with a kick.

ASPARAGUS, ZUCCHINI
AND LEEK KUGEL

MOROCCAN SPICED
SHORT RIBS

BEET AND BUTTERNUT
SQUASH SALAD

Beet and Butternut Squash Salad

MAKES 8 servings **PREP** 15 minutes
ROAST at 400° for 1 hour **COOL** 30 minutes

SALAD

- 3 medium red beets
- 3 medium golden beets
- 2 cups butternut squash, cut into 1-inch cubes
- 2 tsp extra-virgin olive oil
- 5 oz arugula (about 6 cups)
- 1 cup loosely packed fresh cilantro leaves, roughly chopped
- ⅓ cup pomegranate seeds (from 1 pomegranate), for garnish

DRESSING

- 2 tbsp extra-virgin olive oil
- 2 tsp balsamic vinegar
- 1 tsp orange zest (from 1 orange)
- 1 tsp fresh orange juice (from zested orange)
- ¼ tsp salt, plus more to taste
  Freshly ground black pepper to taste

■ Heat oven to 400°.

■ **Salad.** Trim beets, then rinse, dry and wrap each beet in aluminum foil. Place on one side of a jelly roll or roasting pan. Place butternut squash on other side of pan, drizzle with oil and toss to coat.

■ Bake at 400° for 20 minutes, until squash is fork-tender. Remove pan from oven and transfer squash to a medium bowl to cool. Return beets to oven and roast at 400° for 30 to 40 minutes, until center of beets can be pierced with a fork. Let cool on pan 30 minutes, until cool enough to handle.

■ Place arugula in a large serving bowl and toss with cilantro and squash.

■ **Dressing.** In a small bowl, whisk all ingredients until combined.

■ When beets are cool, put on gloves and unwrap golden beets. You will be able to slide peels off them. Cut beets into 1- to 1½-inch cubes and scatter over greens. Repeat with red beets; scatter over salad. Whisk dressing, drizzle over salad and toss. Scatter pomegranate seeds on top.

Moroccan Spiced Short Ribs

MAKES 6 servings **PREP** 5 minutes
MARINATE 8 hours or overnight
COOK 7 minutes per batch
BAKE at 325° for 2 hours 30 minutes

- 4 long strips (3½ to 4 lb) top rib (flanken)
- 1 tbsp light brown sugar
- 1 tbsp ground cumin
- 1 tsp ground turmeric
- 1 tsp ground thyme
- 1 tsp ground cinnamon
- ½ tsp salt
- ½ tsp black pepper, plus more to taste
- 2 tsp extra-virgin olive oil
- ¾ cup barbecue sauce
- ⅓ cup hot water

■ Place meat in a 13 x 9 x 2-inch baking pan. In a small bowl, mix brown sugar, cumin, turmeric, thyme, cinnamon, salt and ½ tsp pepper until well combined. Rub spice mix all over meat. Cover pan with plastic wrap and refrigerate at least 8 hours or overnight.

■ Heat oven to 325°. Heat oil in a large heavy frying pan over medium-high. Brown meat, in batches, on all sides, 5 to 7 minutes per batch.

■ Combine barbecue sauce and water in a small bowl; pour over meat. Season with pepper to taste. Cover pan with aluminum foil and bake at 325° for 2 hours 30 minutes. To serve, cut ribs into 3-inch pieces.

Asparagus, Zucchini and Leek Kugel

MAKES 12 to 15 servings **PREP** 30 minutes
COOK 7 minutes **COOL** 15 minutes
BAKE at 375° for 45 minutes

- 3 tbsp vegetable oil
- 1 leek, white and light green parts only, halved and cut into ¼-inch-thick slices
- 1 medium onion, cut in half and thinly sliced
- 3 cloves garlic, crushed
- 1 bunch (1 lb) asparagus (choose thicker stalks), trimmed, halved lengthwise and cut into thirds
- 1 medium zucchini, not peeled, shredded on the large holes of a box grater (about 2 cups)
- 1 cup spinach leaves, stacked and sliced into ⅓-inch-thick ribbons
- 2 scallions, cut into ¼-inch-thick slices
- 1 tbsp slivered fresh basil leaves
- 3 large eggs, lightly beaten
- ¼ cup matzoh meal
- ¼ tsp salt, plus more to taste
  Freshly ground black pepper to taste

■ Heat oven to 375°. Heat 2 tbsp oil in a large frying pan over medium. Add leek and onion; cook 3 minutes. Add garlic and asparagus; cook 4 minutes. Turn off heat. Add zucchini, spinach and scallions and stir to combine. Scoop into a large bowl and let cool 15 minutes.

■ Add basil, eggs, matzoh meal, salt and pepper; stir to combine. Grease a 13 x 9 x 2-inch baking dish with 1 tbsp oil. Scoop batter into baking dish and spread evenly. Bake kugel at 375° for 45 minutes or until browned on top.

SUPPER SAVINGS

Tuck into ten $10 dinners you can really bank on.

BLACK BEAN
AND CHEESE
QUESADILLAS

Black Bean and Cheese Quesadillas

MAKES 4 servings **PREP** 15 minutes
COOK 4 minutes **BAKE** at 350° for 3 minutes
BROIL 2 minutes

- ½ **cup chopped onion**
- 1 **tbsp vegetable oil**
- 1 **pkg (10 oz) frozen corn, thawed**
- 1 **pkg (10 oz) frozen chopped spinach, thawed**
- 1 **can (15.5 oz) black beans, drained and rinsed**
- 1½ **tsp chili powder**
- ¾ **tsp cumin**
- ¼ **tsp salt**
- ⅛ **tsp black pepper**
- 4 **burrito-size flour tortillas**
- 1½ **cups shredded Mexican-blend cheese**
- ½ **cup sour cream**
  Spanish Rice (recipe follows; optional)

■ Heat oven to 350°. In a large skillet, cook onion in oil 3 minutes. Add corn and spinach. Stir in beans, chili powder, cumin, salt and pepper. Heat through, mashing beans slightly. On one half of each of the flour tortillas, layer 3 tbsp cheese, ¼ of the bean mixture and 3 tbsp more cheese. Fold in half and place on a baking sheet. Bake at 350° for 3 minutes. Broil 1 minute; flip and broil until crisp. Cut into wedges. Serve with sour cream and Spanish Rice, if desired.

PER SERVING 516 **CAL**; 24 g **FAT**; 23 g **PRO**; 53 g **CARB**; 10 g **FIBER**

Spanish Rice

■ In a saucepan, cook ½ cup chopped onion in 1 tbsp olive oil 3 minutes. Add 1 cup white rice, 2 cups chicken broth, 1 can (8 oz) tomato sauce, ¼ tsp each garlic salt and cumin and ⅛ tsp black pepper. Simmer, covered, 15 minutes.

QUICK-FIX POTATO SALAD

SOUTHWEST TURKEY BURGERS

Southwest Turkey Burgers

MAKES 4 servings **PREP** 15 minutes **COOK** 6 minutes

- 1 **lb ground turkey**
- ¼ **cup bread crumbs**
- ¼ **cup milk**
- ½ **cup salsa**
- 1¼ **tsp chili powder**
- 1 **tsp cumin**
- ½ **tsp salt**
- ¼ **tsp black pepper**
- 4 **slices pepper Jack cheese**
- ¼ **cup mayonnaise**
- 4 **hamburger rolls, toasted**
  Lettuce
  Quick-Fix Potato Salad (recipe follows; optional)

■ In a large bowl, combine turkey, bread crumbs, milk, ¼ cup salsa, 1 tsp chili powder, cumin, salt and pepper. Form into 4 patties. Cook 3 minutes; turn, add 1 slice cheese to each and cook 3 additional minutes. Combine mayonnaise, ¼ cup salsa and ¼ tsp chili powder. Serve burgers on toasted hamburger rolls with lettuce and salsa mayonnaise. Serve with Quick-Fix Potato Salad, if desired.

PER SERVING 466 **CAL**; 25 g **FAT**; 31 g **PRO**; 31 g **CARB**; 2 g **FIBER**

Quick-Fix Potato Salad

■ Cut 2¼ lb potatoes into ½-inch pieces; add to a large pot of lightly salted water and cook 10 minutes. Drain. In a large bowl, whisk 2 tbsp olive oil, 1 tbsp white vinegar, ½ tsp each salt and sugar and ¼ tsp black pepper. Stir in ½ cup each sliced celery rib and pimiento. Gently fold in potatoes.

ROPA VIEJA

Spinach and Sausage Pie

MAKES 6 servings **PREP** 15 minutes
COOK 7 minutes **BAKE** at 350° for 1 hour
20 minutes

Piecrust

½ **lb crumbled sweet Italian sausage**

10 **oz chopped frozen spinach, thawed**

2 **cups shredded mozzarella**

½ **lb seeded and diced plum tomatoes**

6 **eggs**

½ **cup milk**

½ **tsp salt**

½ **tsp onion powder**

½ **tsp dried oregano**

¼ **tsp black pepper**

Tossed Salad with Apricots and Almonds (recipe follows; optional)

■ Heat oven to 350°. Fit a prepared piecrust into a 9-inch pie plate and line with foil, pressing down. Bake at 350° for 10 minutes. Remove foil and bake 10 minutes. In a skillet, sauté sausage 5 minutes; stir in spinach, and cook 2 minutes. Spread 1 cup mozzarella over crust; add sausage mixture and tomatoes. Sprinkle 1 cup mozzarella over tomatoes. Whisk eggs, milk, salt, onion powder, oregano and pepper. Pour over pie and bake at 350° for 1 hour. Serve with Tossed Salad with Apricots and Almonds if desired.

Tip: For a Tex-Mex take on the pie, substitute spicy jalapeño sausage for the sweet Italian and shredded taco-blend cheese for the mozzarella. Add a pinch of chili powder to the egg mixture.

PER SERVING 418 **CAL**; 27 g **FAT**; 23 g **PRO**;
23 g **CARB**; 2 g **FIBER**

Tossed Salad with Apricots and Almonds

■ In a bowl, whisk 2 tbsp each olive oil and white wine vinegar, ½ tsp Dijon mustard, ¼ tsp salt and ⅛ tsp black pepper. Toss with 8 cups salad greens and ⅓ cup each sliced dried apricots and sliced almonds.

Ropa Vieja

MAKES 6 servings **PREP** 15 minutes **SLOW COOK** on HIGH for 5 hours or LOW for 8 hours

2 **lb boneless, skinless chicken thighs**

½ **tsp salt**

1 **can (28 oz) fire-roasted diced tomatoes**

4 **chopped garlic cloves**

2 **tbsp cider vinegar**

2 **tsp cumin**

⅛ **tsp cayenne pepper**

3 **seeded and sliced green or red sweet peppers**

1 **large sliced onion**

¼ **cup chopped pitted green olives**

¼ **cup chopped cilantro**

3 **cups cooked brown rice**

Lime wedges

■ Add chicken thighs to a 5-qt slow cooker and season with salt. Combine tomatoes, garlic, vinegar, cumin and cayenne; pour over chicken. Add peppers and onion. Cover and cook on HIGH for 5 hours or LOW for 8 hours. Add olives during last 30 minutes. Shred chicken and stir in cilantro. Serve with brown rice and lime for squeezing.

PER SERVING 373 **CAL**; 11 g **FAT**; 30 g **PRO**;
35 g **CARB**; 5 g **FIBER**

SPINACH AND
SAUSAGE PIE

TOSSED SALAD
WITH APRICOTS
AND ALMONDS

ROASTED ZUCCHINI AND TOMATOES

CHICKEN AND BACON STUFFED POTATOES

Make it old-school: Replace shrimp with cubed boneless chicken and use 2 tsp poultry seasoning instead of curry powder.

Curried Rice and Shrimp

MAKES 4 servings **PREP** 15 minutes
COOK 4 minutes **BAKE** at 350° for 50 minutes

2	tbsp butter
1	cup white rice
2	chopped scallions
3	chopped garlic cloves
1	tbsp curry powder
2	cups vegetable broth
1	pkg (10 oz) frozen peas, thawed
1	pkg (10 oz) frozen broccoli, thawed
¼	tsp salt
¼	tsp black pepper
½	lb shrimp
	Lemon

■ Heat oven to 350°. Heat butter in a large skillet. Add rice, scallions and garlic; cook 3 minutes. Stir in curry powder and cook 1 minute. Add broth, peas, broccoli, salt and pepper. Bring to a simmer. Add to a large casserole and bake at 350°, covered, for 35 minutes. Add shrimp and bake, covered, an additional 15 minutes. Squeeze lemon over shrimp.

PER SERVING 358 **CAL**; 7 g **FAT**; 19 g **PRO**; 53 g **CARB**; 7 g **FIBER**

Chicken and Bacon Stuffed Potatoes

MAKES 4 servings **PREP** 15 minutes **BAKE** at 400° for 1 hour 10 minutes

4	large potatoes
1	cup milk
4	oz cream cheese
2	oz crumbled feta
2	chopped scallions
½	tsp salt
½	tsp dried oregano
¼	tsp black pepper
2½	cups diced cooked chicken
8	slices chopped cooked bacon

■ Heat oven to 400°. Bake potatoes at 400° for 50 minutes or until tender. Cut in half lengthwise and spoon flesh into a bowl. Mash with milk, cream cheese, 1 oz feta, scallions, salt, oregano and pepper. Stir in chicken and half of bacon. Fill each potato skin with an equal amount of potato and chicken mixture. Top each with 1 oz feta and remaining bacon. Bake at 400° for 20 minutes. Serve with Roasted Zucchini and Tomatoes, if desired.

PER SERVING 549 **CAL**; 23 g **FAT**; 41 g **PRO**; 46 g **CARB**; 3 g **FIBER**

Roasted Zucchini and Tomatoes

■ Heat oven to 400°. Cut 1½ lb zucchini into 1½-inch pieces and 1 lb plum tomatoes into quarters. Place on a greased rimmed baking sheet; toss with 3 sliced garlic cloves, 2 tbsp olive oil, ½ tsp each salt and dried Italian seasoning and ¼ tsp black pepper. Roast at 400° for 30 minutes, turning once.

CURRIED RICE
AND SHRIMP

EASY MANICOTTI

SAUTÉED
ESCAROLE

Easy Manicotti

MAKES 6 servings **PREP** 25 minutes
COOK 8 minutes **BAKE** at 400° for 40 minutes

- 1 box (8 oz) manicotti shells
- 1 container (16 oz) reduced-fat ricotta
- 1 pkg (10 oz) frozen spinach, thawed
- 1½ cups shredded mozzarella
- ⅓ cup grated Parmesan plus 2 tbsp
- 2 eggs, lightly beaten
- ½ cup chopped basil
- ¼ tsp salt
- ¼ tsp black pepper
- ¼ tsp nutmeg
- ⅛ tsp cayenne
- 3 cups marinara sauce
- ½ cup water

■ Heat oven to 400°. Cook manicotti shells following package directions (about 8 minutes). In a large bowl, combine ricotta, spinach, ½ cup mozzarella, ⅓ cup Parmesan, eggs, basil, salt, pepper, nutmeg and cayenne. Combine marinara sauce and water; spread ½ cup in bottom of a 13 x 9 x 2-inch baking dish. Fill manicotti shells with ricotta mixture and place in baking dish. Spoon remaining marinara over top; sprinkle with 1 cup mozzarella and 2 tbsp Parmesan. Cover and bake at 400° for 30 minutes. Uncover and bake 10 minutes more. Serve with Sautéed Escarole, if desired.

PER SERVING 501 **CAL**; 19 g **FAT**; 31 g **PRO**; 52 g **CARB**; 5 g **FIBER**

Sautéed Escarole

■ In a large skillet, heat 2 tbsp olive oil; add ½ sliced onion and 2 sliced garlic cloves. Cook 3 minutes. Stir in 1 head chopped escarole. Season with salt and red pepper. Cook 6 minutes.

QUICK CASSOULET

Quick Cassoulet

MAKES 4 servings **PREP** 15 minutes **COOK** 10 minutes **BAKE** at 350° for 20 minutes

- 1 tbsp vegetable oil
- ½ lb kielbasa, cut into ½-inch pieces
- 3 cups diced celery
- 1 cup diced carrot
- 1 cup chopped onion
- 4 chopped garlic cloves
- 1 lb thick-cut boneless pork chops, cut into 1-inch pieces
- 1 can (15.5 oz) drained white beans
- 1 can (15.5 oz) drained pink beans
- 1½ cups reduced-sodium beef broth
- ¼ cup tomato paste
- 1 tsp dried thyme
- 1 tbsp bread crumbs

■ Heat oven to 350°. Heat oil in a large skillet. Add kielbasa, celery, carrot, onion and garlic. Cook over medium-high 7 minutes. Add pork chops and cook 3 minutes. Stir in white beans, pink beans, broth, tomato paste and thyme. Simmer 2 minutes. Spoon into a large casserole and sprinkle bread crumbs on top. Bake at 350° for 20 minutes.

PER SERVING 605 **CAL**; 26 g **FAT**; 42 g **PRO**; 52 g **CARB**; 15 g **FIBER**

MISO-ROASTED
ASPARAGUS,
PAGE 114

MAY

113

119

128

GET FRESH

Artichokes. Peas. Asparagus. A field guide to what's best right now.

GRILLED CHICKEN AND
BABY ARTICHOKES

After months of hearty and warming winter food, the light and fresh green foods of spring are a welcome break.

Grilled Chicken and Baby Artichokes

MAKES 4 servings **PREP** 25 minutes
MARINATE 30 minutes **GRILL** 35 minutes

- 1 **chicken, cut into 8 pieces**
- ⅓ **cup extra-virgin olive oil, plus more for drizzling**
- ⅓ **cup fresh lemon juice, plus more for drizzling**
- ¼ **cup chopped parsley**
- 2 **tsp lemon zest**
- 1 **tsp salt**
- ½ **tsp black pepper**
- 12 **baby artichokes**

■ Pat chicken dry and place in a large resealable plastic bag. Whisk olive oil, lemon juice, parsley, lemon zest, ½ tsp salt and the pepper. Pour half over chicken, making sure to coat each piece. Seal and marinate 30 minutes at room temperature.

■ Meanwhile, heat grill or grill pan to medium. Trim stems and cut off top third of artichokes; peel off several layers of leaves until light-green part is visible. Slice in half and toss in remaining marinade.

■ Grill artichokes over medium heat 8 to 10 minutes, flipping once, until tender. Grill chicken 20 to 25 minutes, flipping once, until it reaches 165° on an instant-read thermometer.

■ Season chicken and artichokes with ½ tsp salt. If desired, drizzle with more olive oil and lemon juice.

PER SERVING 380 **CAL**; 23 g **FAT**; 36 g **PRO**; 6 g **CARB**; 3 g **FIBER**

SPRING PEA TART

Spring Pea Tart

MAKES 8 side-dish servings **PREP** 15 minutes **COOK** 2 minutes **BAKE** at 400° for 47 minutes

- 1 **refrigerated piecrust**
- 2 **cups shelled English peas**
- 1 **container (15 oz) ricotta**
- 3 **eggs**
- ¼ **cup plus 2 tbsp grated pecorino cheese**
- ¾ **tsp salt**
- ¼ **tsp black pepper**
- ¼ **cup finely chopped chives**

■ Heat oven to 400°. Roll out piecrust on a lightly floured surface and fit into a 10-inch tart pan with a removable bottom. Pierce crust all over with a fork. Place a piece of parchment paper over crust and fill with dried beans or pie weights. Bake at 400° for 12 minutes. Carefully remove beans or weights and paper.

■ Meanwhile, blanch peas by cooking them in salted water 2 minutes and rinsing under cold water.

■ Using a hand mixer, beat ricotta, eggs, ¼ cup pecorino, salt and pepper for 1 minute. Fold in peas and chives. Transfer to crust, smoothing top. Sprinkle with 2 tbsp pecorino. Bake at 400° for 30 to 35 minutes, until set.

PER SERVING 270 **CAL**; 16 g **FAT**; 13 g **PRO**; 18 g **CARB**; 2 g **FIBER**

ARTICHOKE COUSCOUS

Ocean Mist Farms—the largest grower of fresh artichokes in the U.S.— suggests slicing off a dime-size portion of each stem and dunking ends in water, then storing artichokes in an airtight container in the fridge up to a week

Artichoke Couscous

MAKES 8 side-dish servings **PREP** 25 minutes
COOK 15 minutes

- **2 cups Israeli couscous**
- **¼ cup plus 1 tsp extra-virgin olive oil**
- **16 baby artichokes**
- **¼ cup minced red onion**
- **2 cloves garlic, minced**
- **2 tbsp red wine vinegar**
- **2 tbsp honey**
- **½ tsp salt**
- **½ tsp black pepper**
- **1 can (14.5 oz) cannellini beans, drained and rinsed**
- **⅔ cup crumbled feta cheese**
- **½ cup fresh mint, chopped**

- Bring a pot of lightly salted water to a boil. Add couscous and 1 tsp oil. Cook 8 minutes. Drain and set aside.

- Trim stems and cut off top third of artichokes; peel off several layers of leaves until light-green part is visible, then quarter. Heat 2 tbsp oil in a large skillet over medium-high. Add artichokes and cook 5 minutes. Stir in onion and garlic; cook 2 minutes.

- Whisk 2 tbsp oil, the vinegar, honey, salt and pepper. Stir in couscous, cooked artichokes, beans, feta and mint.

PER SERVING 300 **CAL**; 10 g **FAT**; 9 g **PRO**; 43 g **CARB**; 6 g **FIBER**

STUFFED ARTICHOKES

Stuffed Artichokes

MAKES 8 appetizer servings **PREP** 15 minutes **COOK** 25 minutes **BAKE** at 400° for 20 minutes

- **2 tbsp lemon juice**
- **4 globe artichokes**
- **1⅓ cups plain bread crumbs**
- **1 cup shredded Asiago cheese**
- **½ cup parsley, chopped**
- **⅓ cup extra-virgin olive oil**
- **4 cloves garlic, minced**
- **1 tbsp chopped thyme**
- **½ tsp salt**
- **½ tsp black pepper**

- Bring a pot of lightly salted water and lemon juice to a boil. Trim stems and cut off top third of artichokes.

Add artichokes to pot and boil 25 minutes. Remove artichokes with a slotted spoon and rinse under cold water. Turn upside down onto paper towels and let drain 5 minutes.

- Meanwhile, heat oven to 400°. To prepare stuffing, combine all remaining ingredients.

- Place drained artichokes in a small baking dish. Divide stuffing evenly among artichokes, filling between leaves. Bake at 400° for 15 to 20 minutes, until golden.

PER SERVING 240 **CAL**; 15 g **FAT**; 8 g **PRO**; 22 g **CARB**; 6 g **FIBER**

GNOCCHI, PEAS AND PROSCIUTTO

SMASHED PEAS WITH HALIBUT

Gnocchi, Peas and Prosciutto

MAKES 4 servings **PREP** 10 minutes **COOK** 8 minutes

- 1 tbsp extra-virgin olive oil
- 3 oz prosciutto, chopped
- 1 cup heavy cream
- ¼ cup shredded Parmesan, plus more for serving
- ¼ tsp salt
- ¼ tsp black pepper
- 1 pkg (17.5 oz) gnocchi
- 1½ cups shelled English peas

■ Bring a pot of lightly salted water to a boil.

■ Heat oil in a large skillet over medium. Add prosciutto and cook 3 to 5 minutes, until crispy. Add heavy cream, bring to a simmer and cook 1 minute, until slightly thickened. Stir in Parmesan, salt and pepper.

■ Add gnocchi and peas to water; cook 2 minutes. Drain and add to cream sauce. Return to a simmer and toss to coat. Sprinkle with Parmesan.

PER SERVING 530 **CAL**; 30 g **FAT**; 16 g **PRO**; 52 g **CARB**; 5 g **FIBER**

Smashed Peas with Halibut

MAKES 4 servings **PREP** 10 minutes **COOK** 12 minutes

- 1 lb (3 cups) shelled English peas
- 3 tbsp extra-virgin olive oil
- 1 small shallot, minced
- ¼ cup packed basil leaves
- 2 tbsp unsalted butter
- 1 tsp salt
- ¼ tsp plus ⅛ tsp black pepper
- 4 halibut fillets (4 oz each)

■ Combine peas and ¼ cup water in a skillet. Simmer 2 minutes. Add 1 tbsp oil and shallot; cook 2 minutes. Transfer to a food processor with basil and blend until well combined but still has texture. Return to skillet and stir in butter, ½ tsp salt and ¼ tsp pepper.

■ Heat 2 tbsp oil in a large skillet over medium-high. Season halibut with ½ tsp salt and ⅛ tsp pepper. Add to skillet, skin sides up. Cook 4 minutes; flip and cook 3 to 4 minutes. Serve over peas.

PER SERVING 340 **CAL**; 18 g **FAT**; 27 g **PRO**; 18 g **CARB**; 6 g **FIBER**

Miso-Roasted Asparagus

MAKES 4 servings **PREP** 10 minutes **ROAST** at 400° for 15 minutes

- 1 tbsp red miso paste
- 1 tbsp extra-virgin olive oil
- 1 tsp sesame oil
- 1 tbsp rice vinegar
- 1 lb asparagus, trimmed
- 1 tsp toasted sesame seeds

■ Heat oven to 400°. Whisk miso paste, oils and vinegar in a bowl and toss with asparagus.

■ Spread on a baking sheet. Roast at 400° for 10 minutes, then flip and roast 5 minutes. Toss with sesame seeds.

PER SERVING 60 **CAL**; 5 g **FAT**; 2 g **PRO**; 4 g **CARB**; 2 g **FIBER**

ASPARAGUS–GOAT CHEESE FLATBREAD

Korean Beef, Asparagus and Tofu

MAKES 4 servings **PREP** 15 minutes
COOK 9 minutes

- 2 **tbsp gochujang (Korean hot chile paste, such as Annie Chun's)**
- 2 **tbsp low-sodium soy sauce**
- 2 **tbsp rice vinegar**
- 1 **tsp cornstarch**
- 2 **tbsp extra-virgin olive oil**
- 3 **cloves garlic, sliced**
- ½ **lb skirt steak, sliced into strips**
- 7 **oz extra-firm tofu, cut into ½ x 2-inch strips**
- 1 **lb asparagus, trimmed and cut on the bias into ½-inch pieces**
- 4 **cups cooked jasmine rice**

■ Whisk ¼ cup water with gochujang, soy sauce, vinegar and cornstarch until smooth.

■ Heat 1 tbsp oil in a large nonstick skillet over medium-high. Stir in garlic and steak; cook 2 minutes. Remove to a plate with a slotted spoon.

■ Add 1 tbsp oil. Stir in tofu. Cook 4 minutes to brown, stirring a few times. Add asparagus and cook 2 minutes.

■ Pour in sauce, bring to a simmer and cook 1 minute. Stir in beef. Serve over rice.

PER SERVING 400 **CAL**; 10 g **FAT**; 13 g **PRO**; 64 g **CARB**; 4 g **FIBER**

Asparagus–Goat Cheese Flatbread

MAKES 8 side-dish servings **PREP** 20 minutes **LET STAND** 30 minutes **BAKE** at 450° for 12 minutes

- 2 **tbsp extra-virgin olive oil, plus more for coating**
- 8 **oz refrigerated pizza dough**
- 1 **lb asparagus, trimmed**
- ¼ **cup chopped pitted Kalamata olives**
- ¼ **cup toasted sliced almonds**
- 1 **tbsp fresh lemon juice**
- ¼ **tsp salt**
- ¼ **tsp black pepper**
- 4 **oz soft herb goat cheese**
- 2 **tbsp milk**

■ Heat oven to 450°. Coat a bowl with a bit of oil. Place dough in bowl and cover with plastic wrap. Let stand at room temperature 30 minutes.

■ Meanwhile, slice asparagus into long strips with a vegetable peeler, holding on to tip of spear. Toss strips, tips, olives and almonds with 1 tbsp oil, lemon juice, salt and pepper.

■ Lightly coat a baking sheet with oil. Form dough into an 8 x 12-inch oval, place on sheet and pierce all over with a fork. Bake at 450° for 10 to 12 minutes, until lightly browned. (Keep an eye on dough; pierce again if it puffs too much.)

■ Using a hand mixer, beat goat cheese with milk 1 minute, until well combined. Spread on flatbread and top with asparagus mixture. Drizzle with 1 tbsp oil.

PER SERVING 190 **CAL**; 11 g **FAT**; 6 g **PRO**; 15 g **CARB**; 2 g **FIBER**

KOREAN BEEF, ASPARAGUS AND TOFU

HEALTHY FAMILY DINNERS

10 easy meals for crazy-busy weeknights.

TOMATILLO CHICKEN
TOSTADAS, PAGE 117

For the flavor of tacos al pastor—a popular Mexican street food— swap ground pork for chicken and finely diced pineapple for the shredded cheese in the Tomatillo Chicken Tostadas.

MINI GYRO BURGERS WITH CUCUMBER-FETA SALAD

Mini Gyro Burgers with Cucumber-Feta Salad

MAKES 4 servings **PREP** 15 minutes
BROIL 6 minutes

- 2 medium peeled, sliced cucumbers
- ¼ cup crumbled seasoned feta
- ¼ cup mint leaves, plus more for garnish
- 1 tbsp olive oil
- 1 tbsp red wine vinegar
- ½ lb ground lamb
- ½ lb lean ground beef
- ¼ cup chopped mint
- ½ tsp dried oregano
- ½ tsp onion powder
-    Salt
- ¼ tsp black pepper
- 8 4-inch pitas
-    Sliced plum tomatoes

■ In a large bowl, combine the first five ingredients. In a medium bowl, combine the next the next seven ingredients. Flatten into 8 patties. Broil 3 minutes per side. Serve in pitas with tomatoes and extra mint leaves. Accompany with cucumber salad.

PER SERVING 470 **CAL**; 24 g **FAT**; 29 g **PRO**; 36 g **CARB**; 3 g **FIBER**

Tomatillo Chicken Tostadas

MAKES 4 servings **PREP** 15 minutes **BAKE** at 350° for 15 minutes **COOK** 10 minutes

- 8 corn tortillas
- 1 tbsp canola oil
- 1 cup chopped red onion
- 1 lb ground chicken
- 1½ cups tomatillo salsa
- ¾ cup shredded taco cheese blend
-    Shredded lettuce
-    Chopped tomato

■ Heat oven to 350°. Place tortillas on a large baking sheet and coat with nonstick cooking spray. Bake at 350° for 15 minutes. Meanwhile, heat oil in a large nonstick skillet over medium-high; add onion and cook 3 minutes. Crumble in chicken; cook 5 minutes, until no longer pink. Stir in salsa; cook 2 minutes, until liquid evaporates. Top tortillas with chicken mixture, cheese, lettuce and tomato.

PER SERVING 430 **CAL**; 22 g **FAT**; 24 g **PRO**; 34 g **CARB**; 5 g **FIBER**

VEGETABLE KORMA

For Meatless Mondays or beyond, try one of these vegetarian dishes inspired by Indian and Mediterranean cuisines.

Fire-Roasted Ratatouille with Linguine

MAKES 4 servings **PREP** 20 minutes
GRILL 16 minutes

- 2 small eggplants
- 2 medium zucchini
- 6 plum tomatoes
- 1 red onion
- 2 sweet red peppers
- 4 tbsp olive oil
- ¾ tsp salt
- ½ tsp black pepper
- ½ lb cooked spinach linguine
- 1 cup sliced basil
- ¼ cup white balsamic vinegar
- 1 can (15 oz) warm drained butter beans

■ Cut eggplants and zucchini into ¼-inch planks. Halve tomatoes. Cut onion into wedges and red peppers into large strips. Brush veggies with 3 tbsp oil; season with salt and pepper. Grill in 2 batches, 4 minutes per side. Coarsely chop veggies and stir into linguine. Add basil, vinegar and beans. Drizzle with 1 tbsp oil.

PER SERVING 462 **CAL**; 12 g **FAT**; 17 g **PRO**; 77 g **CARB**; 12 g **FIBER**

Vegetable Korma

MAKES 4 servings **PREP** 15 minutes **COOK** 18 minutes

- 2 tbsp vegetable oil
- 2 sliced onions
- 2 tbsp chopped ginger
- 4 tsp curry powder
- 1 can (15.5 oz) diced tomatoes
- 6 cups cauliflower florets
- ½ cup yellow lentils
- ¾ tsp salt
- 1 cup hot water
- 1 bag (6 oz) baby spinach
- 1 can (15.5 oz) drained chickpeas
- 1 cup plain Greek yogurt
- ½ cup chopped honey-roasted almonds
- Basmati rice and naan (optional)

■ Heat oil in a large pot over medium. Add onions and ginger; cook 3 minutes. Stir in the next six ingredients. Simmer, covered, 15 minutes, stirring occasionally. Stir in spinach until wilted, then chickpeas and yogurt. Top with almonds. Serve with basmati rice and naan, if desired.

PER SERVING 483 **CAL**; 20 g **FAT**; 25 g **PRO**; 58 g **CARB**; 18 g **FIBER**

FIRE-ROASTED
RATATOUILLE WITH
LINGUINE

HONEY SOY SALMON
WITH CUMIN-INFUSED
POTATOES

ROTINI WITH SAUSAGE, CHARD AND PINE NUTS

Don't toss those Swiss chard stems. Cook the stalks like asparagus— they're especially delicious when roasted.

Honey Soy Salmon with Cumin-Infused Potatoes

MAKES 4 servings **PREP** 15 minutes
COOK 13 minutes **ROAST** at 450° for 15 minutes

- 2 tbsp reduced-sodium soy sauce
- 2 tbsp honey
- 2 cloves chopped garlic
- 4 salmon fillets (5 oz each)
- 1 tbsp vegetable oil
- ¾ tsp cumin seeds
- 1½ lb peeled Yukon gold potatoes, cut into ½-inch cubes
- ½ tsp salt
- ¼ tsp black pepper
- Steamed green beans (optional)

■ In a shallow dish, combine the first four ingredients. Place fillets, skin sides up, in dish. In a large nonstick skillet, heat oil over medium-high; add cumin and cook 1 minute. Stir in potatoes, salt, pepper and ¼ cup water. Cook 12 minutes, stirring frequently, until tender. Add 1 tbsp of water as needed. Turn salmon over and place dish in oven. Roast at 450° for 12 to 15 minutes, basting a few times, until fish is cooked through. Serve with steamed green beans, if desired.

PER SERVING 432 **CAL**; 14 g **FAT**; 36 g **PRO**; 42 g **CARB**; 4 g **FIBER**

Rotini with Sausage, Chard and Pine Nuts

MAKES 6 servings **PREP** 10 minutes **COOK** 9 minutes

- 1 tbsp olive oil
- 1 lb turkey sausage
- 3 cloves sliced garlic
- 1 lb trimmed and sliced rainbow chard
- ½ cup golden raisins
- ¼ cup toasted pine nuts
- ¼ tsp salt
- ¼ tsp black pepper
- 1 lb rotini
- ½ cup grated Parmesan

■ Heat oil in a large nonstick skillet over medium-high; crumble in sausage and garlic. Cook 6 minutes, stirring occasionally. Add chard and cook 3 minutes. Stir in raisins, nuts and salt and pepper. Meanwhile, cook rotini following package directions. Drain and reserve 1 cup cooking water. Toss pasta with sausage mixture and enough reserved water to create a sauce. Stir in Parmesan.

PER SERVING 493 **CAL**; 14 g **FAT**; 25 g **PRO**; 66 g **CARB**; 4 g **FIBER**

PORK AND PEACH-CHERRY-CHIPOTLE CHUTNEY

Pork and Peach-Cherry-Chipotle Chutney

MAKES 4 servings **PREP** 15 minutes **COOK** 15 minutes

- 4 **tbsp olive oil**
- ½ **chopped onion**
- 2 **cups chopped thawed frozen peaches**
- 1 **cup thawed frozen cherries**
- 2 **tbsp red wine vinegar**
- 2 **tbsp brown sugar**
- ½ **tsp chipotle chile powder**
- ¾ **tsp salt plus a pinch**
- 1 **lb thinly sliced boneless pork chops**
- ¼ **tsp black pepper**
  Flour
- 3 **cups cooked red quinoa**

■ Heat 1 tbsp oil in a large nonstick skillet over medium. Add onion; cook 5 minutes. Add the next five ingredients and a pinch of salt. Cook 10 minutes, stirring often. Meanwhile, season chops with ¾ tsp salt and pepper. Lightly coat with flour. Heat 3 tbsp oil in a large nonstick skillet over medium-high. Cook chops 3 minutes per side. Serve with chutney and quinoa.

PER SERVING 476 **CAL**; 15 g **FAT**; 31 g **PRO**; 55 g **CARB**; 7 g **FIBER**

One good skillet can turn out a multitude of wonderful meals.

Chicken with White Beans and Rosemary

MAKES 4 servings **PREP** 15 minutes
BAKE at 375° for 20 minutes **COOK** 14 minutes

- 2 **lb skinless bone-in chicken thighs**
- ¼ **tsp salt**
  Black pepper
- 1 **tbsp olive oil**
- 4 **slices chopped bacon**
- 4 **cloves sliced garlic**
- 1 **sprig rosemary**
- 1 **cup reduced-sodium chicken broth**
- 2 **cans (15.5 oz each) drained white beans**
- 2 **tbsp chopped parsley**

■ Heat oven to 375°. Season thighs with salt and pepper. Heat oil in a large skillet over medium-high. Add chicken; cook 4 minutes per side. Place on a baking sheet; bake at 375° for 20 minutes. Add bacon to skillet; cook 5 minutes, until crisp. Stir in garlic and rosemary; cook 1 minute. Pour in broth, white beans and parsley. Return chicken to skillet. Serve with sautéed spinach.

PER SERVING 429 **CAL**; 23 g **FAT**; 42 g **PRO**; 18 g **CARB**; 5 g **FIBER**

CHICKEN WITH WHITE
BEANS AND ROSEMARY

FAR EAST FARE

Throw your slow cooker an exotic curve with delicious Asian-inspired dishes.

Indian-Spiced Chicken Thighs

MAKES 6 servings **PREP** 20 minutes **SLOW COOK** on HIGH for 4 hours or LOW for 8 hours

- **2** small onions, thinly sliced (about 1 cup)
- **2** tbsp quick-cooking tapioca
- **8** cloves garlic, minced
- **12** boneless, skinless chicken thighs (about 2 lb total)
- **1** tbsp ground cumin
- **2** tsp curry powder
- **1½** tsp salt
- **1½** tsp ground coriander
- **½** tsp ground cinnamon
- **¼** tsp ground cloves
- **¼** tsp cayenne pepper
- **¼** tsp black pepper
- **1** can (14 oz) reduced-sodium chicken broth
- **1** container (6 oz) plain yogurt
- **3** cups hot cooked basmati rice
- Snipped fresh mint (optional)
- Finely shredded lemon peel (optional)
- **3** tbsp toasted slivered almonds (optional)

■ Place onions in a 4- to 5-qt slow cooker; sprinkle with tapioca and garlic. Top with chicken. Sprinkle with next 8 ingredients. Pour broth over chicken mixture.

■ Cover and cook on HIGH for 3½ to 4 hours or LOW for 7 to 8 hours.

■ Transfer chicken to a serving platter. Cover and keep warm. Whisk yogurt into onion mixture in slow cooker; spoon over chicken and serve with basmati rice. Sprinkle with last 3 ingredients, if using.

PER SERVING 337 **CAL**; 6 g **FAT**; 35 g **PRO**; 33 g **CARB**; 1 g **FIBER**

INDIAN-SPICED
CHICKEN THIGHS

Thai-Style Vegetable Rice

MAKES 6 servings **PREP** 20 minutes
SLOW COOK on HIGH for 2½ hours or LOW for 5 hours, then on HIGH for 15 minutes

- 4 cups vegetable broth
- 3 cups frozen shelled edamame
- 2 medium sweet potatoes, peeled and cut into 1-inch pieces
- 1½ cups thinly sliced carrots
- 3 cloves garlic, minced
- 1½ tsp curry powder
- ½ tsp ground cumin
- ½ tsp ground ginger
- 3 cups instant brown rice
- ¾ cup unsweetened light coconut milk
- 3 tbsp snipped fresh cilantro
- ⅓ cup chopped cashews

■ Combine broth, edamame, potatoes, carrots, garlic, curry powder, cumin and ginger in a 4-qt slow cooker. Cover and cook on HIGH for 2 to 2½ hours or LOW for 4½ to 5 hours.

■ If cooking on LOW, turn to HIGH. Stir in rice. Cover and cook 10 to 15 minutes, until rice is tender. Stir in coconut milk and cilantro. Sprinkle each serving with cashews.

PER SERVING 364 **CAL**; 11 g **FAT**; 15 g **PRO**; 53 g **CARB**; 9 g **FIBER**

INDONESIAN BEEF CURRY

THAI-STYLE VEGETABLE RICE

Indonesian Beef Curry

MAKES 6 servings **PREP** 15 minutes **COOK** 6 minutes **SLOW COOK** on HIGH for 6 hours or LOW for 8 hours

- 2 tbsp vegetable oil
- 2 lb beef chuck, cut into 2-inch chunks
- ½ tsp salt
- ¼ tsp black pepper
- 1 large onion, peeled and thinly sliced
- ¾ lb small potatoes, about 2 inches in diameter, quartered
- ¼ lb peeled baby carrots
- 1 can (13.6 oz) light coconut milk
- 2 tbsp curry powder
- 1 tbsp reduced-sodium soy sauce
- ½ tsp ground ginger
- ½ tsp garlic powder
- ¼ tsp cayenne pepper
- 3 large pitas or flatbreads, cut into wedges

Chopped parsley, low-fat plain yogurt and lime wedges (optional)

■ Coat slow cooker with nonstick cooking spray.

■ Heat oil in a large nonstick skillet over medium-high. Season beef with ¼ tsp salt and the pepper and add to skillet. Sauté 3 minutes per side.

■ Transfer beef to slow cooker. Layer in onion, potatoes and carrots. In a medium bowl, whisk next 6 ingredients. Pour over beef and vegetables in slow cooker.

■ Cover and cook on HIGH for 6 hours or LOW for 8 hours. Gently stir in ¼ tsp salt. Serve over flatbread wedges with parsley, yogurt and lime, if using.

PER SERVING 517 **CAL**; 17 g **FAT**; 41 g **PRO**; 50 g **CARB**; 4 g **FIBER**

ASIAN CHICKEN
LETTUCE WRAPS

Asian Chicken Lettuce Wraps

MAKES 6 servings **PREP** 25 minutes **COOK** 6 minutes
SLOW COOK on HIGH for 2 hours 30 minutes or LOW for 5 hours

- 2 **lb ground chicken breast**
- 3 **green onions**
- 1 **can (8 oz) water chestnuts, drained and chopped**
- 2 **medium carrots, shredded (about 1 cup)**
- 1 **cup frozen edamame**
- 4 **tsp reduced-sodium soy sauce**
- 1 **tbsp Chinese-style hot mustard**
- 2 **tsp reduced-sodium teriyaki sauce**
- 1 **tsp rice vinegar**
- ½ **tsp black pepper**
- 1 **can (14.5 oz) reduced-sodium chicken broth**
- 2 **tbsp hoisin sauce**
- 12 **leaves butterhead (Bibb or Boston) lettuce or iceberg lettuce**
  Asian chili sauce (optional)
  Sesame seeds (optional)

■ Lightly coat a large nonstick skillet with nonstick cooking spray. Heat skillet over medium-high. Add chicken and cook until no longer pink, breaking up with a wooden spoon, about 6 minutes. Thinly slice white parts of green onions; set aside. Cut green parts of green onions into slivers; set aside.

■ In a 3½- or 4-qt slow cooker, combine cooked chicken, white parts of green onions, water chestnuts and next 7 ingredients. Pour broth over all in cooker.

■ Cover and cook on HIGH for 2 to 2½ hours or LOW for 4 to 5 hours.

■ Strain mixture, discarding cooking liquid. Stir hoisin sauce and green onion slivers into chicken mixture. Serve with lettuce leaves and, if using, Asian chili sauce and sesame seeds.

PER SERVING 258 **CAL**; 4 g **FAT**; 40 g **PRO**; 13 g **CARB**; 3 g **FIBER**

Thai Brisket Sandwiches

MAKES 6 servings **PREP** 10 minutes
SLOW COOK on HIGH for 5 hours
LET REST 20 minutes

- 2½ **lb flat-cut brisket**
- 6 **scallions**
- ¼ **cup mirin (rice wine)**
- 3 **tbsp Thai red curry paste**
- 1 **cup beef broth**
- 1½ **baguettes**
  Fresh cilantro
  Shredded carrot
  Mayonnaise
  Sriracha

■ Place brisket in a slow cooker, fat side up. Slice scallions into 1-inch pieces and add to slow cooker. Whisk next 3 ingredients and pour over brisket. Cover and cook on HIGH until meat is tender, 5 hours.

■ Transfer meat to a cutting board and let rest 20 minutes before slicing. Meanwhile, pour sauce into a measuring cup and skim off fat. Slice baguettes into 6 pieces. Serve meat on baguettes with sauce, cilantro, carrot, mayonnaise and sriracha.

PER SERVING 460 **CAL**; 25 g **FAT**; 41 g **PRO**; 17 g **CARB**; 1 g **FIBER**

THAI BRISKET
SANDWICHES

Teriyaki Pork with Asian Slaw

MAKES 8 servings **PREP** 25 minutes
SLOW COOK on HIGH for 3 hours or LOW for 6 hours

- 2 **pork tenderloins (about 12 oz each)**
- ½ **cup reduced-sodium soy sauce**
- ¼ **cup rice vinegar**
- 3 **tbsp packed brown sugar**
- 2 **tbsp canola oil**
- 2 **tsp grated fresh ginger**
- 2 **cloves garlic, minced**
- ¼ **tsp black pepper**
  Toasted sesame seeds (optional)
  Asian Slaw (recipe follows)

■ Trim fat from meat. Place in a 3½- or 4-qt slow cooker. In a small bowl, whisk next 7 ingredients. Pour over meat.

■ Cover and cook on HIGH for 2½ to 3 hours or LOW for 5 to 6 hours.

■ Transfer pork to a cutting board, reserving cooking liquid. Cut into ½-inch slices.

■ To serve, drizzle meat with cooking liquid. Sprinkle with sesame seeds, if using. Serve with Asian Slaw.

Asian Slaw

■ In a medium bowl, combine 5 cups shredded napa cabbage, 1 cup yellow sweet pepper strips, ½ cup shredded carrot, ½ cup fresh snow pea pods sliced lengthwise and 2 sliced green onions. For dressing, in a screw-top jar combine 3 tbsp rice vinegar, 2 tbsp canola oil, 1 tbsp toasted sesame oil, 1 tbsp reduced-sodium soy sauce and ¼ tsp each salt and freshly ground black pepper. Cover and shake well. Drizzle over cabbage mixture; toss to coat.

PER SERVING 239 **CAL**; 11 g **FAT**; 21 g **PRO**; 14 g **CARB**; 2 g **FIBER**

TERIYAKI PORK WITH ASIAN SLAW

PEANUT
BUTTER FUDGE,
PAGE 151

RASPBERRY
CHIP,
PAGE 151

MINT
CHOCOLATE
COOKIE,
PAGE 152

JUNE

136

141

155

LATIN HEAT

Fire up your grill with a fiesta of flavors.

MAHI MAHI WITH GRILLED PLANTAINS AND AVOCADO

Plantains are in the banana family. They're starchy when green and very sweet when dark brown.

Mahi Mahi with Grilled Plantains and Avocado

MAKES 4 servings **PREP** 10 minutes
GRILL 12 minutes

- ¼ **cup extra-virgin olive oil**
- ¼ **cup fresh lime juice**
- 2 **tbsp agave syrup**
- ¾ **tsp salt**
- ¼ **tsp black pepper**
- 2 **firm-ripe (yellow and spotted) plantains, peeled, halved lengthwise and crosswise**
- 2 **firm-ripe avocados, peeled, pitted and halved**
- 4 **mahi mahi fillets (1 inch thick, about 4 oz each)**
-    **Cooked white rice (optional)**
-    **Parsley (optional)**

■ Heat a grill or grill pan to medium-high. In a bowl, whisk oil, lime juice, agave, ½ tsp salt and the pepper. Toss all but 2 tbsp with plantains and avocados; brush fish with remaining dressing and season with ¼ tsp salt.

■ Grill plantains and avocados 2 minutes per side, leaving extra dressing in bowl. Grill fish 3 to 4 minutes per side, until cooked through. Serve over rice, if desired. Drizzle with extra dressing from bowl and sprinkle with parsley, if using.

PER SERVING 520 **CAL**; 29 g **FAT**; 24 g **PRO**; 46 g **CARB**; 9 g **FIBER**

CHICKEN WITH
PEPITA CREMA

Chicken with Pepita Crema

MAKES 4 servings **PREP** 15 minutes **GRILL** 28 minutes

- 4 **bone-in chicken thighs (about 2 lb total)**
- 1 **tbsp extra-virgin olive oil**
- ¾ **tsp salt**
- ¼ **tsp plus ⅛ tsp black pepper**
- ⅔ **cup light sour cream**
- ½ **cup plus 1 tbsp raw, hulled unsalted pepitas**
- 1 **scallion, chopped**
- 1 **clove garlic, chopped**

■ Heat grill or grill pan to medium. Rub chicken with oil, then season with ½ tsp salt and ¼ tsp pepper. Grill 12 to 14 minutes per side, until internal temperature reaches 165° on an instant-read thermometer.

■ Meanwhile, combine sour cream, ½ cup pepitas, the scallion, garlic, ¼ tsp salt and ⅛ tsp pepper in a blender. Process until smooth.

■ Spoon sauce over chicken. Scatter 1 tbsp pepitas over top.

PER SERVING 400 **CAL**; 27 g **FAT**; 33 g **PRO**; 6 g **CARB**; 1 g **FIBER**

YUCA FRIES

POBLANO-BLACK
BEAN TORTA

Asado is an Argentine cookout with an array of meats grilled over an open fire.

Poblano-Black Bean Torta

MAKES 4 servings **PREP** 10 minutes **COOK** 5 minutes **GRILL** 17 minutes

- 3   **tbsp extra-virgin olive oil**
- ¼   **cup diced yellow onion**
- 2   **cloves garlic, minced**
- ¼   **tsp ground cumin**
- ⅛   **tsp cayenne pepper**
- 1   **can (15.5 oz) black beans, rinsed and drained**
- 1   **tsp lime juice**
- ⅛   **tsp salt**
- 4   **poblano peppers**
- ¼   **cup mayonnaise**
- 4   **kaiser rolls, split**
- 1   **large vine tomato, cut into 8 slices**
- 4   **oz queso fresco, cut into planks**
      Yuca Fries (recipe follows; optional)

■ Heat 2 tbsp oil in a medium skillet over medium. Stir in next 4 ingredients; cook 3 minutes. Stir in beans; cook 2 minutes. Transfer ¾ of the beans to a bowl and mash; stir back into pan with lime juice and salt.

■ Heat a grill or grill pan to medium-high. Toss poblanos with 1 tbsp oil.

Grill 10 to 12 minutes, turning once, until charred. Place in a bowl covered with plastic wrap 3 minutes. Seed, stem and peel, scraping off skin with a knife. Slice each pepper in half.

■ Reduce grill to medium heat. Spread 1 tbsp mayonnaise on bottom half of each roll. Spoon on ¼ of the bean mixture, then add 2 poblano halves, 2 tomato slices, ¼ of the cheese and top of roll. Wrap each torta tightly in foil and grill 5 minutes, turning once. Slice and serve with Yuca Fries, if desired.

PER SERVING 440 **CAL**; 16 g **FAT**; 17 g **PRO**; 57 g **CARB**; 11 g **FIBER**

Yuca Fries

■ In a large heavy-bottomed pot, heat 3 cups vegetable oil to 350°. Peel and slice 1 yuca (2 lb) into 3 x ¼-inch matchsticks. Carefully add ⅓ of the yuca to oil; fry 3 minutes, until golden. Remove to a paper-towel-lined plate with a slotted spoon and season with kosher salt. Repeat twice, making sure to keep temperature as close to 350° as possible. Serves 6.

Argentine Asado-Style Dinner

MAKES 10 servings **PREP** 10 minutes **GRILL** 32 minutes

- 1   **lb uncooked chorizo sausages (5 or 6 links)**
- 2   **lb grass-fed flank steak (can be 2 pieces)**
- ¼   **cup plus 1 tbsp extra-virgin olive oil**
- 1¾   **tsp coarse salt**
- 3   **lemons, halved**
- ½   **cup packed parsley**
- ½   **cup packed cilantro**
- 2   **tbsp fresh oregano**
- 1   **to 2 cloves garlic**
- 2   **tbsp red wine vinegar**
- ⅛   **tsp red pepper flakes**

■ Heat grill or grill pan to medium. Grill sausages about 20 minutes, turning, until temperature reaches 165°. Place on a cutting board and cover with foil to keep warm. Increase heat to medium-high. Rub steak with 1 tbsp oil and season on both sides with 1½ tsp salt. Grill 5 minutes per side for medium-rare. Place on cutting board and let rest 5 minutes. Meanwhile, grill lemons, cut sides down, for 2 minutes, until charred.

■ To make chimichurri, in a food processor, combine ¼ cup oil, ¼ tsp salt, the parsley and next 5 ingredients. Blend until combined.

■ Slice sausages into coins and steak against the grain. Serve family-style with grilled lemons and chimichurri.

PER SERVING 310 **CAL**; 22 g **FAT**; 25 g **PRO**; 1 g **CARB**; 0 g **FIBER**

CUBAN-STYLE
PORK LOIN

Make this simple loin for a crowd or scale back and grill chops for a weeknight dinner.

Cuban-Style Pork Loin

MAKES 8 servings **STAND** 45 minutes
PREP 15 minutes **GRILL** 30 minutes
LET REST 10 minutes

2	**lb pork loin**
½	**cup fresh orange juice**
2	**tbsp fresh lime juice**
1	**tsp salt**
1	**tsp onion powder**
½	**tsp garlic powder**
¼	**tsp ground coriander**
¼	**tsp black pepper**
⅛	**tsp ground oregano**
1	**flavor injector***
1	**tbsp extra-virgin olive oil**

■ Allow pork to sit 45 minutes at room temperature. Heat gas grill for direct and indirect heat by setting up two zones, one at medium-high and one at medium-low. Or light charcoal grill for indirect heat by stacking coals on one side and leaving the other side empty.

■ Whisk orange and lime juices, ½ tsp salt and next 5 ingredients. Inject pork with mixture, piercing all over. Rub outside with olive oil and season with ½ tsp salt.

■ Grill on hot (direct) side of grill 5 minutes per side, turning 3 times (20 minutes total).

■ Transfer to cooler (indirect) side of grill; temperature of grill should now hold steady at 300°. Grill pork 8 to 10 minutes or until internal temperature reaches 140° on an instant-read thermometer. Let rest 10 minutes before slicing; temperature of meat will increase to 145°.

*Available in most houseware departments

PER SERVING 150 **CAL**; 4 g **FAT**; 24 g **PRO**;
2 g **CARB**; 0 g **FIBER**

JICAMA SLAW

CUBAN-STYLE
PORK CHOPS

Cuban-Style Pork Chops

MAKES 4 servings **PREP** 15 minutes **MARINATE** 1 hour **GRILL** 20 minutes **LET REST** 5 minutes

4	**bone-in pork chops (1 inch thick, about 2 lb total)**
1	**small onion, cut into eighths**
2	**large cloves garlic, roughly chopped**
¾	**cup fresh orange juice**
3	**tbsp fresh lime juice plus 1 tbsp zest**
1	**cup cilantro**
1	**tbsp fresh oregano**
1	**tbsp extra-virgin olive oil**
1	**tsp salt**
¼	**tsp black pepper**
	Jicama Slaw (recipe follows; optional)

■ Place pork chops, onion and garlic in a large resealable plastic bag. Whisk remaining ingredients and pour over pork chops, tossing to coat. Marinate 1 hour at room temperature.

■ Heat grill or grill pan to medium. Remove pork chops from marinade. Grill 8 to 10 minutes per side, until internal temperature reaches 140° on an instant-read thermometer. Let rest 5 minutes before serving; temperature will increase to 145°. Serve with Jicama Slaw, if desired.

PER SERVING 230 **CAL**; 11 g **FAT**; 29 g **PRO**;
2 g **CARB**; 0 g **FIBER**

Jicama Slaw

■ Peel and slice 1 jicama (about 1¼ lb) into matchsticks. Toss with 1 cup finely diced pineapple, 1 seeded and diced jalapeño, ⅔ cup chopped cilantro, 2 tbsp each pineapple juice and lime juice and ¼ tsp salt. Cover and refrigerate at least 3 hours. Serves 8.

HEALTHY FAMILY DINNERS

Enjoy a delicious, nutritious, quick-to-fix meal on even the busiest nights.

**BUCATINI WITH BABY
SPINACH, MUSHROOMS
AND FONTINA**

If you can't find Fontina, try another semisoft cow's milk cheese, such as provolone, gouda or havarti in this pasta dish.

LOW-COUNTRY SHRIMP

Bucatini with Baby Spinach, Mushrooms and Fontina

MAKES 6 servings **PREP** 10 minutes
COOK 10 minutes

- 1 lb bucatini
- 2 tbsp olive oil
- 1 lb sliced mixed mushroom blend
- 1 sliced medium onion
- 4 cloves sliced garlic
- 1 can (28 oz) crushed tomatoes
- 3 sliced hot cherry peppers
- ½ tsp salt
- 5 oz baby spinach
- 1½ cups shredded Fontina cheese

■ Cook bucatini following package directions. Drain, reserving 1 cup cooking water. Meanwhile, heat oil in a large nonstick skillet over medium-high; add mushroom blend, onion and garlic. Cook 5 minutes, stirring occasionally. Stir in tomatoes, peppers and salt; simmer 5 minutes. Toss bucatini with tomato sauce and stir in spinach and 1 cup cheese. Add reserved cooking water to thin sauce, as needed. Serve with ½ cup cheese sprinkled over top.

PER SERVING 549 **CAL**; 18 g **FAT**; 24 g **PRO**;
75 g **CARB**; 7 g **FIBER**

Low-Country Shrimp

MAKES 4 servings **PREP** 10 minutes **COOK** 15 minutes

- 3 tbsp olive oil
- 1 medium chopped onion
- 3 ribs sliced celery
- 1 seeded and chopped green sweet pepper
- 3 cloves chopped garlic
- 1 can (14.5 oz) stewed tomatoes
- ½ cup water
- 1 lb peeled and deveined large shrimp
-    Pinch of cayenne
- 4 cups cooked brown rice and quinoa blend

■ Heat oil in a large skillet over medium-high. Add onion, celery, pepper and garlic. Cook 6 minutes, stirring occasionally. Stir in tomatoes and water; simmer, covered, 6 minutes. Add shrimp and cayenne; cook 3 minutes or until shrimp are cooked through. Serve with brown rice and quinoa blend.

PER SERVING 452 **CAL**; 13 g **FAT**; 22 g **PRO**;
62 g **CARB**; 6 g **FIBER**

ZITI WITH SWISS
CHARD AND WALNUTS

To change the flavor, switch broccoli rabe for chard and diced smoked mozzarella for ricotta.

Ziti with Swiss Chard and Walnuts

MAKES 6 servings **PREP** 10 minutes
COOK 9 minutes

- 1   **lb ziti**
- 4   **tbsp olive oil**
- 3   **cloves chopped garlic**
- 1½ **lb trimmed and sliced Swiss chard**
- 1¼ **tsp salt**
- ¼   **tsp black pepper**
- ½   **cup chopped toasted walnuts**
- ¼   **cup grated Parmesan**
- ½   **cup ricotta**

■ Cook ziti following package directions. Drain and reserve 1 cup cooking water. Meanwhile, heat 2 tbsp oil in a large nonstick skillet over medium-high; add garlic and cook 1 minute. Stir in chard and ¼ tsp salt and pepper; cook 8 minutes, until tender. Toss pasta with chard, walnuts, Parmesan, 2 tbsp oil, 1 tsp salt and enough cooking water to create a sauce. Stir in ricotta.

PER SERVING 526 **CAL**; 23 g **FAT**; 18 g **PRO**; 62 g **CARB**; 5 g **FIBER**

ARCTIC CHAR WITH LEMON BUTTER SAUCE

Arctic Char with Lemon Butter Sauce

MAKES 4 servings **PREP** 10 minutes **COOK** 20 minutes **BROIL** 6 minutes

- 1½ **lb cubed yellow waxy potatoes (such as Yukon gold)**
- ½   **cup warm milk**
- 4   **tbsp butter**
- 1   **tsp salt**
- ¼   **tsp black pepper plus a pinch**
- 4   **pieces (5 oz each) Arctic char**
- 4   **lemon slices**
- 1   **tbsp olive oil**
- 1   **tbsp lemon juice**
- 1   **tbsp capers**
- 1   **tbsp chopped parsley**
     Steamed Broccolini

■ Place potatoes in a saucepan and cover with lightly salted water. Simmer 20 minutes, until tender. Drain and mash with milk, 2 tbsp butter, ¾ tsp salt and ¼ tsp pepper. Meanwhile, season char with ¼ tsp salt and a pinch of pepper and top each piece with a lemon slice. Broil 6 minutes. In a small saucepan, melt 2 tbsp butter with oil, lemon juice, capers and parsley. Drizzle sauce over fish and serve with potatoes and Broccolini.

PER SERVING 496 **CAL**; 26 g **FAT**; 36 g **PRO**; 31 g **CARB**; 2 g **FIBER**

BEEF AND BEEFSTEAK TOMATO SALAD

Sambal oelek is an Asian chile paste made from cayenne chiles, vinegar, salt and sugar. Add it during cooking for some zing or use as a condiment. Sriracha is a fine substitute.

Sambal Pork and Green Beans

MAKES 4 servings **PREP** 15 minutes
COOK 12 minutes

2	tbsp vegetable oil
1	lb thinly sliced pork tenderloin
1	sliced large onion
1	lb green beans, cut into 2-inch pieces
1	sweet red pepper, seeded and cut into 2-inch pieces
¾	cup chicken broth
2	tsp cornstarch
3	tbsp low-sodium soy sauce
1	tbsp sambal oelek
½	tsp ground ginger
7	oz cooked rice stick noodles

■ Heat 1 tbsp oil in a large nonstick skillet over medium-high. Add pork; stir-fry 5 minutes. Transfer to a plate. Add 1 tbsp oil, onion, beans and pepper to skillet. Stir-fry 6 minutes, adding 2 to 3 tbsp water, if needed. Combine broth, cornstarch, soy sauce, sambal oelek and ginger. Add pork back to skillet along with broth mixture. Simmer 1 minute, until thickened. Serve with noodles.

PER SERVING 476 **CAL**; 12 g **FAT**; 32 g **PRO**; 62 g **CARB**; 9 g **FIBER**

Beef and Beefsteak Tomato Salad

MAKES 4 servings **PREP** 15 minutes **GRILL** 8 minutes

½	lb orzo
¼	cup olive oil
2	tbsp lemon juice
¾	tsp garlic salt
½	tsp black pepper
1	lb beefsteak tomatoes cut into chunks
4	oz fresh mozzarella, cut into cubes
1	sliced small sweet onion
¼	cup sliced basil
1¼	lb boneless sirloin

■ Cook orzo following package directions. Drain and cool. Whisk oil, lemon juice and ¼ tsp each garlic salt and pepper. Stir into orzo. Add beefsteak tomatoes, mozzarella, sweet onion and basil. Season sirloin with ½ tsp garlic salt and ¼ tsp pepper. Grill or broil 4 minutes per side for medium-rare. Slice and serve over orzo.

PER SERVING 513 **CAL**; 24 g **FAT**; 35 g **PRO**; 39 g **CARB**; 3 g **FIBER**

SAMBAL PORK AND GREEN BEANS

SAIGON-STYLE
GREEN VEGETABLES

TANDOORI FLOUNDER AND SAMOSA-STYLE POTATO SALAD

For a crunchier texture, cut firm tofu into 1-inch pieces and sauté in vegetable oil until browned.

Saigon-Style Green Vegetables

MAKES 4 servings **PREP** 20 minutes
COOK 10 minutes **BROIL** 2 minutes

- 2   tbsp canola oil
- 1   sliced leek
- 4   sliced scallions
- 4   cloves sliced garlic
- 1   sweet red pepper, seeded and sliced
- 1   lb asparagus
- ½   lb thin green beans, each cut into 1-inch pieces
- ½   cup vegetable broth
- 2   tbsp soy sauce
- 3   tbsp lime juice
- 1   tsp sugar
- ½   cup mint
- 2   tbsp chopped peanuts
- 12 oz Asian-flavor baked tofu

■ Heat oil in a large nonstick skillet over medium-high. Add leek, scallions, garlic, pepper, asparagus and beans. Stir-fry 8 minutes. Partially cover halfway through cooking. Combine broth, soy sauce, lime juice and sugar; add to skillet and stir-fry 2 minutes. Stir in mint and top with peanuts. Meanwhile, broil tofu 2 minutes; cut into 1-inch pieces. Serve vegetables topped with tofu.

PER SERVING 477 **CAL**; 20 g **FAT**; 23 g **PRO**; 58 g **CARB**; 10 g **FIBER**

Tandoori Flounder and Samosa-Style Potato Salad

MAKES 4 servings **PREP** 15 minutes **COOK** 14 minutes **BAKE** at 450° for 12 minutes

- 1¼ lb quartered small red-skinned potatoes
- ¾   tsp salt
- ½   tsp turmeric
- ¼   tsp cayenne
- ¼   tsp black pepper
- 3   tbsp olive oil
- ½   chopped small red onion
- 1   tsp curry powder
- 1   cup thawed frozen peas
- ½   cup cilantro leaves
- 1½ lb flounder fillets
- ½   tsp cumin
- ½   tsp dried thyme
- 2   tbsp melted butter
- 1   tbsp lemon juice

■ Heat oven to 450°. Place potatoes in a saucepan and cover with lightly salted water; simmer 12 minutes. Drain and place in a bowl. Combine salt, turmeric, cayenne and pepper. In the same saucepan, heat 1 tbsp oil over medium; add onion, curry and half the salt mixture. Cook 2 minutes, then fold into potatoes. Stir in peas, cilantro and 2 tbsp oil. Place fillets in a baking dish. To remaining salt mixture, add cumin and thyme. Rub over top of fillets. Drizzle with butter and lemon juice. Bake at 450° for 12 minutes, until cooked through.

PER SERVING 410 **CAL**; 22 g **FAT**; 23 g **PRO**; 30 g **CARB**; 5 g **FIBER**

GOAT CHEESE-AND-
APRICOT-STUFFED
CHICKEN

Goat Cheese-and-Apricot-Stuffed Chicken

MAKES 4 servings **PREP** 15 minutes **COOK** 6 minutes **BAKE** at 375° for 12 minutes

- **2 oz goat cheese**
- **4 tbsp chopped pistachios**
- **6 chopped dried apricots**
- **4 boneless chicken breasts (about 6 oz each)**
- **½ cup bread crumbs**
- **1 beaten egg**
- **½ tsp salt**
- **¼ tsp black pepper**
- **2 tbsp vegetable oil**
- **1 cup couscous**
- **1 cup vegetable broth**
- **Salt and black pepper**
- **2 cups coarsely chopped baby arugula**

■ Heat oven to 375°. Combine cheese, 2 tbsp pistachios and apricots. Slit 1 side of breasts to create a pocket and stuff with cheese mixture. Combine bread crumbs and 2 tbsp pistachios. Dip chicken in egg and coat with bread crumbs; season with ½ tsp salt and ¼ tsp pepper. Heat oil in a large nonstick skillet over medium-high. Cook chicken 3 minutes per side. Place in a baking dish and bake at 375° for 12 minutes. Cook couscous in broth with salt and pepper to taste. Stir in arugula.

PER SERVING 555 **CAL**; 20 g **FAT**; 47 g **PRO**; 45 g **CARB**; 4 g **FIBER**

It's easier to make pockets in chicken breasts for stuffing if you place them in the freezer for 5 minutes before cutting into them.

Chicken Sausage, Peppers, Sweet Onion and Potatoes

MAKES 4 servings **PREP** 15 minutes
ROAST at 400° for 45 minutes

- **4 fresh chicken sausages (about ¾ lb)**
- **2 lb small tricolor potatoes**
- **3 seeded and sliced red sweet peppers**
- **1 sliced sweet onion**
- **4 cloves sliced garlic**
- **3 tbsp olive oil**
- **½ tsp salt**
- **½ tsp Italian seasoning**
- **¼ tsp black pepper**

■ Heat oven to 400°. On a lightly greased large rimmed sheet pan, add sausages, potatoes, peppers, onion and garlic. Toss with oil, salt, seasoning and black pepper. Roast at 400° for 45 minutes, until vegetables are tender. Serve vegetables with sliced sausage.

PER SERVING 475 **CAL**; 22 g **FAT**; 29 g **PRO**; 44 g **CARB**; 6 g **FIBER**

CHICKEN SAUSAGE, PEPPERS, SWEET ONION AND POTATOES

CONE ZONE

Get ready to make some seriously awesome ice cream.

PEANUT
BUTTER
FUDGE

MINT
CHOCOLATE
COOKIE,
PAGE 152

RASPBERRY CHIP

Raspberry Chip

MAKES 8 servings **PREP** 25 minutes
COOK 10 minutes
REFRIGERATE 4 hours or overnight
PROCESS 30 minutes **FREEZE** at least 3 hours

- ⅔ **cup sugar**
- 1 **tbsp cornstarch**
- 2 **cups milk**
- 1 **cup heavy cream**
- ¼ **cup cream cheese**
- 1 **tsp vanilla extract**
- 1½ **cups frozen raspberries**
- 2 **oz semisweet chocolate**

■ In a heavy saucepan, combine sugar and cornstarch. Stir in next 3 ingredients. Whisk constantly over medium-high until mixture is smooth and begins to simmer, about 7 minutes. Simmer 2 to 3 more minutes, until mixture has thickened. Remove from heat; add vanilla and 1 cup raspberries. Stir until fruit bursts and mixture is pink.

■ Transfer mixture to a bowl set over an ice bath. Let stand, stirring occasionally, until completely cool, then strain through a fine-mesh strainer to remove seeds. Cover and refrigerate at least 4 hours or overnight.

■ Transfer mixture to an ice cream maker and process according to manufacturer's instructions. Meanwhile, chop chocolate and melt in the microwave in 30-second intervals, stirring each time. Slowly drizzle in chocolate and ½ cup raspberries during the last few churns. Transfer to a container. Cover and freeze at least 3 hours or up to 1 week.

PER SERVING 280 **CAL**; 18 g **FAT**; 3 g **PRO**; 29 g **CARB**; 3 g **FIBER**

Peanut Butter Fudge

MAKES 10 servings **PREP** 15 minutes
REFRIGERATE 4 hours or overnight
PROCESS 30 minutes **FREEZE** at least 3 hours

- 2½ **cups half-and-half**
- ½ **cup heavy cream**
- 1 **cup smooth peanut butter**
- ¾ **cup sugar**
- ¼ **tsp salt**
- 1 **tsp vanilla extract**
- ⅓ **cup jarred fudge sauce**

■ In a blender, combine first 6 ingredients. Blend on medium-high speed until smooth, about 1 minute. Transfer to a container. Cover and refrigerate at least 4 hours or overnight.

■ Transfer mixture to an ice cream maker and process according to manufacturer's instructions.

■ Place ⅓ of the ice cream in a container. Drizzle with a few tbsp of the fudge. Cover with another ⅓ of the ice cream and drizzle with more fudge. Repeat with remaining ice cream and fudge. Cover and freeze at least 3 hours or up to 1 week.

PER SERVING 360 **CAL**; 24 g **FAT**; 9 g **PRO**; 28 g **CARB**; 2 g **FIBER**

Blackberry Lemon Custard

MAKES 8 servings **PREP** 10 minutes
REFRIGERATE 4 hours or overnight
PROCESS 30 minutes **FREEZE** at least 3 hours

- 2 **cups half-and-half**
- 1 **cup heavy cream**
- 1 **cup jarred lemon curd**
- ½ **cup sugar**
- 6 **oz fresh blackberries**

■ Combine first 4 ingredients in a blender. Blend until smooth, about 1 minute. Transfer to a container. Cover and refrigerate at least 4 hours or overnight.

■ Transfer mixture to an ice cream maker and process according to manufacturer's instructions.

■ Coarsely chop blackberries and fold into ice cream to create a swirl effect. Place ice cream in a container. Cover and freeze at least 3 hours or up to 1 week.

PER SERVING 440 **CAL**; 24 g **FAT**; 5 g **PRO**; 54 g **CARB**; 0 g **FIBER**

You may not be able to offer 31 flavors, but every one of these is so delicious it won't matter.

Midnight Mocha Almond

MAKES 8 servings **PREP** 20 minutes
COOK 4 minutes
REFRIGERATE 4 hours or overnight
MICROWAVE 2 minutes **PROCESS** 30 minutes
FREEZE at least 3 hours

ICE CREAM

- 2 **cups heavy cream**
- 1 **cup milk**
- 2 **tbsp instant coffee or espresso powder**
- ⅔ **cup sugar**
- 1 **cup semisweet chocolate chips**
- 1 **tsp vanilla extract**
- ⅔ **cup slivered almonds, toasted**

FROZEN FUDGE

- ¼ **cup milk**
- 1 **tbsp sugar**
- ¼ **cup semisweet chocolate chips**
- ½ **cup mini marshmallows**

■ **Ice Cream.** Combine first 4 ingredients in a medium saucepan. Stir over medium until coffee and sugar dissolve, about 2 minutes. Add chocolate chips and continue cooking until chocolate is melted and incorporated, about 2 minutes. Remove from heat and add vanilla.

■ Transfer mixture to a bowl set over an ice bath. Let stand, stirring occasionally, until completely cool. Cover and refrigerate at least 4 hours or overnight.

■ **Frozen Fudge.** Meanwhile, in a microwave-safe bowl, combine all ingredients. Microwave until hot, 1 to 2 minutes. Stir until marshmallows are melted and fudge is smooth. Pour into a foil-lined bowl and place in the freezer.

■ Transfer coffee mixture to ice cream maker and process according to manufacturer's instructions. During the last few churns, add almonds. Working quickly, place ⅓ of the ice cream in a container. Spoon bits of frozen fudge over top. Cover with another ⅓ of the ice cream and place more fudge bits over top. Repeat with remaining ice cream and fudge. Cover and freeze at least 3 hours or up to 1 week.

PER SERVING 520 **CAL**; 37 g **FAT**; 6 g **PRO**; 45 g **CARB**; 38 g **TOTAL SUGARS**; 3 g **FIBER**

Mint Chocolate Cookie

MAKES about 10 servings **PREP** 5 minutes
COOK 10 minutes
REFRIGERATE 4 hours or overnight
PROCESS 30 minutes **FREEZE** at least 3 hours

- ⅔ **cup sugar**
- 1 **tbsp cornstarch**
- 2 **cups milk**
- 1 **cup heavy cream**
- ¼ **cup cream cheese**
- 1 to 1¼ **tsp mint extract**
- 8 to 10 **drops green food coloring**
- 1½ **cups chopped Oreo cookies (about 10 cookies)**

■ In a heavy saucepan, mix sugar and cornstarch. Stir in next 3 ingredients over medium-high. Whisk constantly until cream cheese has melted and mixture is smooth and begins to simmer, about 7 minutes. Simmer 2 to 3 minutes, until mixture has thickened. Remove from heat and add mint extract and green food coloring to reach desired color.

■ Strain mixture through a fine-mesh sieve into a bowl over an ice bath. Let stand until completely cool. Cover and refrigerate at least 4 hours or overnight.

■ Transfer mint mixture to ice cream maker and process according to manufacturer's instructions. During the last few churns, add cookies and mix to incorporate. Transfer ice cream to a container and freeze at least 3 hours or up to 1 week.

PER SERVING 240 **CAL**; 15 g **FAT**; 3 g **PRO**; 26 g **CARB**; 21 g **TOTAL SUGARS**; 0 g **FIBER**

RASPBERRY
CHIP, PAGE 151

BLACKBERRY
LEMON CUSTARD,
PAGE 151

MINT CHOCOLATE
COOKIE

PEANUT BUTTER
FUDGE, PAGE 151

MIDNIGHT MOCHA
ALMOND

LENTILS 4 WAYS

Try a different lentil—red, green, black and brown—in each of these recipes.

LENTIL, BARLEY AND CHERRY SALAD

LENTIL BURGERS

RED LENTIL DIP

LENTIL AND SPINACH BURRITOS

Red Lentil Dip

MAKES 10 servings **PREP** 10 minutes
COOK 22 minutes

- 1 small diced onion
  Olive oil
- 1½ tsp curry powder
- ½ tsp ground cumin
- 1⅓ cups dried red lentils
- 1½ cups water
  Salt and black pepper
- ⅓ cup Greek yogurt
- 2 tbsp tomato paste
- 2 tbsp chopped cilantro
  Pita chips

■ In a saucepan, cook onion in oil for 2 minutes. Stir in curry and cumin; cook 2 minutes. Add lentils, water and ½ tsp salt. Bring to a boil; cover, reduce heat and simmer until tender, about 20 minutes. Puree with yogurt and tomato paste. Stir in cilantro; season with salt and pepper and drizzle with olive oil. Serve with pita chips.

PER ¼ CUP DIP 105 **CAL**; 2 g **FAT**; 7 g **PRO**; 14 g **CARB**; 4 g **FIBER**

Lentil, Barley and Cherry Salad

MAKES 6 servings **PREP** 20 minutes
COOK 25 minutes

- 1 cup dried French green lentils
- 2½ cups water
- 2 cups cooked barley
- ½ lb fresh cherries, pitted and halved
- ½ cup crumbled feta
- ½ cup fresh basil leaves, chopped
- 3 tbsp lemon juice
- 2 tsp honey
- 1 tsp mustard

- 1¼ tsp salt
- ¼ cup olive oil
  Black pepper

■ Combine lentils with water. Bring to a boil; reduce heat, cover and simmer until tender, about 25 minutes. Drain and rinse; toss with barley, cherries, feta and basil. Whisk lemon juice, honey, mustard and ¾ tsp salt. Whisk in oil and add dressing to barley mixture with ½ tsp salt and a pinch of pepper.

PER 1 CUP SALAD 308 **CAL**; 13 g **FAT**; 10 g **PRO**; 41 g **CARB**; 7 g **FIBER**

Lentil and Spinach Burritos

MAKES 6 servings **PREP** 15 minutes
COOK 30 minutes **BAKE** at 400° for 15 minutes

- 1 cup dried black beluga lentils
- 2¼ cups water
- ⅔ cup medium salsa
- ½ tsp salt
- 6 large flour tortillas
- 1½ cups shredded Mexican-blend cheese
- 2 cups hot cooked brown or white rice
- 3 cups shredded baby spinach
  Salsa
  Sour cream

■ Heat oven to 400°. Bring lentils, water and salsa to a boil. Reduce heat and simmer until tender, 30 to 45 minutes. Drain; season with salt. Divide among tortillas and top each with ¼ cup cheese, ⅓ cup rice and ½ cup spinach. Fold up and bake at 400° for 15 minutes. Serve with salsa and sour cream.

PER BURRITO 538 **CAL**; 15 g **FAT**; 22 g **PRO**; 79 g **CARB**; 11 g **FIBER**

Lentil Burgers

MAKES 4 servings **PREP** 20 minutes
COOK 38 minutes

- 1 cup dried brown lentils
- 4 cups salted water
- ¾ cup plain bread crumbs
- 3 finely chopped scallions plus more for garnish
- 2 beaten eggs
- ¼ cup grated Parmesan
- 1 tsp garlic salt
- ½ tsp black pepper
  Oil (for frying)
- ¼ cup sun-dried tomato pesto
- 2 tbsp mayonnaise
  English muffins

■ Boil lentils in water until tender, 30 to 45 minutes. Drain and mash lentils. Stir in bread crumbs, scallions, eggs, Parmesan, garlic salt and pepper. Shape into 4 patties and fry in oil for 8 minutes, flipping once. Blend pesto and mayonnaise. Serve burgers open-faced on English muffins, topped with sun-dried tomato mayonnaise and chopped scallions.

PER BURGER 529 **CAL**; 23 g **FAT**; 24 g **PRO**; 60 g **CARB**; 13 g **FIBER**

RED VELVET
DOUGHNUTS,
PAGE 163

171

176

179

#BESTCHICKENSANDWICHEVER
One bite and you'll know exactly why.

It doesn't get much better than crunchy-on-the-outside, juicy-on-the-inside buttermilk-dipped chicken thighs topped with crunchy slaw on toasted buns slathered with a little mayo and spiked with spicy pickled peppers.

Fried Chicken Sandwiches

MAKES 4 servings **PREP** 20 minutes **FRY** 16 minutes

SLAW

- 2 **cups thinly sliced red cabbage**
- 2 **cups thinly sliced green cabbage**
- ⅓ **cup shredded carrots**
- 1 **thinly sliced shallot**
- 4 **sliced scallions**
- 3 **tbsp mayonnaise**
- 2 **tbsp cider vinegar**
- **Salt and black pepper to taste**

SANDWICHES

- 1½ **cups all-purpose flour**
- 1 **tsp salt**
- 1 **tsp freshly ground black pepper**
- ½ **tsp cayenne pepper**
- 1½ **cups low-fat buttermilk**
- 4 **boneless, skinless chicken thighs (about 1⅓ lb total)**
- 4 **cups oil, for frying**
- 4 **sandwich rolls, toasted**
- **Mayonnaise**
- **Pickled jalapeños (optional)**

■ **Slaw.** Toss together cabbage, carrot, shallot, and scallions. Whisk mayonnaise and vinegar and fold into cabbage mixture. Season with salt and pepper; refrigerate.

■ **Sandwiches.** In a bowl, combine flour, salt, black pepper, and cayenne pepper. Pour buttermilk into another bowl. Trim excess fat from chicken. Coat chicken with flour mixture, dip in buttermilk (allowing excess to drip off) and coat again with flour mixture. Place on a baking sheet fitted with a wire rack.

■ In a deep, heavy skillet, heat oil to 350°. Add 2 pieces of chicken. Cook 4 minutes, turn and cook another 4 minutes, until cooked through. Transfer to a paper-towel-lined plate and repeat with remaining chicken.

■ Spread each roll with some mayonnaise. Top with a piece of chicken, some slaw and, if desired, a few pickled jalapeños.

PER SANDWICH 730 **CAL**; 33 g **FAT**; 38 g **PRO**; 67 g **CARB**; 6 g **FIBER**

OH SAY CAN YOU SWEET

Create fireworks-worthy desserts for your Fourth of July celebration.

WATERMELON
BOMB POPS

These red, white and blue desserts will keep you cool no matter how many people you have at your summer party.

PATRIOTIC
PARFAITS

Watermelon Bomb Pops

MAKES 12 pops **PREP** 30 minutes
FREEZE 2 hours, then overnight

- ½   **cup sugar**
- 2   **tbsp lemon juice**
- 1¼   **cups vanilla Greek yogurt**
       Blue food coloring
- ¼   **tsp raspberry-flavor extract (optional)**
- 12   **rocket pop molds (such as Tovolo)**
- 5   **cups diced seedless watermelon**

■ In a small saucepan, combine sugar and ½ cup water. Bring to a simmer and stir until sugar is dissolved. Cool and stir in lemon juice.

■ Stir ¼ cup sugar syrup into yogurt. Mix 8 drops of blue food coloring and raspberry extract, if using, into ½ cup yogurt mixture. Spoon about 2 tsp blue yogurt mixture into each rocket pop mold and freeze for 1 hour. Spoon remaining yogurt mixture into molds (about 3 tsp each) and freeze for 1 hour.

■ Place watermelon in a food processor and add ¾ cup sugar syrup. Process until smooth. Spoon about 3 tbsp watermelon mixture into each mold. Insert handles into molds and freeze overnight.

■ To serve, run mold under warm water and slide each pop out.

PER POP 75 **CAL**; 3 g **FAT**; 2 g **PRO**; 13 g **CARB**; 12 g **TOTAL SUGARS**; 0 g **FIBER**

Patriotic Parfaits

MAKES 6 servings **PREP** 30 minutes **COOK** 15 minutes **LET STAND** 6 minutes
REFRIGERATE 3 hours, then overnight

- 3   **pkg (6 oz each) fresh raspberries**
- 1¼   **cups sugar**
- 2   **envelopes unflavored gelatin**
- 1¼   **cups whole milk**
- ¾   **cup half-and-half**
- ½   **tsp vanilla extract**
- 1½   **cups fresh blueberries**

■ Mash raspberries in a medium saucepan. Add 1 cup sugar and bring to a simmer over medium heat. Cook 7 minutes and strain through a fine-mesh sieve into a medium bowl. Discard solids.

■ Sprinkle 1 envelope gelatin over ½ cup cold water in a small bowl and let stand 3 minutes to soften. Stir into raspberry sauce until gelatin is dissolved. Spoon half the mixture into six 6-oz glasses (2½ to 3 tbsp per glass) and refrigerate 1 hour. Keep remaining raspberry mixture at room temperature. Meanwhile, make the white layer: Place milk, half-and-half and ¼ cup sugar in a medium saucepan. Heat until steaming (just before mixture comes to a simmer), about 8 minutes, stirring frequently to prevent scorching. Remove from heat and stir in vanilla. Sprinkle 1 envelope gelatin over ¼ cup cold water and let stand 3 minutes to soften. Stir into milk mixture until gelatin is dissolved. Keep at room temperature.

■ Remove glasses from refrigerator after 1 hour. Stir milk mixture to blend and spoon 3 tbsp into each glass. Refrigerate 1 hour. Top milk layer in each glass with 2½ to 3 tbsp raspberry mixture, using all remaining mixture. Refrigerate 1 hour. Top with final layer of milk mixture, 3 tbsp per glass. Refrigerate parfaits overnight.

■ Just before serving, top each parfait with ¼ cup blueberries.

PER SERVING 306 **CAL**; 6 g **FAT**; 5 g **PRO**; 61 g **CARB**; 53 g **TOTAL SUGARS**; 6 g **FIBER**

RASPBERRY LINZER STARS

Gingered Triple Berry Bars

MAKES 12 bars **PREP** 15 minutes
BAKE at 325° for 55 minutes

2½	**cups all-purpose flour**
1½	**cups rolled oats**
⅔	**cup packed brown sugar**
¾	**cup (1½ sticks) unsalted butter, melted**
1	**tsp ground ginger**
1	**tsp vanilla extract**
½	**tsp ground cinnamon**
½	**tsp salt**
2	**cups strawberries, sliced**
1	**cup raspberries**
1	**cup blueberries**
⅓	**cup granulated sugar**
2	**tbsp lemon juice**
1	**tbsp cornstarch**
1	**tbsp candied ginger**

■ Heat oven to 325°. Coat a 13 x 9 x 2-inch baking dish with nonstick cooking spray.

■ In a large bowl, combine first 8 ingredients. Press half the flour mixture into prepared baking dish.

■ Combine berries with remaining ingredients. Spoon evenly over flour mixture in baking dish. Crumble remaining flour mixture over berry mixture and press down gently.

■ Bake at 325° for 45 to 55 minutes, until top is browned and fruit filling is bubbling. Cool completely and cut into 12 bars.

PER BAR 330 **CAL**; 13 g **FAT**; 5 g **PRO**; 50 g **CARB**; 21 g **TOTAL SUGARS**; 3 g **FIBER**

Raspberry Linzer Stars

MAKES 24 sandwich cookies **PREP** 30 minutes **REFRIGERATE** 3 hours
BAKE at 350° for 14 minutes **LET STAND** 30 minutes

2¾	**cups all-purpose flour**
1¼	**cups finely ground blanched almonds**
¼	**tsp salt**
¾	**cup (1½ sticks) unsalted butter, softened**
1	**cup confectioners' sugar, plus 1 tbsp for dusting**
2	**eggs**
1	**tsp vanilla extract**
½	**tsp almond extract**
¾	**cup seedless raspberry preserves**

■ In a bowl, combine flour, ground almonds and salt. In a second bowl, beat butter and 1 cup confectioners' sugar until smooth. Add eggs and extracts and beat until combined. Beat in flour mixture until just combined.

■ Form into 2 thick disks. Wrap in plastic wrap and refrigerate 3 hours.

■ Heat oven to 350°. Coat 2 baking sheets with nonstick cooking spray.

■ Roll out one disk to ³⁄₁₆-inch thickness. Using a 2½-inch star cutter, cut out cookies and place on prepared baking sheets. Repeat with second disk. Reroll scraps to make a total of 48 cookies.

■ Using a 1¼-inch star cutter, cut out and remove centers from half the cookies. Bake at 350° for 13 to 14 minutes, until they begin to turn golden around edges. Bake centers, if desired. Remove cookies to a wire rack and let cool.

■ Dust tops of cutout cookies with confectioners' sugar. Spread a generous tsp of preserves on each cookie without a cutout. Press a cutout cookie onto each cookie spread with preserves. Let stand 30 minutes, until set.

PER COOKIE 191 **CAL**; 10 g **FAT**; 4 g **PRO**; 22 g **CARB**; 10 g **TOTAL SUGARS**; 1 g **FIBER**

GINGERED TRIPLE BERRY BARS

To prevent red coloring from seeping through the white glaze, wait a few hours before serving to dip doughnuts.

Red Velvet Doughnuts

MAKES 12 doughnuts **PREP** 15 minutes
BAKE at 350° for 13 minutes

- 2 **cups all-purpose flour**
- 1 **cup sugar**
- 3 **tbsp cocoa powder**
- 2 **tsp baking powder**
- ½ **tsp salt**
- ½ **tsp ground cinnamon**
- 2 **eggs**
- ¾ **cup plus 3 tbsp half-and-half**
- 2 **tbsp melted butter**
- 1 **tbsp red food coloring**
- 1 **tsp vanilla**
- 4 **oz cream cheese, softened**
- ½ **cup confectioners' sugar**
- **Colored sprinkles**

■ Heat oven to 350°. Coat 2 doughnut baking pans with nonstick cooking spray.

■ In a bowl, combine the first six ingredients. In a second bowl, whisk eggs, ¾ cup half-and-half, butter, food coloring and vanilla. Beat egg mixture into flour mixture on low speed until all ingredients are moistened. Beat 1 minute on medium-high.

■ Divide batter between pans. Bake at 350° for 13 minutes or until a wooden toothpick inserted in centers of doughnuts comes out clean. Turn out onto a wire rack and cool completely. Loosen edges with a knife if necessary.

■ Beat cream cheese, confectioners' sugar and 3 tbsp half-and-half until smooth. Dip top of doughnuts into cream cheese glaze and place on wire rack until set. Decorate with colored sprinkles.

PER DOUGHNUT 208 **CAL**; 7 g **FAT**; 5 g **PRO**; 35 g **CARB**; 18 g **TOTAL SUGARS**; 1 g **FIBER**

RED VELVET DOUGHNUTS

HEALTHY FAMILY DINNERS

It's nice to be in and out of the kitchen fast even on the lazy days of summer.

GRILLED VEGGIE
MUFFULETTA

An overnight stint in the fridge lets the flavors meld in this fantastic, filling sandwich.

Grilled Veggie Muffuletta

MAKES 8 servings **PREP** 10 minutes
GRILL 28 minutes **REFRIGERATE** overnight

- ¼   cup extra-virgin olive oil
- ¼   cup red wine vinegar
- 1   lb portobello mushrooms
- 1   lb eggplant, sliced into ¼-inch planks
- 1   sweet red pepper
- ½   small red onion
- 1   cup shredded carrots
- ½   cup parsley
- ⅓   cup roughly chopped pitted mixed olives
- ⅓   cup pepperoncini
- 1   round sourdough loaf (1 to 1¼ lb)
- 8   oz thinly sliced provolone

■ Whisk oil and vinegar. Brush 2 tbsp on mushrooms, eggplant, pepper and onion. Grill mushrooms (turning once) and pepper (turning 3 times) 20 minutes. Grill eggplant and onion 8 minutes, turning once. Quarter pepper and thinly slice onion.

■ In a food processor, combine carrots, parsley, olives, pepperoncini and remaining oil and vinegar. Pulse until combined. Slice loaf in half lengthwise (bottom should be slightly thicker) and spread mixture on bottom. Layer with 4 oz provolone, grilled vegetables and 4 oz more provolone. Wrap tightly with plastic wrap, place on a baking sheet and top with a heavy cast-iron pan to flatten the sandwich. Refrigerate overnight. To serve, slice into 8 wedges.

PER SERVING 431 **CAL**; 18 g **FAT**; 18 g **PRO**; 49 g **CARB**; 5 g **FIBER**

CHICKEN, HEIRLOOM TOMATOES AND AVOCADO

Chicken, Heirloom Tomatoes and Avocado

MAKES 4 servings **PREP** 15 minutes **GRILL** 8 minutes

- 3   tbsp extra-virgin olive oil
- 2   tbsp balsamic vinegar
- 1   tsp Dijon mustard
- ¼   tsp salt
- ¼   tsp black pepper
- 2   lb heirloom tomatoes
- 1   avocado
- ⅓   cup fresh mint
- 1¼ lb chicken cutlets
      French baguette

■ Whisk 2 tbsp oil, vinegar, mustard, salt and pepper. Slice tomatoes and avocado and arrange on a platter. Scatter mint on top and season with salt and pepper. Rub 1 tbsp oil on cutlets; season. Grill on medium-high 6 to 8 minutes, turning once. Arrange chicken over tomatoes and avocado and drizzle with dressing. Serve with a French baguette.

PER SERVING 390 **CAL**; 22 g **FAT**; 35 g **PRO**; 14 g **CARB**; 6 g **FIBER**

SALMON AND
SQUASH NOODLES

Mint and basil are everywhere in the summertime. They'll stay fresh longer in your fridge if you place stems in a glass jar filled with an inch of water.

Salmon and Squash Noodles

MAKES 4 servings **PREP** 15 minutes
COOK 10 minutes

- 1 **lb zucchini**
- 1 **lb yellow squash**
- 2 **tbsp extra-virgin olive oil**
- ¼ **cup chopped pistachios**
- ¼ **cup chopped basil**
- ¾ **tsp salt**
- ½ **tsp freshly cracked black pepper**
- 4 **(4 oz) salmon fillets**
   Sautéed grape tomatoes

■ Spiralize zucchini and squash. Heat oil in a large nonstick skillet over medium-high. Add squash and cook 2 minutes. Stir in pistachios, basil, salt and pepper. Transfer to a bowl and cover. Season fillets with salt. In the same pan, cook, skin sides up, over medium-high 4 minutes; turn and cook 4 more minutes. Serve over squash with a side of tomatoes.

PER SERVING 330 **CAL**; 19 g **FAT**; 31 g **PRO**; 9 g **CARB**; 3 g **FIBER**

HAWAIIAN
GRAIN SALAD

Hawaiian Grain Salad

MAKES 4 servings **PREP** 10 minutes **COOK** 15 minutes **GRILL** 12 minutes

- 1½ **cups quick-cook wheat berries**
- 4 **cups water**
- 1 **tsp extra-virgin olive oil**
- 1 **sweet orange pepper**
- 3 **links (9 oz total) pineapple and bacon chicken sausage or jalapeño chicken sausage**
- 12 **oz fresh pineapple rings**
- ⅓ **cup Bolthouse Farms Caramelized Sweet Onion dressing**
- ¼ **cup chopped parsley**
- ½ **tsp salt**
- ¼ **tsp black pepper**

■ Combine berries with water; bring to a boil. Reduce to a simmer, cook 15 minutes and drain. Rub oil on orange pepper. Grill on medium with sausage 8 minutes, turning. Grill pineapple 4 minutes, turning once. Slice sausage on the bias, dice pepper (discarding stem and seeds) and pineapple, and toss with berries, dressing, parsley, salt and pepper.

PER SERVING 430 **CAL**; 10 g **FAT**; 20 g **PRO**; 64 g **CARB**; 12 g **FIBER**

For a steakhouse-quality meal, cook sirloin over medium-high and don't flip until a crust has formed.

Steak with Berry Sauce

MAKES 4 servings **PREP** 10 minutes
COOK 20 minutes

1	**lb boneless sirloin**
½	**tsp salt**
¼	**tsp freshly cracked black pepper**
1	**tbsp extra-virgin olive oil**
¼	**cup thinly sliced shallots**
½	**tsp chopped fresh thyme**
¾	**cup blueberries**
¾	**cup roughly chopped fresh blackberries**
½	**cup unsalted beef stock**
¼	**cup dry red wine**
2	**tbsp balsamic vinegar**
1	**tbsp unsalted butter**
	Baby spinach and feta salad (optional)

■ Season sirloin with ½ tsp salt and the ¼ tsp freshly cracked black pepper. Heat oil in a large stainless-steel skillet over medium-high. Cook steak 12 minutes, turning once, for medium-rare. Transfer steak to a cutting board to rest 10 minutes.

■ Meanwhile, reduce heat to medium. In the same skillet, add shallots and thyme; sauté 1 minute. Stir in blueberries and blackberries, stock, wine and vinegar. Season with salt and pepper. Bring to a simmer and cook 8 minutes, until berries burst and sauce is thickened. Stir in butter and season with salt and pepper. Slice steak and serve with sauce and baby spinach and feta salad, if desired.

PER SERVING 270 **CAL**; 15 g **FAT**; 22 g **PRO**; 10 g **CARB**; 2 g **FIBER**

CURRIED CHICKEN MEATBALLS

Curried Chicken Meatballs

MAKES 4 servings **PREP** 15 minutes **BAKE** at 400° for 12 minutes

1	**lb ground chicken**
1	**cup roughly chopped cilantro**
¼	**cup currants**
¼	**cup sliced scallions**
1	**tsp Madras curry powder**
¾	**tsp salt**
⅛	**tsp cayenne**
	Cooked basmati rice
	Jarred mango chutney
	Yogurt

Sautéed garlicky bok choy (optional)

■ Heat oven to 400°. Combine chicken, cilantro, currants, scallions, curry powder, salt and cayenne. Form into 12 meatballs and place on a foil-lined baking sheet coated with nonstick cooking spray. Bake at 400° for 12 minutes. Serve with rice, chutney, yogurt and bok choy, if desired.

PER SERVING 370 **CAL**; 10 g **FAT**; 24 g **PRO**; 46 g **CARB**; 2 g **FIBER**

STEAK WITH
BERRY SAUCE

SHRIMP AND ROASTED
RED PEPPER ZITI

SOUTHERN PORK AND COLLARD GREENS

Quick-thaw frozen shrimp in a colander under cool running water.

Shrimp and Roasted Red Pepper Ziti

MAKES 6 servings **PREP** 10 minutes **COOK** 9 minutes

- 1 **lb ziti**
- 2 **tbsp extra-virgin olive oil**
- 1 **lb peeled, deveined small shrimp**
- 1 **cup diced yellow onion**
- 2 **cloves chopped garlic**
- 1 **jar (16 oz) roasted red peppers, drained and diced**
- ½ **cup unsalted chicken stock**
- ¼ **cup heavy cream**
- ¾ **tsp salt**
- ¼ **tsp black pepper**
- ¼ **cup chopped parsley**

■ Bring a pot of salted water to a boil, stir in ziti and cook 9 minutes. Drain.

■ Meanwhile, heat 1 tbsp oil in a large skillet over medium-high. Add shrimp and cook 2 minutes. Remove with a slotted spoon. Reduce heat to medium and add 1 tbsp oil. Sauté onion and garlic 3 minutes. Stir in red peppers and stock. Bring to a simmer. Carefully transfer to a blender and process until smooth. Return to pan, stir in shrimp, cream, salt and black pepper. Bring to a simmer and cook 1 minute, then stir in cooked ziti and parsley.

PER SERVING 460 **CAL**; 11 g **FAT**; 24 g **PRO**; 64 g **CARB**; 4 g **FIBER**

Southern Pork and Collard Greens

MAKES 4 servings **PREP** 10 minutes **COOK** 12 minutes **GRILL** 4 minutes

- 2 **tbsp extra-virgin olive oil**
- 1 **pkg (16 oz) frozen chopped collard greens, thawed**
- ¼ **cup thinly sliced red onion**
- ⅓ **cup water**
- 1 **tbsp cider vinegar**
- 1 **tbsp sweet paprika**
- 1 **tsp mustard powder**
- 1 **tsp garlic powder**
- 1 **tsp onion powder**
- 1 **tsp black pepper**
- ½ **tsp ground coriander**
- ½ **tsp salt**
- 1¼ **lb thin-cut pork chops**

■ Heat a grill or grill pan to medium-high. In a large skillet, heat 1 tbsp oil. Add greens and onion; cook 2 minutes. Pour in water; cook 10 minutes. Stir in vinegar and season with salt and pepper. Combine paprika, mustard, garlic, onion powder, pepper, coriander and salt.

■ Brush 1 tbsp oil on chops, then rub on spice mixture. Grill over medium-high until cooked through, about 2 minutes per side. Serve over greens.

PER SERVING 290 **CAL**; 13 g **FAT**; 33 g **PRO**; 10 g **CARB**; 5 g **FIBER**

*When you can't decide
between your two favorite
things for dinner, Pizza
Burgers topped with
melty cheese are the
perfect option.*

Scallops with Warm Corn-Chorizo Salad

MAKES 4 servings **PREP** 15 minutes
COOK 14 minutes

- 2 **tbsp extra-virgin olive oil**
- ¼ **cup diced cured Spanish-style chorizo**
- 1 **cup diced red onion**
- 2 **cloves sliced garlic**
- 4 **ears of corn, kernels removed**
- 6 **cups packed baby spinach**
- 1 **lb scallops**
- **Salt**
- **Black pepper**

■ Heat 1 tbsp oil in a large skillet over medium heat. Add chorizo and cook 5 minutes. Add onion and garlic; sauté 2 minutes. Stir in kernels from ears of corn. Cook 3 minutes. Wilt in spinach. Season and remove to a bowl. Season scallops with salt and pepper. Increase heat in the same skillet to medium-high and add 1 tbsp oil. Sear scallops 4 minutes, turning once. Serve over warm corn-chorizo salad.

PER SERVING 330 **CAL**; 10 g **FAT**; 24 g **PRO**; 43 g **CARB**; 8 g **FIBER**

Pizza Burgers

MAKES 4 servings **PREP** 15 minutes **MICROWAVE** 30 seconds **BROIL** 6 minutes

- 1 **cup pizza sauce**
- ¼ **cup torn basil**
- 1 **lb lean ground beef**
- 2 **oz (½ cup) diced turkey pepperoni**
- ⅓ **cup grated onion**
- 1 **clove grated garlic**
- ½ **cup chopped basil**
- ½ **tsp chopped oregano**
- ¼ **tsp salt**
- ¼ **tsp black pepper**
- 4 **focaccia bread rounds (use a 3½-inch cutter to remove from a loaf)**
- 4 **oz thinly sliced fresh mozzarella**

■ In a microwave, heat sauce 30 seconds; stir in basil. Combine beef, pepperoni, onion, garlic, basil, oregano, salt and pepper. Form into 4 patties and place on a baking sheet. Broil 2 minutes per side. Carefully place focaccia rounds on baking sheet and use a spatula to place patties on top. Top each with 2 tbsp pizza sauce and 1 oz mozzarella. Broil 2 minutes on top oven rack, until cheese is melted and lightly browned. Serve with remaining pizza sauce alongside.

PER SERVING 342 **CAL**; 17 g **FAT**; 34 g **PRO**; 15 g **CARB**; 1 g **FIBER**

SCALLOPS WITH WARM
CORN-CHORIZO SALAD

SUPER-COOL NO-COOK MEALS

When it's too hot to turn on the oven—or even the grill—chill out with these tasty dishes.

Thai Beef Noodle Bowl

MAKES 4 servings **PREP** 25 minutes

- 6 oz glass (cellophane) noodles
- ¼ cup fresh lime juice plus 4 lime wedges
- ¼ cup fish sauce
- 1 tsp sesame oil
- 1 tsp sugar
- 12 oz thinly sliced roast beef, chopped
- 1 medium cucumber, thinly sliced into half-moons
- 1 large carrot, peeled and grated
- 1 red sweet pepper, thinly sliced
- 6 scallions, thinly sliced (¾ cup)
- ½ cup chopped cilantro
- ½ cup chopped basil
- ½ cup chopped mint
- ½ cup chopped roasted salted peanuts
- 1 serrano chile, sliced and seeded (optional)

■ Soak noodles in a large bowl of very hot tap water until tender, about 10 minutes; drain well. Using kitchen scissors, snip to shorten.

■ In a small bowl, whisk lime juice, fish sauce, sesame oil and sugar until sugar dissolves.

■ Arrange noodles, roast beef, cucumber, carrot, pepper and scallions in 4 bowls; drizzle with dressing. Sprinkle with next 4 ingredients and chile, if using. Serve with lime wedges.

PER SERVING 430 **CAL**; 15 g **FAT**; 24 g **PRO**; 50 g **CARB**; 5 g **FIBER**

THAI BEEF NOODLE BOWL

ZUCCHINI LASAGNA
WITH LEMON-PEA
PESTO

Black Bean Tacos with Spicy Peach Salsa

MAKES 4 servings **PREP** 25 minutes

- 1 **large peach, diced (about 1 cup)**
- ¾ **cup chopped cilantro**
- 2 **scallions, thinly sliced**
- 1 **tbsp finely chopped, seeded jalapeño (optional)**
- ⅛ **tsp salt**
- 1 **can (15 oz) black beans, drained and rinsed**
- 2 **tbsp olive oil**
- 2 **tbsp fresh lime juice plus 4 lime wedges**
- ½ **tsp ground cumin**
- 12 **corn tortillas (6-inch)**
- 1⅓ **cups shredded savoy cabbage**
- ½ **cup (4 oz) crumbled feta**
- 4 **small radishes, thinly sliced**
   Hot sauce (optional)

■ In a bowl, toss peach, ¼ cup cilantro and the scallions, jalapeño and salt.

■ In a second bowl, partially mash together beans, ¼ cup cilantro and the oil, lime juice and cumin.

■ Warm tortillas in a microwave or skillet per package instructions.

■ Top tortillas with bean mixture, peach salsa, cabbage, feta and radishes. Sprinkle with ¼ cup cilantro. Serve with lime wedges and hot sauce, if using.

PER SERVING 340 **CAL**; 13 g **FAT**; 12 g **PRO**; 47 g **CARB**; 9 g **FIBER**

Zucchini Lasagna with Lemon-Pea Pesto

MAKES 4 servings **PREP** 35 minutes

- 1 **lemon**
- 1 **pkg (10 oz) frozen peas, thawed**
- ¾ **cup basil**
- 3 **tbsp plus 1 tsp olive oil**
- 1 **small clove garlic, chopped**
- ¾ **tsp salt**
- 3 **pints heirloom cherry tomatoes, halved**
- 2 **medium zucchini (about 1 lb)**
- 1 **cup (8 oz) fresh ricotta**
   Freshly ground black pepper

■ Finely zest lemon and squeeze 2 tsp juice. Pulse zest and juice in a food processor with peas, ½ cup basil, 2 tbsp oil, 2 tbsp water, the garlic and ½ tsp salt.

■ Tear ¼ cup basil and toss with tomatoes, 1 tbsp oil and ¼ tsp salt.

■ Using a mandoline, slice zucchini lengthwise into ⅛-inch-thick strips. Place 2 zucchini strips overlapping slightly on a serving plate. Dot with 2 tbsp pea pesto, 1 tbsp ricotta and 8 to 10 tomato halves. Repeat twice. Top with another layer of zucchini strips. Repeat to make 4 servings.

■ Drizzle 1 tsp oil over each lasagna and sprinkle with salt and pepper. Serve with remaining tomatoes.

PER SERVING 320 **CAL**; 21 g **FAT**; 14 g **PRO**; 25 g **CARB**; 7 g **FIBER**

GRILLED CHICKEN TABBOULEH SALAD WITH SPICED YOGURT DRESSING

Slaw can be made up to one day ahead and BBQ sauce up to three days ahead. Just cover and refrigerate.

BBQ Chicken "Slawiches"

MAKES 4 servings **PREP** 25 minutes

SLAW AND CUCUMBERS

- ½ cup red onion, thinly sliced
- 2 tbsp plus 1 tsp red wine vinegar
- ¾ tsp salt
- 3 cups thinly sliced red cabbage
- 2 tbsp olive oil
- 1 small cucumber, thinly sliced
- ¼ cup chopped dill

BBQ CHICKEN

- ½ cup ketchup
- 2 tbsp packed dark brown sugar
- 2 tbsp red wine vinegar
- 1 tsp Worcestershire sauce
- ¼ tsp dry mustard
- ¼ tsp smoked paprika
- 3 dashes hot sauce
- 2 cups shredded cooked chicken
- 8 Bibb lettuce leaves
- 4 hamburger buns, split, lightly toasted

■ **Slaw and Cucumbers.** In a large bowl, combine onion, 2 tbsp vinegar and ½ tsp salt. Let stand 10 minutes, stirring occasionally. Add cabbage and oil; toss to combine well.

■ In a second bowl, toss cucumber, dill, 1 tsp vinegar and ¼ tsp salt.

■ **BBQ Chicken.** Whisk first 7 ingredients and 2 tbsp water. Add chicken and toss to combine.

■ Divide lettuce, chicken, slaw and about ½ the cucumber among buns. Press down lightly to compress. Serve extra cucumber on the side.

PER SERVING 600 **CAL**; 20 g **FAT**; 28 g **PRO**; 77 g **CARB**; 3 g **FIBER**

Grilled Chicken Tabbouleh Salad with Spiced Yogurt Dressing

MAKES 4 servings **PREP** 35 minutes

- ½ cup bulgur
- ½ cup 2% Greek yogurt
- ¾ cup finely chopped mint
- ¼ cup fresh lemon juice
- 1 small garlic clove, finely chopped
- ¾ tsp salt
  Pinch of cayenne pepper
- 1 medium cucumber, seeded and diced
- 1½ cups cherry tomatoes, halved
- 4 scallions, thinly sliced
- ½ cup finely chopped parsley
- 3 tbsp olive oil
- ¼ tsp black pepper
- 1 heart romaine, coarsely chopped
- 12 oz grilled chicken, thinly sliced

■ In a heatproof bowl, pour ¾ cup boiling water over bulgur. Cover with plastic wrap and let stand at room temperature until tender, 20 to 25 minutes.

■ Meanwhile, whisk yogurt, ¼ cup mint, 3 tbsp water, 1 tbsp lemon juice, the garlic, ¼ tsp salt and the cayenne. Cover and refrigerate.

■ Firmly press bulgur through a fine-mesh strainer to remove excess water. In a large bowl, toss bulgur, cucumber, tomatoes, scallions, parsley, oil, black pepper, ¼ cup mint, 3 tbsp lemon juice and ½ tsp salt.

■ Make salads with tabbouleh, Romaine and chicken. Drizzle with yogurt dressing and sprinkle with ¼ cup mint.

PER SERVING 370 **CAL**; 15 g **FAT**; 34 g **PRO**; 27 g **CARB**; 7 g **FIBER**

BBQ CHICKEN
"SLAWICHES"

STRAWBERRIES 4 WAYS

Summer's favorite berry takes turns both sweet and savory.

**BERRY
ICEBOX
CAKE**

**PORK WITH
BERRY SALSA**

**STRAWBERRY-
COCONUT ICE**

Berry Icebox Cake

MAKES 9 servings **PREP** 30 minutes
REFRIGERATE 4 hours

- 1½ lb (2½ cups) strawberries
- 1 tbsp granulated sugar
- 1½ cups heavy cream
- ¼ cup confectioners' sugar
- ½ tsp vanilla extract
- 12 chocolate wafer cookies
  Dark chocolate

■ Hull and thinly slice strawberries and toss with granulated sugar. Beat heavy cream with confectioners' sugar and vanilla to stiff peaks. Spread 1 cup whipped cream in an 8-inch square baking dish. Top with cookies, ⅓ of the berries and 1 cup whipped cream. Repeat twice, ending with whipped cream. Cover and refrigerate at least 4 hours or overnight. Shave chocolate on top before serving.

PER SERVING 300 **CAL**; 19 g **FAT**; 3 g **PRO**; 32 g **CARB**; 19 g **TOTAL SUGARS**; 2 g **FIBER**

Strawberry-Coconut Ice

MAKES 10 servings **PREP** 15 minutes
FREEZE overnight

- 1 can (14 oz) coconut milk
- ¼ cup honey
- 1 tsp fresh lemon juice
- 8 oz strawberries, hulled and coarsely chopped (about 1½ cups)
  Greek yogurt

■ Whisk coconut milk, honey and lemon juice. Stir in 8 oz strawberries. Spoon into 2 ice cube trays and freeze overnight. Pulse frozen cubes in a food processor until crushed. Spoon into small bowls and serve with more sliced strawberries and a dollop of yogurt.

PER SERVING 120 **CAL**; 9 g **FAT**; 2 g **PRO**; 10 g **CARB**; 8 g **TOTAL SUGARS**; 0 g **FIBER**

Pork with Berry Salsa

MAKES 4 servings **PREP** x minutes
GRILL 15 minutes

- 10 oz strawberries (2 cups)
- 3 tbsp fresh lime juice
- 2 tbsp chopped cilantro
- ¼ cup diced red onion
- 1 seeded and minced jalapeño
- ¼ tsp salt
- ¼ tsp black pepper
- 1 pork tenderloin (about 1¼ lbs)
  Rice or couscous

■ Hull and chop strawberries. Combine with lime juice, cilantro, onion, jalapeño, salt and pepper. Grill tenderloin on medium-high about 15 minutes, turning twice, for medium. Let rest 5 minutes. Slice pork and spoon salsa on top. Serve with rice or couscous.

PER SERVING 180 **CAL**; 4 g **FAT**; 30 g **PRO**; 7 g **CARB**; 2 g **FIBER**

Chunky Chicken and Berry Salad

MAKES 6 servings **PREP** 15 minutes

- 8 oz strawberries (about 1½ cups)
- ¾ lb diced cooked chicken breast
- 1 cup diced celery
- ¾ cup chopped toasted walnuts
- ½ cup crumbled blue cheese
- ⅓ cup mayonnaise
- 2 tbsp white wine vinegar
- ¼ tsp salt
- ¼ tsp black pepper
- ¼ cup sliced scallions

■ Halve or quarter strawberries. Toss with chicken, celery, walnuts, cheese, mayonnaise, vinegar, salt and pepper. Top with sliced scallions.

PER SERVING 330 **CAL**; 25 g **FAT**; 23 g **PRO**; 6 g **CARB**; 2 g **FIBER**

CHUNKY CHICKEN AND BERRY SALAD

MOLASSES-GLAZED
GRILLED SPARERIBS,
PAGE 184

AUGUST

189

200

201

JAMAICAN-STYLE DINNER

Try a little island spice with these festive party recipes and inspiration.

RICE AND PEAS

MOLASSES-GLAZED
GRILLED SPARERIBS,
PAGE 184

CREOLE-SPICED
SLAW, PAGE 184

The flavors of Jamaican cooking—chiles, garlic, ginger, thyme, allspice and coconut—infuse this simple dish of rice and legumes. If you can't find pigeon peas, substitute black-eyed peas.

Rice and Peas

MAKES 12 servings **PREP** 10 minutes
COOK 20 minutes **LET STAND** 10 minutes

- 3 cans (15 oz each) pigeon peas, drained and rinsed
- 2 cups uncooked jasmine rice
- 1 can (13.5 oz) coconut milk
- 4 scallions, chopped, whites and greens kept separate
- 2 medium serrano chiles
- 1 clove garlic, smashed and peeled
- 1 tbsp peeled and finely chopped fresh ginger
- 1½ tsp salt
- ¼ tsp black pepper
- ¼ tsp dried thyme
- ⅛ tsp ground allspice

■ In a lidded 4- to 5-qt heavy saucepan, combine all ingredients except scallion greens. Stir in 2¼ cups water. Bring to a boil, stirring occasionally, then reduce heat to low, cover and cook until liquid is absorbed and rice is tender, about 20 minutes. Let stand off heat, covered, 10 minutes. Fluff with a fork. Remove and discard chiles. Stir in scallion greens.

PER SERVING 290 **CAL**; 8 g **FAT**; 9 g **PRO**; 46 g **CARB**; 7 g **FIBER**

ROASTED SALMON WITH CITRUS GINGER AIOLI

Roasted Salmon with Citrus Ginger Aioli

MAKES 8 servings **PREP** 15 minutes **REFRIGERATE** 1 to 4 hours **ROAST** at 500° for 15 minutes, then at 425° for 10 minutes

- 2 oranges
- 3 tbsp olive oil
- 2 tbsp fresh lime juice (from 1 large lime)
- 2 tbsp chopped fresh rosemary
- 4 cloves garlic, smashed and peeled, plus 1 tsp minced garlic
- ½ tsp salt
- 1 tbsp plus 1 tsp peeled, finely chopped fresh ginger
- ½ tsp black pepper
- 2½ lb salmon fillet, in one piece, skin on
- 1 cup mayonnaise
- 1 tsp Dijon mustard

■ Zest 1 orange, then juice; set aside 1½ tsp zest and 1 tbsp juice. Whisk remaining orange juice and zest, oil, lime juice, rosemary, garlic cloves, salt, 1 tbsp ginger and ¼ tsp pepper.

Place salmon in a baking dish, skin side down; pour marinade on top. Cover and refrigerate at least 1 hour or up to 4 hours.

■ Meanwhile, whisk mayonnaise, mustard, minced garlic, 1 tsp ginger, reserved zest and juice and ¼ tsp pepper. Refrigerate, covered, until ready to use.

■ Heat oven to 500°. Cut remaining orange into ⅛-inch-thick slices. Remove and discard seeds. Transfer fish, skin side down, to a rimmed baking sheet or large roasting pan (discard marinade). Top with orange slices. Roast 15 minutes; reduce oven temperature to 425° and continue roasting until fish is cooked through, 5 to 10 minutes. Serve with roasted orange slices and aioli.

PER SERVING 510 **CAL**; 37 g **FAT**; 35 g **PRO**; 7 g **CARB**; 2 g **FIBER**

BOOZY LIMEADE

What would a Jamaican feast be without a splash of rum? Here, it spikes the limeade and adds flavor to the glaze for the ribs.

Boozy Limeade

MAKES 16 servings   PREP 10 minutes
REFRIGERATE at least 1 hour

- 4 cups cold water
- 1 bottle (750 ml) dark rum
- ¾ cup packed dark brown sugar
- ¾ cup fresh lime juice (from 5 to 7 limes)
  Lime slices

■ Combine water, rum, sugar and juice in a pitcher or punch bowl. Refrigerate at least 1 hour (or up to 1 day) before serving. Serve over ice with lime.

PER SERVING 140 CAL; 0 g FAT; 0 g PRO; 11 g CARB; 0 g FIBER; 3 mg SODIUM

Creole-Spiced Slaw

MAKES 8 servings   PREP 30 minutes

- 6 tbsp fresh lime juice (from 2 to 3 limes)
- 2 tbsp toasted sesame oil
- 2 tbsp honey

- 1 tsp soy sauce
- ¼ cup canned coconut milk
- ½ tsp salt
- ½ tsp black pepper
- 1 small red cabbage (about 1¾ lb), cored and shredded
- 1 large mango, thinly sliced
- 1 small red onion, thinly sliced
- 2 sweet peppers (red, orange or yellow), thinly sliced
- 1 medium jalapeño, seeded and thinly sliced
- ½ cup chopped mint
- ½ cup chopped cilantro
- ½ cup toasted coconut flakes

■ Whisk first 5 ingredients and ¼ tsp each salt and black pepper in a bowl. Add cabbage, mango, onion, peppers, jalapeño, mint, cilantro, ¼ cup coconut and ¼ tsp each salt and pepper. Toss to combine. Sprinkle with ¼ cup coconut.

PER SERVING 367 CAL; 16 g FAT; 3 g PRO; 56 g CARB; 1 g FIBER

Molasses-Glazed Grilled Spareribs

MAKES 8 servings   PREP 10 minutes
COOK 1 hour   GRILL 10 minutes

- 4 lb baby back ribs or pork spareribs, cut into ribs
- 1 cup fresh orange juice
- 6 tbsp hoisin sauce
- ⅓ cup packed brown sugar
- ¼ cup distilled white vinegar
- ¼ cup water or dark rum
- 3 tbsp molasses
- 2 tbsp soy sauce
- 2 tbsp chili garlic sauce or sriracha
- 1 1-inch piece ginger, peeled and thinly sliced
- 2 tsp dried thyme
- ¼ cup chopped cilantro

■ Bring a large pot of lightly salted water to a boil. Add ribs and gently simmer 1 hour.

■ Meanwhile, in a medium saucepan, whisk remaining ingredients except cilantro. Bring to a boil over medium-high, then reduce to a low simmer. Cook until glaze is thickened and reduced to 1 cup, 45 to 50 minutes.

■ Heat a gas grill to medium-high or the coals in a charcoal grill to medium-hot.

■ Drain and transfer ribs to a large cutting board. Generously brush with glaze. Grill 5 minutes per side, brushing with more glaze as needed, until ribs are nicely browned. Sprinkle with cilantro. Serve with remaining glaze on the side.

PER SERVING 620 CAL; 40 g FAT; 27 g PRO; 30 g CARB; 1 g FIBER

Beef Patties with Chutney and Cheese

MAKES 8 servings **PREP** 30 minutes
COOK 10 minutes **BAKE** at 375° for 20 minutes

- 2 tsp olive oil
- ½ cup finely chopped yellow onion
- 1 medium serrano chile, seeded and finely chopped
- 1 clove garlic, finely chopped
- ⅓ lb 90% lean ground beef
- 1½ tsp low-sodium soy sauce
- ¼ tsp dried thyme
- ⅛ tsp salt
- ⅛ tsp black pepper
- 1 box (14.1 oz) refrigerated piecrusts
- All-purpose flour, for dusting
- ¼ lb Gruyère or Swiss cheese, grated (1 cup)
- ⅓ cup banana or mango chutney
- 1 large egg, beaten with 1 tbsp water

■ Heat oil in a large skillet over medium. Stir in onion, chile and garlic; cook 5 minutes, until softened. Add beef, soy sauce, thyme, salt and pepper. Increase heat to medium-high and cook, stirring to break into small bits with a wooden spoon, until browned, about 5 minutes. Cool completely. (Filling can be refrigerated for up to 2 days. Bring to room temperature before filling patties.)

■ Heat oven to 375°. Line 2 baking sheets with parchment paper. Roll out both piecrusts from box on a lightly floured surface to ¹⁄₁₆ inch thick. Using a 4½-inch round cutter, remove 16 rounds, rerolling scraps as needed. Transfer rounds to prepared baking sheets.

■ Spoon 1 tbsp each beef and cheese and 1 scant tsp chutney onto one side of each round, leaving ½-inch border. Fold dough over filling, then crimp edges with a fork. Slice a few vents in top with a paring knife and brush with egg.

■ Arrange patties on baking sheets. Bake, rotating pans once halfway through, until patties are light golden, 18 to 20 minutes. Serve warm.

PER SERVING 331 **CAL**; 22 g **FAT**; 10 g **PRO**; 27 g **CARB**; 1 g **FIBER**

BEEF PATTIES WITH CHUTNEY AND CHEESE

TWICE-FRIED PLANTAINS WITH
JAMAICAN SALSA VERDE

Crispy-fried plantains are classic Jamaican fare. Plantains look like bananas but are starchier and less sweet—and have to be cooked in order to be eaten.

Twice-Fried Plantains with Jamaican Salsa Verde

MAKES 8 servings PREP 15 minutes FRY 9 minutes per batch

- 2 cups coarsely chopped parsley
- ½ cup coarsely chopped cilantro, plus more for serving
- 1 small serrano chile, halved and seeded
- ⅓ cup olive oil
- 1 clove garlic, peeled
- 1 tbsp peeled, finely chopped fresh ginger
- ½ cup chopped scallions
- ½ cup fresh lime juice (from 5 to 6 limes)
- ¼ tsp plus ⅛ tsp salt
- 4 large firm-ripe green plantains (about 2½ lb total)

  Vegetable oil, for frying (about 2 cups)

■ Combine parsley, cilantro, chile, oil, garlic, ginger, ¼ cup scallions, 3 tbsp lime juice, salt and 3 tbsp water in a blender. Process until smooth. Transfer to a bowl and set aside.

■ Cut off ends of plantains, then score skins lengthwise in 3 places; remove and discard peels. Cut plantains crosswise into 1-inch-thick pieces. Heat ½ inch vegetable oil in a large skillet over medium until hot enough to sizzle when a plantain piece is added.

■ Fry plantains in batches, without crowding, until tender and just golden, 2 to 3 minutes per side. Using tongs or a slotted spoon, transfer plantains to a paper-towel-lined plate.

■ Remove skillet from heat, reserving oil. With the bottom of a heavy saucepan, flatten plantains to ⅓ inch thick.

■ Heat reserved oil over medium until hot but not smoking. Refry plantains in batches, without crowding, until golden, about 3 minutes. With a slotted spoon, transfer to a paper-towel-lined plate and season with salt. Serve immediately with salsa.

PER SERVING 380 CAL; 31 g FAT; 2 g PRO; 32 g CARB; 3 g FIBER

No-Bake Ginger Lychee Trifle

MAKES 8 servings PREP 30 minutes
LET STAND 10 minutes
REFRIGERATE at least 3 hours

- 4 navel oranges
- 3 tbsp dark rum
- 1¼ cups heavy cream
- 3 tbsp sugar
- 1 store-bought pound cake (10.75 oz)
- 1 can (20 oz) whole lychees in syrup, drained and quartered
- ¾ cup sliced almonds, toasted
- ¾ cup toasted coconut flakes
- ½ cup chopped candied ginger

■ Segment 3 oranges. Cut segments in half crosswise. Squeeze ⅓ cup juice from remaining orange. In a bowl, combine juice and 2 tbsp rum.

■ In another bowl, using an electric mixer, beat cream and sugar to medium-stiff peaks. Gently fold in 1 tbsp rum.

■ Cut cake into ½-inch-thick slices; brush both sides of slices with juice mixture. Let stand 10 minutes, then cut into ½-inch cubes. Place ⅓ of the cubes in a 3-quart trifle dish. Gently spread ⅓ of the whipped cream on top, then layer with ⅓ of the orange segments, lychees, almonds, coconut and ginger. Repeat to make 2 more layers. Refrigerate, covered, at least 3 hours or overnight. Before serving, let stand at room temperature 45 minutes.

PER SERVING 517 CAL; 12 g FAT; 6 g PRO; 55 g CARB; 3 g FIBER

NO-BAKE GINGER
LYCHEE TRIFLE

HEALTHY FAMILY DINNERS

10 easy meals for those crazy-busy weeknights.

SOUTHEAST ASIAN CHICKEN BURGER WITH PICKLED CARROT AND RADISH

For the flavor of tacos al pastor—a popular Mexican street food—swap ground pork for chicken and finely diced pineapple for the shredded cheese.

Southeast Asian Chicken Burger with Pickled Carrot and Radish

MAKES 4 servings **PREP** 20 minutes
REFRIGERATE 1 hour **COOK** 8 minutes

1½	**cups thinly sliced carrot**
1½	**cups thinly sliced radish**
½	**cup distilled white vinegar**
1	**tbsp sugar**
⅛	**tsp salt**
1¼	**lb ground chicken**
2	**tbsp lime juice**
1	**tbsp soy sauce**
1	**tbsp chopped fresh ginger**
2	**cloves chopped garlic**
2	**tsp fish sauce**
6	**tsp mayonnaise**
4	**toasted buns**
	Sliced cucumber
	Cilantro

■ Combine carrot, radish, vinegar, sugar and salt. Cover and refrigerate 1 hour. Combine chicken, juice, soy sauce, ginger, garlic and fish sauce. Form into 4 patties and refrigerate 30 minutes. Cook in a nonstick skillet over medium-high 4 minutes per side, until cooked through. Spread 1½ tsp mayonnaise on each bun; place a burger on each and top with cucumber and cilantro.

PER SERVING 409 **CAL**; 18 g **FAT**; 32 g **PRO**; 33 g **CARB**; 4 g **FIBER**

CHARRED PORK THAI SALAD

Charred Pork Thai Salad

MAKES 4 servings **PREP** 20 minutes **GRILL** 12 minutes

1½	**lb pork tenderloin**
4	**tbsp reduced-sodium soy sauce**
4	**cloves chopped garlic**
1	**bunch trimmed scallions**
5	**tbsp peanut butter**
3	**tbsp warm water**
1	**tbsp lemon juice**
¼	**tsp red pepper flakes**
¼	**tsp ground ginger**
8	**cups shredded iceberg lettuce**
1	**sliced cucumber**
1	**thinly sliced sweet red pepper**
¼	**cup chopped peanuts**

■ Rub tenderloin with 2 tbsp soy sauce and garlic. Grill on medium-high 6 minutes per side for medium. Add scallions during last 5 minutes of grilling. Combine peanut butter, water, 2 tbsp soy sauce, lemon juice, pepper flakes and ginger. Combine lettuce, cucumber and red pepper. Toss with dressing and serve with sliced pork and scallions. Sprinkle with peanuts.

PER SERVING 373 **CAL**; 17 g **FAT**; 43 g **PRO**; 15 g **CARB**; 5 g **FIBER**

ORECCHIETTE WITH
NO-COOK HEIRLOOM
TOMATO SAUCE

LEMONY PISTACHIO PESTO TUNA

Toasting nuts first intensifies their flavor and crunchiness.

Orecchiette with No-Cook Heirloom Tomato Sauce

MAKES 6 servings **PREP** 15 minutes **COOK** 10 minutes

- 2 lb heirloom tomatoes
- 5 tbsp olive oil
- 3 tbsp white balsamic vinegar
- 1½ tsp salt
- ½ tsp black pepper
  Orecchiette
- 4 cups baby arugula
- 8 oz fresh bocconcini
- ¼ cup grated Parmesan

■ Cut tomatoes into 1-inch pieces and toss with oil, vinegar, salt and pepper. Cook orecchiette following package directions, about 10 minutes. Drain and place in a serving bowl. Stir in arugula until wilted. Add bocconcini and Parmesan. Serve warm or at room temperature.

Note: A tablespoon of capers adds a nice briny tang to this pasta.

PER SERVING 515 **CAL**; 23 g **FAT**; 18 g **PRO**; 61 g **CARB**; 4 g **FIBER**

Lemony Pistachio Pesto Tuna

MAKES 4 servings **PREP** 15 minutes **GRILL** 8 minutes

- ⅓ cup shelled pistachios
- 3 cloves garlic
- 3 cups fresh basil
  Juice and zest of 1 lemon
- 1 tsp salt
- ¼ tsp black pepper
- 4 tbsp olive oil
- 2 tbsp grated Parmesan
- 4 tuna steaks (about 6 oz each)
- 8 cups baby greens
- 1 cup heirloom cherry tomatoes
- 1 diced cucumber

■ In a food processor, mix pistachios, garlic, basil, lemon juice and zest, ¾ tsp salt and pepper. Process while gradually adding 3 tbsp olive oil. Stir in Parmesan. Brush tuna with 1 tbsp olive oil and season with ¼ tsp salt. Grill on medium-high 4 minutes per side (light pink in center). Combine greens, tomatoes, cucumber and ½ cup pesto. Serve tuna warm or at room temperature with salad and remaining ¼ cup pesto spooned on top.

PER SERVING 415 **CAL**; 20 g **FAT**; 49 g **PRO**; 12 g **CARB**; 5 g **FIBER**

BARLEY, PLUM AND CHICKEN SALAD

Barley, Plum and Chicken Salad

MAKES 4 servings **PREP** 15 minutes **COOK** 20 minutes

- 2 cups pearl barley
- 2 cups chicken broth
- 2 cups water
- 1 can (15½ oz) drained chickpeas
- 3 cups cooked diced chicken
- 3 oz crumbled feta
- ¼ cup olive oil
- ¼ cup chopped dill
- ¼ cup red wine vinegar
- ¼ tsp salt
- ¼ tsp black pepper
- 2 cups sliced plums

■ Place barley, broth and water in a saucepan. Simmer about 20 minutes, until tender, and let cool. In a bowl, combine barley, chickpeas, chicken, feta, oil, dill, vinegar, salt and pepper. Gently stir in plums.

Note: To make it vegetarian, use vegetable broth instead of chicken broth and double the amount of chickpeas and feta.

PER SERVING 551 **CAL**; 20 g **FAT**; 35 g **PRO**; 60 g **CARB**; 11 g **FIBER**

This easy herb-butter sauce is a riff on the famous Zip Sauce served in Detroit steakhouses.

Flatiron Steak with Fresh Herb Butter Sauce

MAKES 4 servings **PREP** 15 minutes
COOK 1 minute **GRILL** 8 minutes

- 1¼ lb flatiron steak
- 2 tbsp chopped parsley
- 2 tsp chopped rosemary
- 2 tsp chopped thyme
- ¼ tsp salt
- ¼ tsp black pepper
- 2 large tomatoes
- ¼ cup butter
- ¼ cup Worcestershire sauce
- 2 cups cooked farro

■ Rub steak with 1 tbsp chopped parsley, 1 tsp each chopped rosemary and thyme, and the salt and pepper. Grill steak on medium-high 4 minutes per side for medium-rare. Cut tomatoes in half horizontally and grill 6 minutes with steak, turning once. Heat butter; add 1 tbsp chopped parsley and 1 tsp each chopped rosemary and thyme. Cook 1 minute. Stir in Worcestershire sauce. Coarsely chop grilled tomato; combine with farro. Serve with steak and sauce.

PER SERVING 530 **CAL**; 24 g **FAT**; 35 g **PRO**; 41 g **CARB**; 4 g **FIBER**

FLATIRON STEAK
WITH FRESH HERB
BUTTER SAUCE

GRILLED SUMMER
VEGETABLE HASH

BEEF FAJITA
STEAKHOUSE SALAD

Make this yummy hash for brunch or for a simple summer supper.

Grilled Summer Vegetable Hash

MAKES 4 servings **PREP** 20 minutes
COOK 12 minutes **GRILL** 8 minutes

1¼	**lb fingerling potatoes**
2	**tbsp red wine vinegar**
1	**tbsp snipped chives**
1	**tsp mustard**
1	**tsp chopped fresh thyme**
1	**tsp salt**
¼	**tsp black pepper**
¼	**cup olive oil**
2	**medium zucchini**
2	**medium summer squash**
8	**fried eggs**

■ Simmer potatoes 12 minutes. Combine vinegar, chives, mustard, thyme, ½ tsp salt and ¼ tsp pepper. Gradually whisk in oil. Slice zucchini and squash into ¼-inch planks. Brush vegetables with dressing and grill 4 minutes per side (use a vegetable basket for potatoes). Season with ½ tsp salt and additional pepper to taste. Top each serving with 2 eggs.

PER SERVING 412 **CAL**; 24 g **FAT**; 19 g **PRO**; 33 g **CARB**; 6 g **FIBER**

Beef Fajita Steakhouse Salad

MAKES 4 servings **PREP** 20 minutes **GRILL** 8 minutes

3	**tbsp lime juice**
3	**tbsp olive oil**
2	**tsp honey**
¾	**tsp salt**
½	**tsp chili powder**
¼	**tsp cumin**
1	**large sweet onion**
¾	**lb skirt steak**
8	**cups sliced romaine hearts**
1	**sliced avocado**
	Warm flour tortillas, sour cream and salsa (optional)

■ Combine lime juice, oil, honey, ½ tsp salt, chili powder and cumin. Cut onion into ½-inch slices and grill on medium-high 4 minutes per side. Brush steak with 2 tbsp dressing and season with ¼ tsp salt. Grill 2 minutes per side for medium-rare; slice thin. Toss romaine and avocado with remaining dressing. Add meat and onion to salad. Serve with warm tortillas, sour cream and salsa, if desired.

PER SERVING 407 **CAL**; 25 g **FAT** ; 17 g **PRO**; 32 g **CARB**; 7 g **FIBER**

MINT-AND-CUMIN-SPICED CHICKEN

Feel free to substitute lump crabmeat or steamed lobster for the shrimp.

Old Bay Shrimp Rolls and Zucchini Fries

MAKES 4 servings PREP 15 minutes
ROAST at 450° for 30 minutes

½	lb cooked medium shrimp
1	cup sliced celery
⅓	cup reduced-fat mayonnaise
2	tsp lemon juice
1	tsp chopped fresh tarragon
1	tsp Dijon mustard
1	tsp Old Bay seasoning
2	medium zucchini
2	beaten egg whites
1	cup panko
	Salt (optional)
	Black pepper (optional)
4	split-top buns
	Zucchini fries

■ Cut shrimp into large chunks. Combine with celery, mayonnaise, juice, tarragon, mustard and seasoning. Refrigerate. Cut zucchini into 2 x ½-inch sticks. Dip in egg and coat in panko. Roast at 450° for 25 to 30 minutes, turning once. Season with salt and pepper, if desired. Divide shrimp mixture equally among buns and serve with zucchini fries on the side.

PER SERVING 379 CAL; 16 g FAT; 19 g PRO; 32 g CARB; 2 g FIBER

Mint-and-Cumin-Spiced Chicken

MAKES 4 servings PREP 15 minutes MARINATE 1 hour BAKE at 400° for 40 minutes

1	quartered onion
1	cup mint leaves
½	cup parsley leaves
2	tbsp tomato paste
1	tbsp olive oil
2	tsp cumin
2	tsp paprika
¾	tsp salt
½	tsp red pepper flakes
4	small skinless chicken thighs
4	small skinless chicken drumsticks
1	cup couscous
	Chicken broth
1	bag (5 oz) baby spinach

■ In a food processor, mix onion, mint, parsley, tomato paste, oil, cumin, paprika, salt and pepper flakes. Process until smooth. Place chicken thighs and drumsticks in a roasting pan. Rub chicken generously with mint-and-cumin mixture. Cover and marinate at least 1 hour. Bake at 400° for 40 minutes or until juices run clear. Prepare couscous with broth, following pkg directions. Stir in spinach until wilted.

PER SERVING 577 CAL; 13 g FAT; 61 g PRO; 45 g CARB; 6 g FIBER

OLD BAY SHRIMP ROLLS
AND ZUCCHINI FRIES

EASY AS PIE

These wow-worthy pizzas are cooked on the grill for a crisp crust and smoky flavor.

For a group, put out bowls of toppings and let guests customize their own pizza. When brushing dough with oil, be generous— you don't want it to stick to the grill.

GRANNY SMITH AND ARUGULA

GRILLED CHICKEN PEPERONATA

SAUSAGE AND TOMATO, PAGE 200

Grilled Pizza Crusts

MAKES 4 servings **PREP** 30 minutes
GRILL 2 minutes

- 1 lb frozen pizza dough,* thawed
  Flour, for dusting
  Olive oil, for grilling

■ Heat grill or large grill pan to medium-high. If using a charcoal grill, arrange coals for direct grilling.

■ Leave pizza dough out on counter 30 minutes. This makes it easier to work with.

■ Dust countertop lightly with flour. Divide dough into 4 pieces and roll or stretch to 7- to 8-inch shapes. Brush each piece with oil. Transfer, oil sides down, to grill grate. Grill 2 minutes, uncovered, until tops puff and appear dry to the touch. Flip onto a large cutting board or baking sheet, so grilled sides face up. Use for pizzas.

*If you can't find raw pizza dough, sub in flatbread or naan, and reduce cooking time by 1 minute per side.

Granny Smith and Arugula

MAKES 4 servings **PREP** 5 minutes
GRILL 2 minutes

- 4 Grilled Pizza Crusts
- 8 thin slices prosciutto (about 4 oz total)
- ¾ cup packed arugula
- ¾ cup crumbled blue or goat cheese
- 1 Granny Smith apple, cored and thinly sliced
  Balsamic glaze (such as Colavita)
  Coarsely ground black pepper

■ Top each crust with 2 slices prosciutto. Divide arugula and cheese evenly among crusts. Scatter apple slices over pizzas. Return pizzas to grill, cover and cook 2 minutes.

■ Remove pizzas from grill, drizzle with balsamic glaze and season with pepper.

PER PIZZA 510 **CAL**; 29 g **FAT**; 21 g **PRO**; 50 g **CARB**; 2 g **FIBER**

Grilled Chicken Peperonata

MAKES 4 servings **PREP** 10 minutes
GRILL 14 minutes

- 1 lb boneless, skinless chicken breasts
- ¼ tsp salt
- ¼ tsp black pepper
- 6 mini red, yellow and orange peppers
- ¾ cup jarred pizza sauce
- 4 Grilled Pizza Crusts
- 8 oz pepper Jack cheese, grated
- 1 scallion, trimmed and sliced
  Coarsely ground salt and black pepper

■ Season chicken breasts with salt and pepper. Thread peppers onto a thin skewer. Grill chicken 12 minutes, turning once, and peppers 4 minutes, turning once. Remove from grill. Cube chicken breasts and slice peppers into rings.

■ Spread 3 tbsp pizza sauce on each crust. Divide cheese among crusts. Top with chicken and pepper rings. Transfer pizzas to grill, cover and cook 2 minutes. Sprinkle with scallion slices and salt and pepper.

PER PIZZA 730 **CAL**; 37 g **FAT**; 42 g **PRO**; 62 g **CARB**; 4 g **FIBER**

CARAMELIZED ONION
AND MUSHROOM

Sausage and Tomato

MAKES 4 servings **PREP** 5 minutes
COOK 5 minutes **GRILL** 2 minutes

- 2 **fresh sweet pork or chicken sausages, casings removed**
- ¾ **cup jarred pizza sauce**
- 4 **Grilled Pizza Crusts**
- 8 **oz fresh mozzarella, sliced**
- 16 **heirloom cherry tomatoes, sliced**
   Basil leaves
   Coarsely ground salt and black pepper

■ Heat a 10-inch nonstick skillet over medium-high. Crumble in sausage and cook 5 minutes, breaking pieces apart with a wooden spoon, until browned and cooked through. Set aside.

■ Spread 3 tbsp pizza sauce on each crust. Divide mozzarella slices among crusts and top with sausage and cherry tomato slices. Return pizzas to grill, cover and cook 2 minutes. Remove from grill, add basil leaves and season with salt and pepper.

PER PIZZA 690 **CAL**; 37 g **FAT**; 32 g **PRO**; 60 g **CARB**; 4g **FIBER**

Caramelized Onion and Mushroom

MAKES 4 servings **PREP** 10 minutes
COOK 24 minutes **GRILL** 2 minutes

- 3 **tbsp unsalted butter**
- 1 **red onion, thinly sliced**
- ⅛ **tsp salt**
- 1 **tsp sugar**
- 2 **cups sliced cremini mushrooms**
- 4 **tbsp creamy goat cheese, softened**
- 4 **Grilled Pizza Crusts**
- 1⅓ **cups shredded Italian cheese blend**
- 2 **tsp chopped fresh oregano**

Coarsely ground salt and black pepper

■ Melt 2 tbsp butter in a large stainless skillet over medium heat. Add onion and salt. Reduce heat to medium-low; cook, stirring frequently, 10 minutes. Sprinkle with sugar and cook 10 minutes. Remove from pan to a bowl.

■ Add 1 tbsp butter to pan; increase heat to medium. Stir in mushrooms and sauté 4 minutes, until browned.

■ Spread 1 tbsp goat cheese on each crust. Top with ⅓ cup shredded cheese, ¼ of the onions and ¼ of the mushrooms. Return pizzas to grill, cover and cook 2 minutes. Sprinkle with oregano and salt and pepper.

PER PIZZA 610 **CAL**; 33 g **FAT**; 19 g **PRO**; 54 g **CARB**; 2 g **FIBER**

HAUTE DOGS

Let's be frank: You're going to love these unexpected, flavor-packed toppings.

All-American

Spoon on warm **chili**, finely shredded **sharp cheddar** and **French's Crispy Fried Onions**.

Oaxacan

Top with thinly sliced **avocado** and **radishes** and crumbled **Cotija cheese**.

Korean

Combine 1½ cups **water**, ½ cup **white wine vinegar**, ¼ cup **sugar** and ½ tsp **salt**. Bring to a boil. Remove from heat and cool. Pour over 1 very thinly sliced **English cucumber**; refrigerate at least 2 hours. Scatter cucumbers on hot dog and finish with **sriracha**.

Caprese

Layer sliced **roma tomatoes** and fresh **mozzarella** along the inside of a hot dog bun. Garnish with chopped fresh **basil**.

Caribbean

Combine 1 finely diced **mango**, ¼ cup each roughly chopped **cilantro** and diced **red onion**, 1 sliced **bird's-eye chile**, 4 tsp **lime juice** and a pinch of **salt**. Spoon onto hot dogs.

BLT

Wrap 1 slice **smoked bacon** around each hot dog. Broil 8 minutes, turning once, until cooked and crisp. Top with chopped **cherry tomatoes** and **romaine**; finish with **mayo**.

CINNAMON-APPLE
WAFFLES À LA MODE,
PAGE 211

SEPTEMBER

217

221

229

APPLE ABUNDANCE

Tuck into the best apple pie ever, plus cupcakes, cookies and more.

SKILLET APPLE-PLUM
COBBLER

Here's an apple dessert that's as easy as 1, 2, 3: Wrap, bake, eat. (Just don't forget the caramel sauce.)

Skillet Apple-Plum Cobbler

MAKES 6 servings **PREP** 30 minutes
BAKE at 400° for 45 minutes

FRUIT

- 1½   **lb apples, such as Cortland, peeled and sliced ⅛ inch thick**
- 1½   **lb plums, sliced ⅛ inch thick**
- ½   **cup sugar**
- ¼   **cup all-purpose flour**
- 2   **tbsp lemon juice**
- ⅛   **tsp salt**

BISCUITS

- 1   **cup all-purpose flour**
- ¼   **cup sugar**
- 1   **tsp baking powder**
- ¼   **tsp baking soda**
- ¼   **tsp salt**
- 4   **tbsp cold unsalted butter, cubed**
- ½   **cup sour cream**
- 1   **tbsp turbinado sugar**

■ Heat oven to 400°.

■ **Fruit.** Carefully combine all ingredients. Place in a 12-inch cast-iron skillet and bake at 400° for 25 minutes.

■ **Biscuits.** Meanwhile, whisk first 5 ingredients. Using hands, add butter until clumps the size of peas are formed. Stir in sour cream. Form into 6 round biscuits.

■ Carefully remove skillet from oven and place biscuits on top. Sprinkle with turbinado sugar. Bake 20 more minutes, until biscuits are browned.

PER SERVING 390 **CAL**; 12 g **FAT**; 4 g **PRO**; 73 g **CARB**; 6 g **FIBER**

FARMHOUSE APPLE DUMPLINGS

Farmhouse Apple Dumplings

MAKES 4 servings **PREP** 15 minutes **BAKE** at 375° for 45 minutes

- 1   **refrigerated piecrust**
- ¼   **cup sugar**
- ½   **tsp ground cinnamon**
- 4   **small Braeburn apples, cored and peeled**
- 2   **tbsp cold butter, cubed**
   Caramel sauce, warmed
   Whipped cream

■ Heat oven to 375°. Place piecrust on a lightly floured surface and cut into 4 equal pieces. Roll each piece into an 8-inch square. Combine sugar and cinnamon in a small bowl.

■ Place an apple in center of each dough square. Sprinkle with half the cinnamon sugar, then dot with butter. Fold edges over apples and pinch closed. Place in an 8 x 8-inch baking dish coated with nonstick cooking spray. Sprinkle remaining cinnamon sugar over dumplings. Bake 45 minutes, until browned.

■ Cool slightly, then serve in a bowl with warm caramel sauce and whipped cream.

PER SERVING 460 **CAL**; 24 g **FAT**; 3 g **PRO**; 66 g **CARB**; 4 g **FIBER**

APPLE-CHERRY CRISP

Pick your favorite apple dessert—a warm crisp topped with ice cream or a go-anywhere oatmeal cookie drizzled with a maple glaze.

Jumbo Apple-Oatmeal Cookies

MAKES 12 cookies PREP 15 minutes
BAKE at 350° for 18 minutes

3	cups rolled oats
¾	cup all-purpose flour
1	tsp pumpkin pie spice
¼	tsp salt
1	stick (½ cup) unsalted butter, softened
1	cup packed brown sugar
2	egg whites
½	tsp maple extract
½	tsp vanilla extract
1	cup cored, peeled and diced McIntosh apple
	Maple Glaze (recipe follows)

■ Heat oven to 350°. Line 2 large baking sheets with parchment paper.

■ Combine oats and next 3 ingredients. In a large bowl, beat butter and next 4 ingredients until smooth. Stir in oat mixture and apple.

■ Drop ¼-cup scoops of dough onto prepared baking sheets. Flatten to 3-inch disks. Bake 15 to 18 minutes, until set. Cool 3 minutes on sheets. Remove cookies to a wire rack and cool completely. Drizzle with Maple Glaze.

Maple Glaze Combine ½ cup confectioners' sugar, 1 tsp maple extract and 1 tbsp water. Stir until smooth.

PER COOKIE 277 CAL; 9 g FAT; 5 g PRO; 44 g CARB; 3 g FIBER

Apple-Cherry Crisp

MAKES 12 servings PREP 25 minutes BAKE at 350° for 55 minutes

FILLING

2½	lb Rome apples, cored, peeled and cut into ½-inch cubes
1½	cups pitted cherries
½	cup packed brown sugar
¼	cup all-purpose flour
¾	tsp ground cinnamon
¼	tsp ground nutmeg

TOPPING

1¾	cups all-purpose flour
½	cup packed brown sugar
½	cup chopped walnuts
½	cup rolled oats
¼	tsp ground cinnamon
⅛	tsp salt
1½	sticks (¾ cup) unsalted butter, melted

Ice cream (optional)

■ Heat oven to 350°. Coat a 12 x 8 x 2-inch baking dish with nonstick cooking spray.

■ **Filling.** Combine all ingredients. Spoon into prepared dish.

■ **Topping.** In a bowl, combine flour and next 5 ingredients. Add melted butter and stir until large clumps form. Scatter over apple-cherry mixture.

■ Bake 45 to 55 minutes, until bubbly and lightly browned. Cool slightly. Serve with ice cream, if desired.

PER SERVING 454 CAL; 27 g FAT; 4 g PRO; 52 g CARB; 4 g FIBER

JUMBO APPLE-
OATMEAL COOKIES

Apple-Ginger Cake

MAKES 16 servings **PREP** 25 minutes
BAKE at 350° for 30 minutes

- 2½ **cups all-purpose flour**
- 1½ **tsp baking powder**
- ½ **tsp baking soda**
- 2 **tsp ground ginger**
- 1 **tsp cinnamon**
- ½ **tsp salt**
- 1¼ **cups sugar**
- 1 **cup apple butter**
- ½ **cup vegetable oil**
- 2 **eggs**
- 1 **tsp vanilla extract**
- ½ **cup buttermilk**
- 1 **cup peeled and chopped Honeycrisp apple**
- **Buttery Cream Cheese Frosting (recipe follows)**
- 1 **Honeycrisp apple, cored and thinly sliced**
- 2 **tbsp apple brandy or apple cider**

■ Heat oven to 350°. Coat two 9-inch round cake pans with nonstick cooking spray. Line bottoms with wax paper; coat paper with cooking spray.

■ Combine flour and next 5 ingredients. In a large bowl, beat sugar and next 4 ingredients until smooth. Beat in flour mixture, alternating with buttermilk, in 3 additions. Beat 2 minutes. Fold in chopped apple. Divide between prepared pans.

■ Bake 27 to 30 minutes, until cake springs back when pressed lightly. Cool 10 minutes. Turn onto a cooling rack, remove wax paper and cool completely.

■ Place one cake layer on a plate and frost top with half the frosting. Add second layer and frost top with remaining frosting.

■ Just before serving, toss sliced apple with brandy and pile on center of cake.

Buttery Cream Cheese Frosting Beat 8 oz softened cream cheese, 1 stick softened butter, ½ tsp vanilla extract and 1 cup confectioners' sugar until smooth.

PER SERVING 354 **CAL**; 18 g **FAT**; 4 g **PRO**; 45 g **CARB**; 1 g **FIBER**

CINNAMON-APPLE WAFFLES À LA MODE

Cinnamon-Apple Waffles à la Mode

MAKES 6 servings **PREP** 15 minutes **COOK** 5 minutes per batch

- 2 **cups all-purpose flour**
- 2 **tbsp sugar**
- 1 **tbsp cinnamon**
- 2 **tsp baking powder**
- ½ **tsp salt**
- 2 **eggs, separated**
- 1 **cup milk**
- ⅓ **cup vegetable oil**
- 1½ **cups peeled and shredded Gala apple**
- 1 **Gala apple, cored, peeled and cut into small cubes**
- 3 **tbsp butter**
- 4 **cups assorted ice cream, such as butter pecan, milk chocolate and strawberry**

■ Combine flour and next 4 ingredients. In a large bowl, whisk egg yolks, milk and oil. Blend into flour mixture. Beat egg whites to soft peaks and fold into batter. Gently fold in shredded apple.

■ Heat a waffle iron. Ladle batter into waffle iron, about ½ cup per waffle. Cook according to manufacturer's instructions, 4 to 5 minutes per waffle. Repeat with remaining batter. (Makes about 6 standard-size waffles.)

■ Meanwhile, sauté apple cubes in butter over medium-high for 3 minutes, until browned.

■ Top each waffle with 3 small scoops ice cream, about ⅔ cup total per waffle, and some caramelized apples.

PER SERVING 599 **CAL**; 31 g **FAT**; 11 g **PRO**; 72 g **CARB**; 4 g **FIBER**

APPLE CUPCAKES WITH SALTED CARAMEL FROSTING

The Best Apple Pie Ever

MAKES 12 servings **PREP** 45 minutes
REFRIGERATE 2 hours + 15 minutes
BAKE at 375° for 1 hour

- 2½ cups plus 3 tbsp all-purpose flour
- 2 sticks (1 cup) unsalted butter, cut into pieces and chilled
- 1 tsp salt
- ½ cup ice water
- 1¼ lb Granny Smith apples, peeled and sliced ¼ inch thick
- 1¼ lb Jonathan apples, peeled and sliced ¼ inch thick
- ⅔ cup sugar
- 3 tbsp lemon juice
- 1 tsp ground cinnamon
- ¼ tsp ground nutmeg
- ¼ tsp ground allspice
- ¼ tsp salt
- 1 egg, beaten
- 1 tbsp turbinado sugar

■ Combine 2½ cups flour, the butter and salt in a food processor. Pulse until crumbs are the size of peas. With machine running, slowly pour in ¼ to ½ cup ice water, until dough just comes together (squeeze a bit between your hands to see if it holds). Form into 2 equal rounds, wrap in plastic wrap and refrigerate 2 hours.

■ Heat oven to 375°. On a lightly floured surface, roll one round of dough to fit inside a 9 x 2-inch deep pie dish. Refrigerate 15 minutes.

■ Combine apples, sugar, 3 tbsp flour, lemon juice, cinnamon, nutmeg, allspice and salt. Transfer to pie dish. Roll out second crust and place on top of pie. Pinch edges of both crusts together, then crimp. Brush top and edges with egg, then sprinkle on turbinado sugar.

■ Bake 30 minutes. Carefully wrap foil around edges of crust to prevent burning, then bake another 30 minutes, until golden brown. Cool completely on a wire rack before slicing.

PER SERVING 310 **CAL**; 16 g **FAT**; 4 g **PRO**; 40 g **CARB**; 2 g **FIBER**

Apple Cupcakes with Salted Caramel Frosting

MAKES 24 cupcakes **PREP** 25 minutes **BAKE** at 350° for 30 minutes

- 3 cups all-purpose flour
- 2 tsp baking soda
- 1 tsp ground cinnamon
- ½ tsp salt
- 1½ sticks (¾ cup) unsalted butter, softened
- ½ cup packed brown sugar
- ½ cup granulated sugar
- 2 eggs
- ½ cup sour cream
- 1 tsp vanilla extract
- ¾ cup heavy cream
- 1½ cups peeled and diced Granny Smith apple

  Salted Caramel Frosting (recipe follows)

  Flaked sea salt for garnish (optional)

■ Heat oven to 350°. Line 2 standard-size muffin pans with paper liners.

■ Combine flour and next 3 ingredients. In a large bowl, beat butter and next 5 ingredients until smooth. Beat in flour mixture in 2 additions, alternating with heavy cream. Fold in apple. Fill liners halfway, about 2 rounded tbsp each.

■ Bake 25 to 30 minutes, until toothpick inserted in center comes out clean. Remove from pan; cool completely on a rack.

■ Spread each cupcake with about 2 tsp frosting while still warm and spreadable. If mixture gets too stiff, heat gently. Sprinkle with sea salt, if using, when cool.

Salted Caramel Frosting In a heavy saucepan, heat 40 caramel candies and 6 tbsp heavy cream over low heat until smooth. Cool slightly.

PER SERVING 268 **CAL**; 13 g **FAT**; 3 g **PRO**; 36 g **CARB**; 1 g **FIBER**

THE BEST
APPLE PIE EVER

APPLE-
RASPBERRY
SLAB PIE

Slab pies are gaining in popularity because they're simple to make and they feed a crowd. Most serve twice the number of a standard round pie.

APPLE-CARDAMOM COFFEE CAKE

Apple-Raspberry Slab Pie

MAKES 16 servings **PREP** 30 minutes
BAKE at 400° for 40 minutes
COOL 45 minutes

3	refrigerated piecrusts (from 2 boxes), at room temperature
2½	lb Fuji apples
2	cups raspberries
¾	cup sugar
¼	cup all-purpose flour
2	tbsp lemon juice
⅛	tsp salt
2	tbsp heavy cream
2	tbsp turbinado sugar

■ Heat oven to 400°. Lightly flour a surface. Unroll 2 piecrusts and stack on top of each other. Use a rolling pin to combine crusts into a 17 x 12-inch rectangle. Place in bottom of a rimmed 15 x 10-inch baking sheet. Roll out third piecrust to a 15 x 12-inch rectangle and cut into long strips. Place on another baking sheet. Refrigerate while preparing filling.

■ Peel and slice apples into ⅛-inch-thick slices. Carefully toss with next 5 ingredients. Remove piecrust from refrigerator and pour filling inside. Arrange strips in a lattice pattern, folding over any edges of bottom crust. Brush with heavy cream and sprinkle with turbinado sugar.

■ Bake 35 to 40 minutes, until crust is browned and filling is bubbling. Cool at least 45 minutes before slicing into squares.

PER SERVING 230 **CAL**; 11 g **FAT**; 2 g **PRO**; 36 g **CARB**; 2 g **FIBER**

Apple-Cardamom Coffee Cake

MAKES 9 servings **PREP** 25 minutes **BAKE** at 375° for 40 minutes

CAKE

1¾	cups all-purpose flour
1	tsp baking powder
½	tsp baking soda
½	tsp ground cardamom
½	tsp salt
⅛	tsp ground cloves
4	tbsp unsalted butter, softened
⅔	cup packed light brown sugar
1	egg
⅔	cup buttermilk
2	cups Gala apple, peeled and diced into ½-inch cubes

STREUSEL TOPPING

¼	cup all-purpose flour
¼	cup light brown sugar
3	tbsp cold unsalted butter, cubed
⅛	tsp ground cardamom
⅛	tsp salt

■ Heat oven to 375°. Coat an 8-inch-square baking dish with nonstick cooking spray; dust with flour on the bottom and sides.

■ **Cake.** Whisk first 6 ingredients. In a separate bowl, beat butter and brown sugar with a hand mixer 2 minutes. Beat in egg and buttermilk. Slowly add flour mixture, beating until just combined. Fold in apple. Transfer to prepared baking dish, spreading into an even layer.

■ **Streusel Topping.** In another bowl, combine all ingredients with hands, breaking up butter into smaller pieces. Scatter over batter. Bake 35 to 40 minutes, until browned and a toothpick inserted in center comes out clean.

PER SERVING 290 **CAL**; 10 g **FAT**; 4 g **PRO**; 47 g **CARB**; 1 g **FIBER**

THE $20 CHALLENGE

Make low-cost meals like a master—a Master Chef, that is. *Family Circle* teamed up with the hit TV show and asked contestants to whip up a healthy family dinner using just one secret ingredient: a $20 bill. Here, we serve up the top three.

PESTO-STUFFED
CHICKEN BREAST OVER
ROASTED ASPARAGUS

"I am living my lifelong dream—being a New York City firefighter and a contestant on MasterChef."

– *Eric Howard, New York City Firefighter*

Pesto-Stuffed Chicken Breast over Roasted Asparagus

MAKES 4 servings **PREP** 20 minutes **COOK** 3 minutes **BAKE** at 350° for 8 minutes, 425° for 32 minutes

PESTO
- ½ cup pine nuts
- 4 cups packed fresh basil
- 2 cups spinach
- ½ cup grated Parmesan
- 1 clove garlic
- Salt and black pepper to taste
- ½ cup extra-virgin olive oil

STUFFING
- 2 tbsp vegetable oil
- 4 cups spinach
- 2 cloves garlic
- 1 shallot, minced

CHICKEN
- 4 bone-in or boneless chicken breasts
- ½ cup plus 2 tbsp grated Parmesan
- Salt and black pepper to taste
- Dried oregano to taste
- ¼ cup extra-virgin olive oil

- 1 bunch asparagus
- 1 clove garlic
- ⅛ tsp smoked paprika

■ **Pesto.** Heat oven to 350°. Spread nuts on a baking sheet. Toast until golden and fragrant, tossing occasionally, 5 to 8 minutes. Set aside to cool. Increase oven to 425°.

■ In a food processor, combine toasted nuts, basil, spinach, Parmesan and garlic. Season with salt and pepper. Process until finely chopped. With processor running, slowly pour in olive oil in a steady stream. Process until smooth. Set aside.

■ **Stuffing.** Heat vegetable oil in a large sauté pan over medium. Add spinach and sauté until wilted, about 3 minutes. Slice garlic and add to pan along with shallot. Set aside.

■ **Chicken.** To create a pocket in each breast, slice parallel ⅓ inch beneath skin without cutting all the way through. Divide stuffing and ½ cup Parmesan among pockets. Add 1 tbsp pesto to each pocket. Season with salt, pepper and oregano. Heat 3 tbsp olive oil in a large oven-safe stainless skillet until hot and you see wisps of smoke. Place chicken, skin sides down, and cook until golden and crispy. Transfer to oven and roast 15 to 20 minutes, until temperature reaches 165°.

■ Coat asparagus in 1 tbsp olive oil. Chop garlic, add to asparagus and season with paprika, salt, pepper and oregano. Sprinkle with 2 tbsp Parmesan. Roast 10 to 12 minutes.

■ Top each piece of chicken with a dollop of pesto and serve with asparagus.

"Some of the most delicious meals can surprisingly be made on a budget."

– *Brandi Mudd*
Irvington, KY
Fifth-grade teacher

Pan-Seared Chicken Thighs over Roasted Bell Pepper Polenta with Citrus Arugula Salad and Red Pepper Gastrique

MAKES 4 servings **PREP** 30 minutes **COOK** 15 minutes **BAKE** at 400° for 15 minutes

CHICKEN

- 4 **boneless chicken thighs (about 1½ lb)**
- 2 **tsp smoked paprika**
- 2 **tsp kosher salt**
- 1 **tsp black pepper**
- ¼ **tsp cayenne pepper**

FRIED GREEN TOMATOES

- 1 **green tomato**
- 1½ **cups all-purpose flour**
- ½ **cup cornstarch**
- ½ **tsp salt**
- 1 **tsp black pepper**
- 1 **cup heavy cream**
- 2 **large eggs**
  Grapeseed oil, for frying

POLENTA

- 4 **cups chicken stock**
- ½ **cup heavy cream**
- 2 **tsp kosher salt**
- 1 **tsp black pepper**
- 1 **cup polenta**
- 2 **cloves garlic, minced**
- 1 **sweet red pepper, seeded and finely chopped**

- 1 **shallot, minced**
- 1 **tbsp olive oil**
- 2 **tbsp unsalted butter**

GASTRIQUE

- 1 **cup sugar**
- ½ **cup apple cider vinegar**
- 1 **small roasted red pepper**
- ½ **tsp kosher salt**
- ¼ **tsp black pepper**

ARUGULA SALAD

- 1 **tbsp cider vinegar**
- 1 **tbsp lemon juice**
- 1 **tbsp lime juice**
- 2 **tbsp sugar**
  Kosher salt and black pepper to taste
- ½ **cup grapeseed oil**
- 1 **cup arugula**

■ **Chicken.** Heat oven to 400°. Season chicken with paprika, salt, black pepper and cayenne. Sear in a cast-iron pan, move to a rack and bake 15 minutes.

■ **Fried Green Tomatoes.** Cut tomato into ½-inch-thick slices. Combine next 4 ingredients in a shallow dish; mix

cream and eggs in a second dish. Coat tomato slices with flour mixture, dip in cream-egg mixture and coat again with flour mixture. Let rest 5 minutes. In a cast-iron skillet, fry in oil until golden.

■ **Polenta.** Heat first 4 ingredients in a pot. Add polenta and whisk until softened, 10 to 12 minutes. Sauté garlic, sweet pepper and shallot in oil. Stir into polenta; whisk in butter.

■ **Gastrique.** Meanwhile, add sugar and vinegar to a heavy medium saucepan. Cook over medium until sugar begins to melt. Stir until sugar dissolves; cook, without stirring, until mixture is thick enough to coat the back of a spoon, 10 to 15 minutes. Puree roasted red pepper in a small food processor or blender and fold into finished gastrique. Season with salt and pepper.

■ **Arugula Salad.** Whisk first 6 ingredients. Slowly add oil; whisk to combine. Toss arugula with dressing.

■ Layer polenta, chicken thighs and tomato. Top with arugula. Drizzle gastrique on plate.

"I brought big, bold flavors and a fine dining experience to the family dinner table."

– Shaun O'Neale
Las Vegas, NV
Deejay

Trout with Almonds, Wax Beans and Snap Peas in Fragrant Fish Broth

MAKES 4 servings **PREP** 30 minutes **COOK** 25 minutes

BROTH

1	tbsp plus 2 tsp olive oil
2	shallots, minced
3	cloves garlic, minced
1	tsp kosher salt
½	tsp black pepper
¾	cup white wine
1	qt. fish stock
1	tsp cayenne pepper or to taste
1	tsp smoked paprika
3	sprigs fresh thyme
1	tsp dried oregano
	Zest and juice from 1 lemon
	Zest from 1 lime

TROUT

	Vegetable oil
4	skin-on trout fillets
1	tsp kosher salt
¼	cup toasted sliced almonds

WAX BEANS

1½	cups wax beans
2	tbsp unsalted butter
	Kosher salt and black pepper to taste

SUGAR SNAP PEAS

1	cup sugar snap peas
2	tbsp unsalted butter
	Kosher salt and black pepper to taste

■ **Broth.** In a large pot, add 1 tbsp oil; sauté shallots and garlic until fragrant. Season with salt and pepper.

■ Deglaze pan with white wine and reduce by half. Add fish stock and next 4 ingredients. Reduce by half, about 20 to 25 minutes. Add lemon zest and juice and lime zest. Remove broth from heat, strain and set aside.

■ **Trout.** Meanwhile, heat oil in a stainless skillet over high. Pat fish skin dry. Score each piece 3 times on skin side and season with salt. Cook, skin

sides down, 1 to 2 minutes, then turn to finish for 15 seconds. Remove fish from pan.

■ **Wax Beans.** Bring a large pot of salted water to a boil. Blanch wax beans 2 minutes, then move to an ice bath to stop cooking. Add butter to a hot pan and sauté beans until tender. Season with salt and pepper; set aside.

■ **Sugar Snap Peas.** Bring a large pot of salted water to a boil. Blanch snap peas 2 minutes, then move to an ice bath. When cool, split snap peas lengthwise with your fingers. Add butter to a hot pan and sauté beans until tender. Season with salt and pepper; set aside.

■ To serve, in each of 4 bowls or deep dishes, ladle about ½ cup broth. Arrange 1 trout fillet and ¼ of the snap peas and wax beans in broth. Sprinkle with toasted almonds.

QUICK CHICK

Count down 20 minutes—or less—to dinnertime with these delicious recipes.

CREAMY
CHICKEN
PICCATA

Pan-seared and served in a creamy sauce, curried, coated in Cajun seasonings or tossed with peppers and pasta, chicken suits every mood, occasion and palate.

Creamy Chicken Piccata

MAKES 8 servings **PREP** 20 minutes
COOK 20 minutes

- 2½ **lb chicken cutlets**
- ½ **tsp salt**
- ¼ **tsp black pepper**
- 1 **cup plus 2 tbsp flour**
- 3 **tbsp olive oil**
- 3 **tbsp butter**
- ½ **cup white wine**
- 2 **cups chicken broth**
   Rind from 1 lemon, thinly sliced
- 2 **tbsp capers**
- ½ **cup whipped cream cheese**
- 2 **tbsp chopped parsley**
   Mashed potatoes

Season chicken with salt and pepper. Dredge in 1 cup flour. In a nonstick skillet, heat oil and butter; sauté chicken 3 minutes per side, in 2 batches if necessary. Remove chicken to a plate. Add 2 tbsp flour to skillet and cook 30 seconds. Add wine and cook 30 seconds, scraping up browned bits from bottom of pan. Stir in broth and lemon rind; simmer 2 minutes. Add chicken and capers to pan; cover and simmer 5 minutes. Remove chicken to a serving platter. Over low, whisk in cream cheese until smooth. Spoon sauce over chicken and top with parsley. Serve over mashed potatoes.

PER SERVING 451 **CAL**; 17 g **FAT**; 38 g **PRO**; 25 g **CARB**; 0 g **FIBER**

CHICKEN MURPHY
OVER PENNE

Chicken Murphy over Penne

MAKES 4 servings **PREP** 15 minutes **COOK** 15 minutes

- 2 **tbsp olive oil**
- 4 **cloves sliced garlic**
- 1 **can (28 oz) whole tomatoes**
- ½ **tsp salt**
- ¼ **tsp black pepper**
- 1½ **lb boneless, skinless chicken breasts, cut into 2-inch chunks**
- 1 **seeded and sliced sweet red pepper**
- 1 **sliced sweet onion**
- 4 **hot cherry peppers, seeds removed, cut in half**
- ½ **lb cooked penne**
- ¼ **cup grated Parmesan**

■ Heat oil in a skillet over medium-high. Add garlic and cook 2 minutes; stir in tomatoes, salt and black pepper. Break up tomatoes and simmer 3 minutes. Add chicken to skillet. Stir in red pepper, onion and cherry peppers. Cook, covered, 10 minutes, turning chicken after 5 minutes. Serve with penne and Parmesan.

PER SERVING 560 **CAL**; 14 g **FAT**; 46 g **PRO**; 62 g **CARB**; 6 g **FIBER**

CHICKEN KORMA

Chicken and Broccolini Aglio e Olio

MAKES 4 servings **PREP** 15 minutes
COOK 20 minutes

- 1 **bunch Broccolini**
- ½ **lb linguine**
- 1½ **lb boneless, skinless chicken breasts**
- ¼ **cup flour**
- ½ **tsp salt**
- ¼ **tsp black pepper**
- 4 **tbsp olive oil**
- 6 **cloves sliced garlic**
- 2 **tbsp capers**
- 1 **tbsp caper brine**
- ¼ **tsp red pepper flakes**
- 2 **tbsp chopped parsley**

■ Cut Broccolini into thirds and boil 3 minutes in a large pot of water. Remove with a slotted spoon; add linguine and cook following package directions (about 8 minutes). Drain, reserving ½ cup cooking water. Meanwhile, cut chicken into 1-inch pieces and coat with flour. Season with ¼ tsp each salt and pepper. Heat 3 tbsp olive oil in a skillet and cook 4 minutes per side. Add garlic, capers, brine and pepper flakes. Cook 1 minute. Add Broccolini and reserved pasta water and bring to a simmer. Add pasta and ¼ tsp salt. Drizzle with 1 tbsp olive oil and sprinkle with parsley.

PER SERVING 507 **CAL**; 16 g **FAT**; 39 g **PRO**; 55 g **CARB**; 9 g **FIBER**

Chicken Korma

MAKES 4 servings **PREP** 15 minutes **COOK** 11 minutes

- ¼ **cup cashews**
- 2 **tbsp vegetable oil**
- 1 **large onion, sliced**
- 1 **tbsp fresh ginger, chopped**
- 2 **cloves garlic, chopped**
- 2 **tsp curry powder**
- 1 **tsp turmeric**
- 1¼ **lb boneless, skinless chicken breasts, cut into 1-inch pieces**
- ½ **cup chicken broth**
- ¼ **cup tomato sauce**
- ¾ **tsp salt**
- ½ **cup plain Greek yogurt**
- 1 **tbsp cornstarch**
- 3 **cups cooked basmati rice**

■ Soak cashews in ¼ cup boiling water 15 minutes.

■ Heat oil in a skillet over medium-high; add onion, ginger and garlic. Cook 3 minutes. Stir in curry powder, turmeric and chicken. Cook 3 minutes. Stir in broth, tomato sauce and salt; simmer 3 minutes.

■ In a food processor, blend cashews, soaking water and yogurt. Blend cornstarch with 1 tbsp water; add to skillet. Stir in cashew mixture and cook 2 minutes. Serve with basmati rice.

PER SERVING 496 **CAL**; 16 g **FAT**; 36 g **PRO**; 53 g **CARB**; 2 g **FIBER**

CHICKEN AND BROCCOLINI AGLIO E OLIO

Chicken with Basil-Tomato Aioli

MAKES 4 servings **PREP** 20 minutes
COOK 14 minutes

- **1 cup light mayo**
- **½ cup basil leaves**
- **1 clove garlic**
- **2 tsp olive oil**
- **1 tsp lemon juice**
- **¾ tsp salt**
- **½ tsp black pepper**
- **5 oil-packed sun-dried tomatoes, cut into strips**
- **4 boneless, skinless chicken breasts (1 lb)**
- **3 cups cooked orzo**

■ Combine mayo, basil, garlic, oil, lemon juice and ¼ tsp each salt and pepper in a food processor. Process until smooth. Spoon into a serving bowl and stir in tomatoes. Season chicken with ½ tsp salt and ¼ tsp pepper. Coat a grill pan with nonstick cooking spray; cook over medium-high 6 to 7 minutes per side, until cooked through. Drizzle pan drippings over chicken. Serve with aioli and orzo.

Note: For more intense flavor, prep and refrigerate aioli a day or two in advance.

PER SERVING 562 **CAL**; 25 g **FAT**; 30 g **PRO**; 50 g **CARB**; 2 g **FIBER**

CAJUN-FRIED CHICKEN WITH RÉMOULADE

Cajun-Fried Chicken with Rémoulade

MAKES 4 servings **PREP** 15 minutes **COOK** 10 minutes

- **½ cup light mayo**
- **3 tbsp sweet pickle relish**
- **2 tbsp chopped parsley**
- **1 tbsp chopped capers**
- **1 tbsp Dijon mustard**
- **1 tbsp lemon juice**
- **¼ tsp hot pepper sauce**
- **1¼ tsp onion salt**
- **½ cup cracker meal**
- **2 tsp chili powder**
- **½ tsp cumin**
- **½ tsp cayenne**
- **4 boneless chicken breasts (about 1½ lb)**
- **3 tbsp flour**
- **2 beaten eggs**
- **¼ cup solid vegetable shortening**
- **Roasted potato wedges**

■ Combine mayo, relish, parsley, capers, mustard, lemon juice, hot pepper sauce and ¼ tsp onion salt. Refrigerate.

■ In a shallow dish, combine cracker meal, chili powder, 1 tsp onion salt, cumin and cayenne.

■ Dip chicken in flour, eggs and cracker meal mixture. Heat shortening in a nonstick skillet over medium-high. Add chicken and cook 5 minutes per side.

■ Remove to a plate and slice on an angle. Serve with rémoulade and potato wedges.

Note: Cracker meal really ramps up the crunch factor, but bread crumbs work well too.

PER SERVING 626 **CAL**; 34 g **FAT**; 40 g **PRO**; 44 g **CARB**; 3 g **FIBER**

FIVE-SPICE CHICKEN SKEWERS

General Tso's Chicken

MAKES 4 servings **PREP** 15 minutes
COOK 8 minutes

- 1 cup chicken broth
- 2 tbsp soy sauce
- 1 tbsp chopped ginger
- 2 tsp rice vinegar
- 2 tsp sugar
- 2 tsp cornstarch
- 1 tsp Asian chili paste
- 2 tbsp canola oil
- 1½ lb boneless, skinless chicken breasts, cut into 1½-inch-thick pieces
- ½ cup sliced scallions
- 2 cups cooked brown rice
- 1 head steamed broccoli

■ Whisk broth, soy sauce, ginger, vinegar, sugar, cornstarch and chili paste. Heat oil in a nonstick skillet. Add chicken to skillet and cook 6 minutes, turning after 3 minutes; remove to a plate. Stir in broth mixture and bring to a simmer; add back chicken and scallions. Stir to coat chicken and simmer 2 minutes. Serve with rice and broccoli.

PER SERVING 414 **CAL**; 11 g **FAT**; 45 g **PRO**; 33 g **CARB**; 3 g **FIBER**

Five-Spice Chicken Skewers

MAKES 4 servings **PREP** 20 minutes **CHILL** 2 hours **GRILL** 14 minutes

- ¼ cup rice wine vinegar
- ¼ cup canola oil
- 3 tbsp soy sauce
- 2 tsp Chinese five-spice powder
- 1 tsp sesame oil
- ½ cup sliced scallions
- 2 tbsp chopped ginger
- 1¼ lb boneless, skinless chicken breasts, cut into 1½-inch chunks
- 2 seeded sweet orange peppers, cut into 1½-inch pieces
- 16 scallions, cut into 2-inch pieces
- Cooked couscous

■ Combine vinegar, canola oil, soy sauce, five-spice powder and sesame oil. Stir in sliced scallions and ginger. Place chicken in a resealable plastic bag. Add peppers and ¾ of the marinade. Refrigerate 2 hours. Heat grill to medium-high. Thread chicken, peppers and cut scallions on 8 skewers. Brush with remaining marinade and grill 7 minutes per side, until chicken is cooked through. Serve with couscous.

PER SERVING 421 **CAL**; 17 g **FAT**; 39 g **PRO**; 26 g **CARB**; 3 g **FIBER**

Arrabbiata Sauce with Chicken and Mushrooms

MAKES 6 servings **PREP** 10 minutes
COOK 15 minutes

- 3 **tbsp olive oil**
- 4 **cups sliced mushrooms**
- 1½ **lb boneless, skinless chicken breasts, cut into 1-inch pieces**
- ¾ **tsp salt**
- 3 **cloves chopped garlic**
- 3 **cans (8 oz each) tomato sauce**
- ¾ **tsp red pepper flakes**
- ½ **lb cooked shells**
- ½ **cup shredded ricotta salata**

■ Heat 2 tbsp olive oil in a skillet over medium-high. Add mushrooms and cook 5 minutes. Push mushrooms to one side of skillet and add chicken. Season with ¼ tsp salt and cook 7 minutes, turning after 4 minutes. Remove to a plate. Add 1 tbsp olive oil and garlic to skillet; cook 1 minute. Stir in sauce, pepper flakes and ½ tsp salt; simmer 2 minutes. Return chicken and mushrooms to skillet and heat through. Add shells and toss with sauce. Top with ricotta salata.

Note: We love this with ricotta salata, but if you can't find it at your grocery store, grated Parmesan is a great substitute.

PER SERVING 571 **CAL**; 13 g **FAT**; 42 g **PRO**; 716 g **CARB**; 4 g **FIBER**

CAPRESE-STYLE CHICKEN

Caprese-Style Chicken

MAKES 8 servings **PREP** 15 minutes **MARINATE** 20 minutes **COOK** 14 minutes

- 1 **pkg (8 oz) low-fat plain yogurt**
- 3 **tbsp plus ¼ cup balsamic vinegar**
- 8 **thinly sliced boneless, skinless chicken cutlets (about 1½ lb)**
- 1 **tbsp olive oil**
- 1 **medium onion, cut into 16 wedges**
- 4 **cups chopped plum tomatoes (about 1 lb)**
- 1 **tsp salt**
- ½ **tsp black pepper**
- 8 **oz cubed fresh mozzarella**
- 1 **cup chopped basil**
  Tossed green salad

■ Combine yogurt and 3 tbsp vinegar in a resealable plastic bag. Add chicken and refrigerate 20 minutes.

Heat oil in a skillet over medium. Add onion and cook 5 minutes. Add ¼ cup vinegar and 2 tbsp water. Simmer 7 minutes, until thickened. Add tomatoes, salt and pepper; cook 2 minutes. Cool slightly and stir in mozzarella and basil. Meanwhile, broil or grill marinated chicken 3 to 4 minutes per side. Spoon about ¼ cup tomato mixture over each cutlet and serve with a tossed green salad.

Note: Switch it up by going Greek: Skip the basil, swap in feta for the mozzarella and add ½ cup pitted and halved Kalamata olives.

PER SERVING 244 **CAL**; 11 g **FAT**; 24 g **PRO**; 6 g **CARB**; 1 g **FIBER**

MORNING RUSH

Get your day off to a great start with these make-ahead mobile eats.

Pumpkin Spice Granola

MAKES 20 servings **PREP** 5 minutes
BAKE 30 minutes at 350°

- 2 **cups rolled oats**
- 1 **cup pecans**
- 1 **cup raw unsalted pumpkin seeds**
- ⅓ **cup extra-virgin olive oil**
- ⅓ **cup honey**
- 2 **tsp pumpkin pie spice**
- ½ **tsp kosher salt**
- 1 **cup dried cranberries**

■ In a large bowl, combine oats, pecans, pumpkin seeds, oil, honey, pie spice and salt. Mix until well combined and spread onto a rimmed baking sheet. Bake at 350° for 30 minutes, stirring halfway. Cool completely on baking sheet, then mix in cranberries.

PER SERVING 170 **CAL**; 12 g **FAT**; 3 g **PRO**; 14 g **CARB**; 1 g **FIBER**

PB&J Overnight Oats

MAKES 4 servings **PREP** 5 minutes
COOK 5 minutes **CHILL** overnight

- 2 **cups milk**
- 1 **cup steel-cut oats (not quick-cook)**
- ⅓ **cup natural chunky peanut butter**
- 2 **tbsp honey**
- ¼ **tsp salt**
- 4 **microwave-safe jars**
- 4 **tbsp strawberry preserves**

■ In a small pot, stir milk, oats, peanut butter, honey and salt. Bring to a simmer. Cook 5 minutes; stir until peanut butter is melted. Cool slightly, then pour into jars and cover with their lids. Refrigerate overnight. Reheat in microwave. Serve each with 1 tbsp strawberry preserves.

PER SERVING 370 **CAL**; 16 g **FAT**; 15 g **PRO**; 47 g **CARB**; 5 g **FIBER**

**PUMPKIN SPICE
GRANOLA**

Chorizo Breakfast Burritos

MAKES 6 servings **PREP** 5 minutes
COOK 10 minutes **HEAT** 2 minutes

- 6 oz (2 links) uncooked chorizo sausage, casings removed
- 1 tbsp extra-virgin olive oil
- 1 chopped vine tomato
- ⅓ cup thinly sliced scallions
- 6 eggs
- ¼ tsp salt
- 6 8-inch flour tortillas
- 6 tbsp shredded sharp cheddar
  Sour cream
  Salsa

■ Cook sausage in oil over medium-high, breaking up with a spoon, until browned, 5 to 7 minutes. Stir in tomato and scallions. Cook 1 minute, scraping bottom of pan.

■ Whisk eggs with salt and pour into pan, stirring until scrambled. Divide mixture among tortillas and top each with 1 tbsp cheddar. Roll tightly and freeze in a resealable plastic bag.

■ When reheating, wrap in a damp paper towel and microwave 2 minutes. Serve with sour cream and salsa.

PER SERVING 320 **CAL**; 17 g **FAT**; 15 g **PRO**; 27 g **CARB**; 1 g **FIBER**

Bacon-Banana Muffins

MAKES 12 servings **PREP** 15 minutes
COOK 5 minutes **BAKE** 30 minutes at 375°

- 8 oz diced bacon
- 2¼ cups all-purpose flour
- 1 tsp baking powder
- ½ tsp salt
- 1 cup packed light brown sugar
- 1 stick (½ cup) unsalted butter, softened
- 2 eggs
- 1 cup (about 3 small) mashed very ripe bananas
- ¼ cup milk
- ½ tsp vanilla extract

■ In a skillet, cook bacon 5 minutes over medium-high, until crispy. Remove to a paper-towel-lined plate with a slotted spoon. Reserve 2 tbsp bacon fat. Whisk flour, baking powder and salt. In a separate bowl, beat sugar with butter and reserved bacon fat. Beat in eggs, bananas, milk and vanilla extract. Beat in flour until combined. Stir in bacon. Place paper liners in a standard 12-cup muffin tin and pour in batter. Bake at 375° for 30 to 35 minutes, until browned and a toothpick inserted in centers comes out clean.

PER SERVING 360 **CAL**; 19 g **FAT**; 6 g **PRO**; 42 g **CARB**; 1 g **FIBER**

Blueberry, Lemon and Poppy Seed Muffins

MAKES 12 servings **PREP** 15 minutes
BAKE 30 minutes at 375°

- 2¼ cups all-purpose flour
- 1 tsp baking powder
- ½ tsp salt
- 1 cup sugar
- 10 tbsp unsalted butter, softened
- 2 eggs
- ¼ cup milk
- ¼ cup lemon juice
- 1 tbsp poppy seeds
- 1 tsp lemon zest
- 1 cup blueberries

■ Whisk flour, baking powder and salt. In a separate bowl, beat sugar with butter. Beat in eggs, milk, lemon juice, poppy seeds and zest. Beat in flour until just combined. Stir in blueberries with a spatula. Place paper liners in a standard 12-cup muffin tin and pour in batter. Bake at 375° for 30 to 35 minutes, until browned and a toothpick inserted in centers comes out clean. Once cool, freeze in a single layer in a resealable plastic bag.

PER SERVING 260 **CAL**; 11 g **FAT**; 4 g **PRO**; 37 g **CARB**; 1 g **FIBER**

CHORIZO
BREAKFAST
BURRITOS

BLUEBERRY,
LEMON AND POPPY
SEED MUFFINS

Carrot-Pineapple Quick Bread

MAKES 12 servings **PREP** 20 minutes
BAKE 50 minutes at 350°

- ¾ cup all-purpose flour
- ¾ cup whole wheat flour
- ½ tsp baking soda
- ½ tsp baking powder
- ¼ tsp ground nutmeg
- ¼ tsp salt
- 1 cup finely shredded carrots
- ⅔ cup packed light brown sugar
- ½ cup vegetable oil
- 1 egg
- 1 can (8 oz) crushed pineapple, drained

■ Line an 8½ x 4½ x 2½-inch loaf pan with foil and coat with nonstick cooking spray. Whisk all-purpose flour, whole wheat flour, baking soda, baking powder, nutmeg and salt.

■ In a separate bowl, combine carrots, sugar, oil, egg and pineapple. Pour dry ingredients into wet ingredients and mix until just combined.

■ Transfer to loaf pan. Bake at 350° for 50 minutes, until a toothpick inserted in center comes out clean. Cool completely on a wire rack before slicing.

PER SERVING 200 **CAL**; 10 g **FAT**; 3 g **PRO**; 27 g **CARB**; 1 g **FIBER**

CARROT-PINEAPPLE QUICK BREAD

Maple-Walnut Chia Pudding

MAKES 4 servings **PREP** 5 minutes
CHILL overnight

- 2 cups unsweetened vanilla almond milk
- ½ cup chia seeds
- ¼ cup pure maple syrup
- 8 tbsp toasted chopped walnuts

■ Combine milk, chia seeds and syrup. Distribute among 4 lidded jars and refrigerate overnight. Just before serving, stir 2 tbsp walnuts into each and drizzle with more syrup.

PER SERVING 260 **CAL**; 16 g **FAT**; 8 g **PRO**; 27 g **CARB**; 13 g **FIBER**

Apricot-Quinoa Bars

MAKES 12 servings **PREP** 15 minutes
BAKE 30 minutes at 350°

- 1 cup uncooked quinoa
- 1 cup uncooked rolled oats
- 1 cup chopped dried apricots
- ½ cup chopped shelled unsalted pistachios
- 3 egg whites
- ½ cup honey
- ¼ cup vegetable oil
- ¼ tsp salt

■ Toast quinoa in a medium skillet for 2 to 3 minutes over medium, until quinoa starts making a popping sound. Toss with oats, apricots and pistachios.

■ In a separate bowl, whisk egg whites, honey, oil and salt. Stir into dry mixture.

■ Line an 8 x 8-inch baking dish with foil and coat with nonstick cooking spray. Spread mixture evenly, pressing down firmly. Bake at 350° for 30 minutes, until lightly browned. Cool completely, then refrigerate. Slice into bars; store in a resealable container.

PER SERVING 260 **CAL**; 8 g **FAT**; 6 g **PRO**; 42 g **CARB**; 4 g **FIBER**

Sausage, Pepper and Cheese Crustless Quiches

MAKES 12 servings **PREP** 10 minutes
COOK 5 minutes **BAKE** 20 minutes at 350°

- 6 oz (2 links) uncooked chicken sausage, casings removed
- 1 tbsp extra-virgin olive oil
- 12 eggs
- ¼ cup milk
- ½ cup shredded Monterey Jack cheese
- ½ cup diced roasted red peppers
- ½ tsp salt
- ¼ tsp black pepper

■ Cook sausage in oil over medium-high, breaking up with a wooden spoon, until browned, 5 to 7 minutes. Cool slightly.

■ In a bowl, whisk eggs, milk, cheese, red peppers, salt and pepper. Stir in sausage. Coat a standard 12-cup muffin tin with nonstick cooking spray. Ladle egg mixture evenly into tin. Bake at 350° for 20 to 22 minutes, until puffed and eggs are cooked.

■ Let muffins cool, then remove from tin and freeze in a single layer in a resealable plastic bag. To reheat, wrap in a damp paper towel and microwave 30 to 45 seconds.

PER SERVING 130 **CAL**; 9 g **FAT**; 10 g **PRO**; 1 g **CARB**; 0 g **FIBER**

Loaded Breakfast Frittata

MAKES 6 servings **PREP** 5 minutes
COOK 10 minutes **BAKE** 10 minutes at 400°
REHEAT 2 minutes

- 7 whole eggs
- 2 egg whites
- ½ cup shredded cheddar
- ¼ tsp salt
- ¼ tsp black pepper
- 6 oz diced bacon
- 2 cups thawed frozen shredded hash brown potatoes
- 1 tbsp olive oil (if needed)
- ½ cup thawed frozen spinach, squeezed dry

LOADED BREAKFAST FRITTATA

■ Whisk eggs, egg whites, ¼ cup cheddar, salt and pepper.

■ Cook bacon in a 10-inch nonstick oven-safe skillet over medium-high. Remove to a paper-towel-lined plate with a slotted spoon. Pour off all but 2 tbsp bacon fat from skillet, reserving the excess.

■ Add hash browns (before adding, squeeze tightly with a clean towel to remove as much moisture as possible). Cook 3 minutes, stirring, until browned. Pour 1 tbsp reserved bacon fat (or use oil if none remains) around perimeter of skillet, then stir in spinach, bacon and eggs. Cook 2 minutes and sprinkle with ¼ cup more shredded cheddar.

■ Bake at 400° for 10 minutes, until eggs are cooked. Use a knife or spatula to release frittata from sides and carefully slide onto a plate.

■ Once cool, slice into 6 wedges, wrap each in plastic and place in a resealable plastic bag. To reheat, wrap in a paper towel and microwave 2 minutes.

PER SERVING 320 **CAL**; 25 g **FAT**; 14 g **PRO**; 10 g **CARB**; 2 g **FIBER**

PEANUT BUTTER CUP
CAKE ROLL,
PAGE 240

OCTOBER

235

245

250

PASTA PRONTO

These 10 dinners go from pot to plate in 15 minutes.

LINGUINE WITH CHICKEN
AND MUSHROOMS

Pasta is an adaptable, easy-to-make and comforting weeknight meal—and there's a noodle and flavor combination here to please everyone in your family.

Linguine with Chicken and Mushrooms

MAKES 6 servings **PREP** 10 minutes
COOK 15 minutes

1	**lb linguine**
3	**tbsp unsalted butter**
2	**pkg (4 oz each) mixed sliced mushrooms**
2	**cups shredded rotisserie chicken**
½	**cup heavy cream**
2	**tbsp chopped fresh parsley**
¼	**cup grated Parmesan**
½	**tsp salt**
	Cracked black pepper
1	**tsp truffle oil**

■ Bring a large pot of salted water to a boil. Add linguine and cook until al dente, 9 minutes. Drain, reserving 1¼ cups pasta water. Melt unsalted butter in a large skillet over medium-high. Add mixed sliced mushrooms and cook 3 minutes. Stir in shredded rotisserie chicken, heavy cream and chopped parsley. Simmer 3 minutes. Toss mushroom mixture with linguine, ¾ cup pasta water, grated Parmesan and salt. If sauce is too thick, add remaining pasta water to loosen. Sprinkle with cracked black pepper and drizzle with truffle oil.

PER SERVING 505 **CAL**; 19 g **FAT** 25 g **PRO**; 59 g **CARB**; 3 g **FIBER**;

NO-BAKE LASAGNA BOWL

No-Bake Lasagna Bowl

MAKES 8 servings **PREP** 10 minutes **COOK** 10 minutes **MICROWAVE** 1 minute

1	**lb lasagna noodles**
1½	**lb ground beef**
1	**tbsp minced garlic**
1	**jar (24 oz) marinara sauce**
¾	**tsp salt**
½	**tsp black pepper**
1	**container (15 oz) ricotta**
¼	**cup grated Parmesan**
¼	**cup fresh basil leaves, chopped**
	Grated Parmesan

■ Bring a large pot of salted water to a boil. Break lasagna noodles into thirds and add to boiling water. Cook until al dente, 8 minutes; drain. Meanwhile, heat a 12-inch skillet over medium-high. Add ground beef and brown, breaking apart with a wooden spoon, 5 minutes. Drain off liquid. Stir minced garlic and marinara sauce, ½ tsp salt and ¼ tsp pepper into skillet. Simmer 3 minutes. In a bowl, stir ricotta, ¼ cup grated Parmesan, chopped basil and ¼ tsp each salt and pepper. Microwave 1 minute until slightly heated. Stir noodles into skillet with meat mixture. Cook 2 minutes. To serve, spoon ⅔ cup noodle mixture into a bowl, top with about ¼ cup ricotta mixture and another ⅔ cup noodle mixture. Sprinkle with grated Parmesan.

PER SERVING 536 **CAL**; 20 g **FAT** 33 g **PRO**; 56 g **CARB**; 4 g **FIBER**

GEMELLI WITH
SAUSAGE AND FENNEL

Cauliflower Parmesan

MAKES 6 servings PREP 10 minutes
COOK 13 minutes BROIL 4 minutes

- **1 lb medium pasta shells**
- **8 cups cauliflower florets (about a 2½-lb head)**
- **2 tbsp plus ¼ cup olive oil**
- **½ tsp salt**
- **¼ tsp black pepper**
- **¼ cup toasted pine nuts**
- **2 tbsp grated Parmesan**
- **½ cup fresh basil leaves, cut into thin strips**

■ Bring 2 pots of salted water to a boil. Add medium pasta shells to one pot. Cook 13 minutes. Drain and return to pot, reserving ¾ cup pasta water. Meanwhile, add cauliflower florets to second pot of water. Cook 4 minutes and drain well. Transfer to a baking sheet and toss with 2 tbsp olive oil, salt and pepper. Push florets close together but in a single layer and top with grated Parmesan. Broil, 3 inches from heat, 3 to 4 minutes, until browned. Toss pasta with cauliflower, ¼ cup olive oil, toasted pine nuts, grated Parmesan, ½ cup reserved pasta water and basil strips. If pasta seems dry, add ¼ cup more pasta water.

PER SERVING 500 CAL; 21 g FAT 16 g PRO; 64 g CARB; 7 g FIBER

Gemelli with Sausage and Fennel

MAKES 6 servings PREP 5 minutes COOK 14 minutes

- **1 lb gemelli**
- **2 tbsp olive oil**
- **1 pkg (1 to 1¼ lb) spicy Italian sausage**
- **1 fennel bulb**
- **1 halved and sliced large sweet onion**
- **2 cups halved cherry tomatoes**
- **¼ cup grated Parmesan**

■ Bring a large pot of salted water to a boil. Add gemelli, cook 9 minutes and drain, reserving ¾ cup pasta water. Meanwhile, heat olive oil in a large skillet over medium-high. When hot, crumble in spicy Italian sausage (casings removed). Sauté 5 minutes, breaking up with a spoon. Trim fennel bulb (reserving fronds, if desired). Cut out core and thinly slice bulb. Add fennel and halved and sliced large sweet onion to sausage. Cook 6 minutes and reduce heat to medium. Add halved cherry tomatoes. Cook 3 minutes. Toss pasta with sausage mixture, reserved pasta water, grated Parmesan and fennel fronds, if using.

PER SERVING 539 CAL; 20 g FAT; 21 g PRO; 67 g CARB; 5 g FIBER

CAULIFLOWER
PARMESAN

PENNE
PEPERONATA

BUCATINI
MARGHERITA

Penne Peperonata

MAKES 6 servings **PREP** 10 minutes
COOK 11 minutes

- 1   lb penne pasta
- 2   tbsp olive oil
- 2   seeded and thinly sliced red, yellow or orange sweet peppers
- 8   oz diced Canadian bacon
- 12 oz halved mixed cherry tomatoes
- 1   can (8 oz) tomato sauce
- ¼   tsp salt
- ¼   tsp black pepper
- ½   cup heavy cream
- ¼   cup grated Parmesan

■ Bring a large pot of salted water to a boil. Add penne pasta and cook until al dente, 10 minutes. Drain. Meanwhile, heat olive oil in a large skillet over medium. Add pepper slices and diced Canadian bacon. Cook 3 minutes. Stir in mixed cherry tomatoes; cook 3 minutes. Stir in tomato sauce, salt and black pepper. Simmer 5 minutes. Remove from heat and stir in heavy cream. Toss sauce with penne and top with grated Parmesan.

PER SERVING 482 **CAL**; 16 g **FAT** 20 g **PRO**; 65 g **CARB**; 5 g **FIBER**

Bucatini Margherita

MAKES 6 servings **PREP** 5 minutes **COOK** 15 minutes

- 3   tbsp unsalted butter
- 2   medium diced onions
- 3   cloves sliced garlic
- 1   can (28 oz) whole peeled San Marzano tomatoes in juice
- 1   can (8 oz) tomato sauce
- 2   tbsp sugar
- ½   tsp salt
- ¼   tsp black pepper
- 1   lb bucatini or thin spaghetti
- 1   cup fresh basil leaves, chopped
      BelGioioso Burrata with Black Truffles

■ Bring a large pot of salted water to a boil. Melt unsalted butter in a large skillet over medium. Add diced onions and sliced garlic. Cook 5 minutes. Pour in tomatoes, breaking them apart with your hands or a wooden spoon. Stir in tomato sauce, sugar, salt and pepper. Simmer 10 minutes over medium-high. Meanwhile, add bucatini or thin spaghetti to boiling water and cook per package directions, about 9 minutes. Drain. Toss bucatini with tomato sauce and chopped basil and top with spoonfuls of BelGioioso Burrata with Black Truffles.

PER SERVING 507 **CAL**; 16 g **FAT**; 18 g **PRO**; 72 g **CARB**; 5 g **FIBER**

GREEN CAVATELLI

LEMONY ORECCHIETTE WITH SHRIMP AND KALE

Lemony Orecchiette with Shrimp and Kale

MAKES 6 servings **PREP** 10 minutes
COOK 9 minutes

- 1 **lb orecchiette pasta**
- 4 **tbsp olive oil**
- 1 **lb cleaned raw shrimp**
- 6 **packed cups trimmed and sliced Tuscan kale**
- 2 **cloves sliced garlic**
- ¼ **tsp red pepper flakes (optional)**
- ¾ **cup crumbled feta cheese**
- 2 **tbsp lemon juice**
- 2 **tsp lemon zest**
- ½ **tsp salt**
- ½ **tsp black pepper**

■ Bring a large pot of salted water to a boil. Add orecchiette pasta. Cook 9 minutes; drain, reserving 1 cup cooking water. Meanwhile, heat 2 tbsp olive oil over medium-high. Add cleaned raw shrimp. Cook 3 to 4 minutes, turning once. Remove to a plate. Add 2 more tbsp olive oil to skillet, along with trimmed and sliced Tuscan kale, garlic and red pepper flakes, if desired. Cook 4 minutes. In a large bowl, toss orecchiette with shrimp, kale mixture, reserved pasta water, crumbled feta cheese, lemon juice, lemon zest, salt and black pepper.

PER SERVING 492 **CAL**; 15 g **FAT**; 29 g **PRO**; 63 g **CARB**; 4 g **FIBER**

Green Cavatelli

MAKES 4 servings **PREP** 12 minutes **COOK** 10 minutes

- 8 **oz trimmed asparagus**
- 8 **oz trimmed green beans**
- 2 **tbsp olive oil**
- 1 **bag (13 oz) frozen ricotta cavatelli**
- 1 **bag (5 oz) spinach and/or arugula**
- ¾ **cup frozen peas**
   Salt
   Black pepper
- ⅓ **cup basil pesto**

■ Bring a large pot of salted water to a boil. Cut trimmed asparagus and trimmed green beans into 1-inch pieces. Add to boiling water and boil 2 minutes. Remove to a large skillet with a slotted spoon. Add olive oil and heat over medium-high. Add frozen ricotta cavatelli to boiling water and cook 5 to 8 minutes. Meanwhile, coarsely chop spinach and/or arugula and add to skillet with asparagus and beans. Cook 2 minutes and stir in frozen peas. Season with salt and pepper to taste. Keep warm. Drain cavatelli and add to skillet along with basil pesto. Toss to combine and serve immediately.

Note: Freeze leftover pesto in 1 tbsp portions in an ice tray, then toss 3 or 4, still frozen, into cooked pasta for a last-minute side.

PER SERVING 364 **CAL**; 17 g **FAT**; 12 g **PRO**; 44 g **CARB**; 7 g **FIBER**

Tortellini Mac and Cheese

MAKES 4 servings **PREP** 5 minutes
COOK 8 minutes

- 2 **pkg (9 oz each) fresh chicken and prosciutto tortellini**
- 1 **cup frozen peas**
- 2 **tbsp unsalted butter**
- 2 **tbsp all-purpose flour**
- 1½ **cups whole milk**
- 1 **tbsp dried minced onion**
- ¼ **tsp pepper**
- 6 **oz shredded sharp white cheddar**

■ Bring a large pot of salted water to a boil. Add fresh chicken and prosciutto tortellini and cook 8 minutes, adding frozen peas for last 3 minutes. Drain. Meanwhile, in a medium pot, melt unsalted butter. Sprinkle with all-purpose flour and cook, whisking, 2 minutes. While whisking, add whole milk. Stir in dried minced onion and pepper. Bring to a simmer over medium-high; simmer 3 minutes. Remove from heat and whisk in shredded sharp white cheddar. Stir tortellini and peas into cheese sauce and serve.

Note: Swap in a seasonal flavor of ravioli, like butternut squash or pumpkin, for the chicken tortellini.

PER SERVING 705 **CAL**; 33 g **FAT**; 34 g **PRO**; 68 g **CARB**; 4 g **FIBER**

SPAGHETTI WITH HAM AND EGGS

TORTELLINI MAC AND CHEESE

Spaghetti with Ham and Eggs

MAKES 6 servings **PREP** 5 minutes **COOK** 9 minutes

- 1 **lb spaghetti**
- ½ **lb thinly sliced ham (cut into strips)**
- 3 **tbsp unsalted butter**
- 4 **eggs**
- ⅓ **cup grated Parmesan**
- ½ **tsp salt**
- **Cracked black pepper**

■ Bring a large pot of salted water to a boil. Add spaghetti and cook 9 minutes. Drain, reserving ¾ cup pasta water. Meanwhile, sauté ham in 1 tbsp butter in a large skillet over medium-high for 2 minutes. Remove to a plate. Add 2 tbsp butter to skillet and crack in eggs. Fry over medium 3 to 4 minutes, until whites are set. Gently flip eggs and remove from heat. Place spaghetti and ham in a large bowl. Place eggs on top of pasta and cut into strips with a serrated knife. Toss everything together, along with reserved pasta water, grated Parmesan, salt and cracked black pepper.

PER SERVING 439 **CAL**; 12 g **FAT**; 22 g **PRO**; 58 g **CARB**; 2 g **FIBER**

CANDY CRUSH

Take your Halloween haul up a notch with these cupcakes, cookies and brownies.

HALLOWEEN SKILLET COOKIE

Can't decide between a baked goodie and your favorite candy? These confection-infused treats deliver both.

STUFFED CHOCOLATE-CARAMEL BROWNIES

Halloween Skillet Cookie

MAKES 12 servings **PREP** 25 minutes
BAKE at 350° for 35 minutes **COOL** 30 minutes

- 2 **cups all-purpose flour**
- 1 **tsp baking powder**
- ¾ **tsp salt**
- 2 **sticks (1 cup) unsalted butter, softened**
- 1 **cup granulated sugar**
- 2 **eggs**
- 1 **tsp vanilla extract**
- ¾ **cup orange, yellow and brown M&M's**
- 1 **tbsp turbinado sugar**

■ Heat oven to 350°. In a bowl, whisk first 3 ingredients. In a separate bowl, beat butter and sugar 3 minutes, until fluffy. Beat in eggs and vanilla. Pour in dry ingredients and beat until just combined. Fold in ½ cup M&M's.

■ Coat a 10-inch cast-iron skillet with nonstick cooking spray. Using an offset spatula, spread batter into skillet. Scatter ¼ cup M&M's on top and sprinkle with turbinado sugar. Bake 25 minutes. Cover with foil, then bake 5 to 10 minutes, until cookie begins to pull away from edges of pan but is still soft.

■ Cool 30 minutes before slicing into wedges.

PER SERVING 360 **CAL**; 19 g **FAT**; 4 g **PRO**; 43 g **CARB**; 1 g **FIBER**

Stuffed Chocolate-Caramel Brownies

MAKES 9 servings **PREP** 25 minutes **BAKE** at 350° for 25 minutes **COOL** 20 minutes

- 3 **pkg (1.79 oz each) Twix bars**
- ½ **cup all-purpose flour**
- ½ **cup unsweetened cocoa powder**
- ½ **tsp salt**
- ¼ **tsp baking powder**
- ½ **stick (¼ cup) unsalted butter, melted**
- ¾ **cup sugar**
- ⅓ **cup milk**
- 2 **eggs**
- 1 **tsp vanilla extract**
- 3 **tbsp caramel sauce, warmed**

■ Heat oven to 350°. Line an 8 x 8-inch baking dish with foil, then coat with nonstick cooking spray. Slice each Twix bar in half crosswise (there are 2 bars per package, for a total of 12 halves).

■ In a bowl, whisk flour and next 3 ingredients. In a separate bowl, combine butter and next 4 ingredients until smooth. Stir dry ingredients into wet until just combined.

■ Pour batter into baking dish, spreading into an even layer. Press 9 Twix halves into batter, evenly spaced so that every brownie will get a half. Spread batter over Twix with a spatula. Bake 20 to 25 minutes, until a toothpick inserted in center comes out clean.

■ Cool 20 minutes. Chop 3 Twix halves and scatter over brownies. Drizzle with caramel sauce and cut into squares.

PER BROWNIE 270 **CAL**; 11 g **FAT**; 4 g **PRO**; 41 g **CARB**; 2 g **FIBER**

CRISPY
CHOCOLATE
CUPCAKES

Crispy Chocolate Cupcakes

MAKES 12 servings **PREP** 30 minutes
BAKE at 350° for 25 minutes

CUPCAKES

1	cup all-purpose flour
½	cup unsweetened cocoa powder
¾	tsp baking soda
½	tsp baking powder
½	tsp salt
6	tbsp unsalted butter, softened
⅔	cup sugar
2	eggs
¾	cup buttermilk
2	Nestlé Crunch bars (1.55 oz each), chopped

GANACHE FROSTING

1½	cups heavy cream
6	oz bittersweet chocolate, chopped
½	cup Rice Krispies cereal

■ **Cupcakes.** Heat oven to 350°. In a bowl, whisk first 5 ingredients. In a separate bowl, beat butter and sugar for 3 minutes, until fluffy. Add eggs and beat until combined. Beat in half the flour mixture, then the buttermilk and half the flour mixture. Fold in chopped Nestlé Crunch bars.

■ Place paper liners in a standard 12-cup muffin pan. Divide batter among cups. Bake 20 to 25 minutes, until a toothpick inserted in center of a cupcake comes out clean. Remove cupcakes to a wire rack and cool completely.

■ **Ganache Frosting.** Heat heavy cream in a small pot until barely simmering. Pour over chocolate in bowl of a stand mixer; stir until smooth. Cool 5 minutes. Beat with whisk attachment on high 10 minutes, until fluffy. Transfer to a piping bag fitted with a star tip.

■ Pipe frosting onto cooled cupcakes, starting on the outside, in a circular pattern. Scatter cereal over cupcakes.

PER CUPCAKE 370 **CAL**; 28 g **FAT**; 7 g **PRO**; 32 g **CARB**; 4 g **FIBER**

Peanut Butter Cup Cake Roll

MAKES 16 servings **PREP** 45 minutes
BAKE at 350° for 14 minutes
REFRIGERATE 2 hours

CAKE

¼	cup all-purpose flour
¼	cup unsweetened cocoa powder
¼	tsp salt
6	eggs, separated
¼	tsp cream of tartar
½	cup granulated sugar
1	tsp vanilla extract
	Confectioners' sugar, for dusting

PEANUT BUTTER FILLING

2½	cups confectioners' sugar
¾	cup creamy peanut butter (such as Jif)
⅓	cup unsalted butter, softened
2	tbsp heavy cream

GANACHE FROSTING

⅔	cup heavy cream
6	oz bittersweet chocolate, chopped
15	Reese's Peanut Butter Cup miniatures

■ **Cake.** Heat oven to 350°. Coat a 15 x 10 x 1-inch rimmed baking sheet (jelly roll pan) with nonstick cooking spray. Line bottom of pan with parchment paper. Coat again with spray.

■ Whisk flour, cocoa and salt. In a second bowl, beat egg whites and cream of tartar with a hand mixer until frothy. Beat in ¼ cup sugar until stiff peaks form. In a third bowl, beat yolks with ¼ cup sugar and vanilla until thickened, about 5 minutes. Fold flour mixture into yolks, then fold combined mixture into whites. Pour into pan, spreading evenly.

■ Bake 14 minutes, until center springs back when gently pressed. Sift confectioners' sugar onto a clean kitchen towel. Immediately invert cake onto towel, removing pan and paper. Dust more confectioners' sugar on cake. Starting from short side, roll up cake inside towel. Cool, seam side down, on a rack.

■ **Peanut Butter Filling.** Meanwhile, beat confectioners' sugar, peanut butter, unsalted butter and 2 tbsp heavy cream 3 minutes, until fluffy.

■ Once cake is cool, carefully unroll. Spread filling on cake, leaving a 1-inch border. Reroll cake without towel and wrap in plastic, seam side down. Refrigerate at least 2 hours.

■ **Ganache Frosting.** Remove cake from refrigerator. Heat heavy cream in a small pot until barely simmering. Pour over chopped chocolate in bowl of a stand mixer; stir until smooth. Let cool 5 minutes. Beat with whisk attachment on high 10 minutes, until fluffy. Let rest 10 minutes. Spread evenly over cake.

■ Unwrap and halve 15 peanut butter cups. Arrange on top of cake.

PER SERVING 370 **CAL**; 23 g **FAT**; 8 g **PRO**; 40 g **CARB**; 3 g **FIBER**

Crunchy Chocolate-Peanut Butter Sundae

MAKES 1 sundae **PREP** 5 minutes

- 2 **scoops chocolate peanut butter ice cream**
- 1 **fun-size Butterfinger bar, chopped**
- 1 **tsp roughly chopped roasted and salted peanuts**

 Chocolate sauce, warmed

■ Scoop ice cream into a bowl and layer with chopped Butterfinger and peanuts. Drizzle with chocolate sauce.

PER SUNDAE 500 **CAL**; 30 g **FAT**; 10 g **PRO**; 49 g **CARB**; 3 g **FIBER**

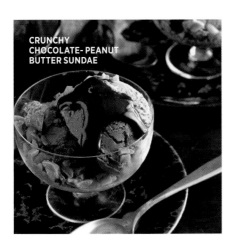

CRUNCHY CHOCOLATE- PEANUT BUTTER SUNDAE

COCONUT-CHOCOLATE CREAM PIE

Coconut-Chocolate Cream Pie

MAKES 12 servings **PREP** 25 minutes **BAKE** at 350° for 15 minutes **COOK** 9 minutes
REFRIGERATE 6 hours or overnight

- 1 **box (9 oz) Nabisco Famous chocolate wafers**
- 1 **stick (½ cup) unsalted butter, melted**
- 1 **cup sweetened flaked coconut, toasted**
- ½ **cup sugar**
- ¼ **cup cornstarch**
- 1 **can (13.5 oz) coconut milk**
- 1 **cup milk**
- ½ **tsp salt**
- 3 **egg yolks**
- ½ **tsp coconut extract**
- 1 **Mounds bar (1.75 oz), chopped**

■ Heat oven to 350°. In a food processor, combine wafers, melted butter and ¼ cup toasted coconut. Pulse until crumbs form. Transfer to a 9-inch pie dish. Firmly press into bottom and up sides. Bake 15 minutes. Set aside.

■ Meanwhile, in a medium pot, whisk sugar and cornstarch until blended. Whisk in coconut milk, milk and salt. Cook over medium-high until bubbling and thick, 5 to 7 minutes. Whisk egg yolks in a large bowl. Slowly pour hot mixture into yolks while constantly whisking. Return to pot and bring to a low simmer for 2 minutes, stirring constantly. Pour through a fine-mesh strainer into a bowl. Stir in coconut extract and ½ cup toasted coconut. Pour into crust. Cover with plastic wrap and refrigerate 6 hours or overnight.

■ Once pie is chilled and set, scatter chopped Mounds bar and ¼ cup toasted coconut over top.

PER SERVING 350 **CAL**; 22 g **FAT**; 4 g **PRO**; 35 g **CARB**; 2 g **FIBER**

HEALTHY FAMILY DINNERS

10 easy meals for crazy-busy weeknights.

MURGH
MAKHANI

*What are you craving?
The worldly flavors offered
here include Indian, Asian,
Mexican and Italian—all
ready in record time.*

Murgh Makhani

MAKES 6 servings **PREP** 15 minutes
SLOW COOK 5 hours on HIGH

	Nonstick cooking spray
1	sliced onion
1¼	lb halved small waxy potatoes (1-inch diameter)
1	seeded and sliced jalapeño
1	cup cilantro leaves
2	lb boneless, skinless chicken thighs
1	tbsp garam masala
1½	tsp cinnamon
1	tsp salt
¼	tsp black pepper
1	can (15 oz) diced tomatoes
3	tbsp unsalted butter
¼	cup heavy cream
¼	cup plain Greek yogurt
3	cups cooked brown rice
	Naan (optional)

■ Coat a slow cooker with nonstick cooking spray. Add sliced onion, halved small waxy potatoes, seeded and sliced jalapeño, cilantro leaves, chicken, garam masala, cinnamon, ½ tsp salt and black pepper. Pour diced tomatoes over top and dot with unsalted butter. Cover and cook on HIGH for 5 hours. Break up chicken into large pieces and stir in ½ tsp salt, heavy cream and plain Greek yogurt. Serve with cooked brown rice. Serve with naan, if desired.

PER SERVING 498 **CAL**; 20 g **FAT**; 32 g **PRO**; 48 g **CARB**; 5 g **FIBER**

RAMEN SHRIMP

Ramen Shrimp

MAKES 4 servings **PREP** 10 minutes **COOK** 10 minutes

4	cups low-sodium vegetable broth
2	pkg ramen noodles
¾	lb shrimp
1	cup water
4	cups coarsely chopped bok choy
3	sliced scallions and more for garnish
2	cups sliced shiitake mushrooms
1	tbsp chopped fresh ginger
1	tbsp soy sauce
1	tsp sriracha
6	hard-boiled eggs
1	cup bean sprouts
	Cilantro
	Lime wedges

■ In a large pot, combine 1 cup low-sodium vegetable broth and the seasoning packet from 1 package ramen noodles. Add shrimp and simmer 2 minutes; remove shrimp with a slotted spoon and reserve. Add 3 cups low-sodium vegetable broth, the water, coarsely chopped bok choy, sliced scallions, sliced shiitake mushrooms and chopped fresh ginger; simmer 5 minutes. Add ramen noodles, break up and cook 3 minutes. Stir in soy sauce and sriracha. Spoon into 4 bowls and add cooked shrimp, 3 hard-boiled egg halves and ¼ cup bean sprouts to each. Garnish with cilantro, sliced scallions and lime wedges for squeezing. Add more soy sauce, if desired.

PER SERVING 342 **CAL**; 13 g **FAT**; 31 g **PRO**; 25 g **CARB**; 4 g **FIBER**

SHEET PAN SMOKED PAPRIKA SALMON

Roasted Vegetable, Crumbled Sausage and Fresh Ricotta Pizza

MAKES 6 servings **PREP** 20 minutes
BAKE 50 minutes at 450°

- 2 cups butternut squash, cut into ¾-inch pieces
- 2 cups zucchini, cut into ½-inch dice
- 4 quartered shallots
- 2 tbsp olive oil
- ½ tsp salt
- ½ tsp black pepper
- ½ lb crumbled fresh sausage
- 1 lb room-temperature pizza dough
- 1½ cups shredded mozzarella
- 1 cup ricotta

■ Heat oven to 450°. On a large rimmed greased baking sheet, place butternut squash, zucchini and quartered shallots. Toss with olive oil, salt and pepper. Roast 15 minutes. Stir and top with crumbled fresh sausage. Roast 15 more minutes. On a floured surface, roll out room-temperature pizza dough into a rectangle and fit into a greased 18 x 12-inch rimmed baking pan. Sprinkle with shredded mozzarella and top with veggies and sausage. Dollop ricotta over vegetables. Bake 15 to 20 minutes, until crust is golden.

PER SERVING 402 **CAL**; 20 g **FAT** 20 g **PRO**; 45 g **CARB**; 4 g **FIBER**

Sheet Pan Smoked Paprika Salmon

MAKES 4 servings **PREP** 15 minutes **BAKE** 45 minutes

Nonstick cooking spray
- 1 lb fingerling potatoes
- 2 cups trimmed Brussels sprouts
- 4 carrots, peeled and cut into 1-inch pieces
- 4 large shallots, cut into wedges
- 2 tbsp olive oil
- 1 tsp salt
- ½ tsp black pepper
- 4 salmon fillets (6 oz each)
- 1 tsp smoked paprika
- ¼ tsp black pepper

■ Heat oven to 450°. Coat a large rimmed baking sheet with nonstick cooking spray. Toss fingerling potatoes, trimmed Brussels sprouts, carrots and shallots with olive oil. Season with ½ tsp each salt and pepper. Bake 30 minutes, turning once. Season salmon fillets with smoked paprika, ½ tsp salt and ¼ tsp pepper. Add to baking sheet and bake 15 minutes.

PER SERVING 558 **CAL**; 20 g **FAT**; 45 g **PRO**; 51 g **CARB**; 11 g **FIBER**

ROASTED VEGETABLE, CRUMBLED SAUSAGE AND FRESH RICOTTA PIZZA

CHARRED HANGER STEAK WITH CHIMICHURRI BUTTER

SEARED PORK CHOPS WITH CURRIED RICE AND APPLES

Charred Hanger Steak with Chimichurri Butter

MAKES 4 servings **PREP** 15 minutes
ROAST 30 minutes **COOK** 4 minutes

3	tbsp softened unsalted butter
2	tbsp chopped cilantro
2	tbsp parsley
1	tbsp chopped onion
1	clove chopped garlic
2	tsp white wine vinegar
1⅛	tsp salt
⅛	tsp black pepper
2	lb peeled sweet potatoes
1	tbsp olive oil
½	tsp black pepper
1	lb hanger steak

■ Combine softened unsalted butter, chopped cilantro, parsley, chopped onion, chopped garlic, white wine vinegar and ⅛ tsp each salt and pepper. Form into a small log and wrap in plastic. Refrigerate. Heat oven to 400°. Cut peeled sweet potatoes into 1-inch-thick wedges. Toss with olive oil and season with ½ tsp salt and ¼ tsp black pepper. Roast 30 minutes, turning once. Meanwhile, season hanger steak with ½ tsp salt and ¼ tsp black pepper. Heat a nonstick skillet over medium-high; add steak and cook 2 minutes per side. Slice steak, serve with sweet potatoes and top with butter mixture.

PER SERVING 473 **CAL**; 23 g **FAT**; 27 g **PRO**; 33 g **CARB**; 5 g **FIBER**

Seared Pork Chops with Curried Rice and Apples

MAKES 4 servings **PREP** 10 minutes **COOK** 21 minutes

½	chopped onion
2	tbsp butter
1¼	cups basmati rice
3	tsp curry powder
1	tsp salt
2	cups reduced-sodium chicken broth
1	peeled, chopped apple
2	tbsp chopped cilantro
1	tbsp vegetable oil
4	bone-in pork chops (8 oz each)
1	tsp cumin
⅛	tsp black pepper

■ In a medium saucepan, cook chopped onion in butter 2 minutes over medium. Add basmati rice, 2 tsp curry powder and ¼ tsp salt; cook 1 minute. Stir in reduced-sodium chicken broth; bring to a simmer and cook, covered, 15 minutes. Stir in chopped apple and chopped cilantro. Meanwhile, heat vegetable oil in a large nonstick skillet over medium-high. Season bone-in pork chops with 1 tsp curry powder, cumin, ¾ tsp salt and pepper. Sauté chops about 3 minutes per side for medium.

PER SERVING 533 **CAL**; 21 g **FAT**; 34 g **PRO**; 52 g **CARB**; 2 g **FIBER**

CHILAQUILES-STYLE CHICKEN

BROCCOLI, TOMATO AND CHICKPEA FRITTATA

Chilaquiles-Style Chicken

MAKES 6 servings **PREP** 20 minutes **BAKE** 8 minutes at 425° **COOK** 15 minutes

12	corn tortillas
	Nonstick cooking spray
1	can (28 oz) diced tomatoes
1	chopped onion
1	seeded jalapeño
½	cup cilantro leaves (additional for serving, if desired)
4	cloves garlic
¾	tsp salt
1	cup chicken broth
2½	lb boneless, skinless chicken breasts
	Lime wedges
	Sliced scallion
	Chopped avocado
	Crumbled Cotija cheese

■ Heat oven to 425°. Cut corn tortillas in half, then into ½-inch strips. Spread on a baking sheet, coat with nonstick cooking spray and bake 8 minutes, turning once. In a food processor, combine diced tomatoes, onion, jalapeño, cilantro leaves, garlic and salt. Process until smooth. Add to a Dutch oven and stir in chicken broth. Bring to a simmer and add boneless, skinless chicken breasts; simmer, covered, 15 minutes or until cooked through. Remove chicken, shred and return to sauce. Bring to a simmer and stir in baked tortilla strips. Serve with lime wedges, additional cilantro, sliced scallion, chopped avocado and crumbled Cotija cheese.

PER SERVING 463 **CAL**; 16 g **FAT**; 46 g **PRO**; 33 g **CARB**; 7 g **FIBER**

Broccoli, Tomato and Chickpea Frittata

MAKES 6 servings **PREP** 10 minutes
COOK 7 minutes **BAKE** 13 minutes at 400°

2	tbsp olive oil
1	small onion, sliced
1½	cups coarsely chopped broccoli florets
8	eggs
½	cup milk
1½	cups shredded Jarlsberg
1	tsp turmeric
½	tsp salt
½	tsp black pepper
1	cup halved grape tomatoes
1	can (15 oz) drained chickpeas

■ Heat oven to 400°. Heat olive oil in a 12-inch ovenproof nonstick skillet. Add onion slices and coarsely chopped broccoli florets; cook 5 minutes. Whisk eggs, milk, 1 cup shredded Jarlsberg, turmeric, salt and pepper. Add halved grape tomatoes and drained chickpeas to skillet. Pour egg mixture over top and cook 2 minutes, stirring once. Bake 13 minutes, until set. Sprinkle ½ cup shredded Jarlsberg over frittata during last 3 minutes.

PER SERVING 350 **CAL**; 20 g **FAT** 21 g **PRO**; 23 g **CARB**; 6 g **FIBER**

Farmers' Market Fall Minestrone

MAKES 6 servings PREP 15 minutes
SLOW COOK 6 hours on HIGH

- Nonstick cooking spray
- 1 chopped onion
- 2 cloves chopped garlic
- 3 cups cubed (¾-inch) butternut squash
- 1½ cups baby carrots, halved on the bias
- 1 cup peeled and diced white turnip
- 3 cups shredded cabbage
- ¾ tsp salt
- ½ tsp black pepper
- 4 cups low-sodium vegetable broth
- 1 can (14.5 oz) stewed tomatoes
- 2 cups water
- 1 can (15 oz) drained red kidney beans
- ½ cup orzo

■ Coat a slow cooker with nonstick cooking spray. Add onion, garlic, butternut squash, baby carrots, white turnip, shredded cabbage, ½ tsp salt and pepper. Pour in low-sodium vegetable broth, stewed tomatoes and the water. Cover and cook on HIGH 6 hours. During last 20 minutes, add drained red kidney beans, orzo and ¼ tsp salt. If desired, serve with basil, grated Parmesan, crusty bread and salad.

PER SERVING 248 CAL; 1 g FAT; 10 g PRO; 49 g CARB; 10 g FIBER

FARMERS' MARKET FALL MINESTRONE

SLICED BEEF TENDERLOIN AND SHIITAKE QUESADILLAS WITH TWO SALSAS

Sliced Beef Tenderloin and Shiitake Quesadillas with Two Salsas

MAKES 4 servings PREP 20 minutes COOK 17 minutes

- 1 cup diced tomatoes
- 1 chopped jalapeño
- 1 clove chopped garlic
- ¾ tsp salt
- ¼ tsp black pepper
- 1 diced avocado
- 2 tbsp chopped onion
- 1 tbsp lime juice
- 2 tbsp vegetable oil
- 2 beef tenderloin steaks (4 oz each)
- 8 oz sliced shiitake mushrooms
- 1 tsp chili powder
- ½ tsp cumin
- ¼ tsp black pepper
- 4 fajita-size 8-inch flour tortillas
- 4 tbsp shredded Monterey Jack

■ Combine diced tomatoes, chopped jalapeño, chopped garlic and ⅛ tsp each salt and pepper. Set aside. Combine diced avocado, chopped onion, lime juice and ⅛ tsp each salt and pepper. Set aside. Heat 1 tbsp vegetable oil in a nonstick skillet over medium-high. Add beef tenderloin steaks and sauté 2 minutes per side. Set aside. Add 1 tbsp vegetable oil, sliced shiitake mushrooms, chili powder and cumin to skillet. Saute 5 minutes, stirring occasionally. Thinly slice steak and add to mushrooms; season with ½ tsp salt and ¼ tsp pepper. Spoon into a bowl; wipe out skillet. Place 8-inch flour tortillas on a work surface. Cover half of each with 2 tbsp shredded Monterey Jack, ¼ of the steak mixture and another 2 tbsp Monterey Jack. Fold uncovered half over filled half and gently press to seal. Coat skillet with nonstick cooking spray and cook 2 minutes per side over medium-high in 2 batches. Serve with tomato and avocado salsas.

PER SERVING 380 CAL; 21 g FAT; 24 g PRO; 27 g CARB; 5 g FIBER

PUMPKIN 4 WAYS

Brighten up your breakfast, lunch or dinner with this fall favorite.

**PUMPKIN-
SHRIMP BISQUE**

**PUMPKIN
CORNBREAD
MUFFINS**

Pumpkin-Shrimp Bisque

MAKES 6 servings

1	**cup sliced celery**
1	**cup leeks**
2	**tbsp extra-virgin olive oil**
½	**cup dry white wine**
2	**tbsp fresh thyme**
3	**cups seafood stock**
1	**can (15 oz) pumpkin**
1	**lb peeled and deveined raw shrimp**
¾	**cup heavy cream**
½	**tsp salt**
½	**tsp black pepper**
1	**tsp lemon juice**
	Chives (optional)

■ In a large pot over medium, cook celery and leeks in olive oil 5 minutes. Stir in wine and thyme; simmer 2 minutes. Stir in seafood stock, pumpkin and ½ lb shrimp. Simmer 2 minutes.

■ Transfer to a blender and puree until smooth. Return to pot, stir in ½ lb more shrimp, heavy cream and salt and pepper. Simmer 2 minutes, until shrimp are cooked. Stir in lemon juice. If desired, garnish with chives and a splash of heavy cream.

PER SERVING 270 **CAL**; 15 g **FAT**; 18 g **PRO**; 14 g **CARB**; 4 g **FIBER**

PUMPKIN-BACON PASTA

Pumpkin-Bacon Pasta

MAKES 6 servings

- 1 lb mezzi rigatoni
- 8 oz diced bacon
- 2 tbsp all-purpose flour
- 2 cups milk
- 1 can (15 oz) pumpkin
- 8 oz (2 cups) shredded smoked Gouda
- ½ tsp salt
- ½ tsp black pepper

■ Cook rigatoni until al dente, about 10 minutes. Drain, reserving ½ cup pasta water.

■ Cook bacon in a skillet over medium 5 minutes, until crispy. Remove with a slotted spoon to a plate. Pour off all but 2 tbsp bacon fat. Whisk in flour; cook 1 minute. Pour in milk, bring to a simmer and cook 5 minutes. Stir in pumpkin and Gouda until smooth. In a large bowl, combine cooked pasta, bacon, sauce, reserved pasta water, salt and pepper.

PER SERVING 600 **CAL**; 26 g **FAT**; 24 g **PRO**; 68 g **CARB**; 6 g **FIBER**

Pumpkin Cornbread Muffins

MAKES 10 servings

- 1 cup canned pumpkin
- 1 cup buttermilk
- 2 eggs
- ¼ cup sugar
- 3 tbsp melted unsalted butter
- 1½ cups cornmeal
- ½ cup all-purpose flour
- 1 tbsp baking powder
- 1 tsp baking soda
- ¾ tsp salt
- ¼ tsp black pepper
  Jarred pumpkin butter

■ Heat oven to 400°. Coat a standard-size square or round nonstick muffin tin with nonstick cooking spray.

■ In a bowl, whisk pumpkin, buttermilk, eggs, sugar and butter. In a separate bowl, whisk cornmeal, flour, baking powder, baking soda, salt and pepper.

■ Stir wet ingredients into dry. Scoop ¼ cup batter into 10 of the 12 muffin cups; fill the last 2 with water. Bake 8 minutes or until a toothpick inserted in center comes out clean. Cool 15 minutes. Serve with jarred pumpkin butter.

PER SERVING 180 **CAL**; 5 g **FAT**; 5 g **PRO**; 31 g **CARB**; 2 g **FIBER**

Pumpkin Chai Smoothie

MAKES 2 servings

- 2 cups ice
- 1 cup canned pumpkin
- 1 cup Tazo Chai Classic Latte tea concentrate
- ½ cup unsweetened cashew milk*
- 1 tbsp honey
  Cinnamon

■ In a blender, combine ice, pumpkin and tea concentrate, cashew milk and honey. Blend until smooth. Pour into 2 glasses and sprinkle cinnamon on top.

*Cashew milk adds a sweet creaminess, but almond or dairy milk will also work well.

PER SERVING 150 **CAL**; 2 g **FAT**; 2 g **PRO**; 35 g **CARB**; 6 g **FIBER**

PUMPKIN CHAI SMOOTHIE

SIMMER DOWN

Come home to a bubbling pot of deliciousness with these slow cooker chilies.

THREE-BEAN CHILI

FIERY GREEN CHILI

TEXAS-STYLE CHILI

Three-Bean Chili

MAKES 8 servings **PREP** 20 minutes
SLOW COOK 4 hours on HIGH or 8 hours on LOW plus 15 minutes on HIGH

- 1 lb lean ground beef
- 2 cans (14.5 oz each) diced fire-roasted tomatoes
- 1 can (15 oz) drained and rinsed black beans
- 1 can (15 oz) drained and rinsed pinto beans
- 1 can (15 oz) drained and rinsed dark red kidney beans
- 1 can (14.5 oz) beef broth
- 3 medium yellow onions, chopped
- 1 can (8 oz) tomato sauce
- 1 tbsp chili powder
- 1 chopped canned chipotle pepper in adobo
- 6 cloves minced garlic
- 1 tsp ground cumin
- ½ tsp ground cinnamon
- ½ tsp coriander
- 2 oz chopped bittersweet or semisweet chocolate
- 1 tbsp honey

  Sour cream and chopped green onions (optional)

■ In a large skillet, cook beef over medium-high until browned, using a wooden spoon to break up meat as it cooks. Drain off fat. Transfer meat to a 4- to 5-qt slow cooker.

■ Stir in tomatoes, black beans, pinto beans, red kidney beans, broth, onions, tomato sauce, chili powder, chipotle pepper, garlic, cumin, cinnamon and coriander.

■ Cover and cook on LOW for 6 to 8 hours or HIGH for 3 to 4 hours. If using LOW, turn to HIGH. Stir in chocolate and honey. Cover and cook about 15 minutes or until heated through. If desired, serve with sour cream and chopped green onions.

PER SERVING 298 **CAL**; 9 g **FAT** 22 g **PRO**; 37 g **CARB**; 8 g **FIBER**

Fiery Green Chili

MAKES 8 servings **PREP** 15 minutes
SLOW COOK 6 hours on HIGH or 8 hours on LOW

- 1 cup low-sodium beef broth
- 1 cup tomatillo salsa
- 1 large sweet green pepper, seeded and diced
- 1 large yellow onion, diced
- 3 cloves garlic, chopped
- 1 tsp cumin
- 1 tsp ancho chile powder
- ¾ tsp salt
- 1 lb ground pork
- 1 lb ground beef
- 1 can (15.5 oz) butter beans, drained and rinsed
- ¼ cup chopped fresh cilantro

  Sliced scallions, lime wedges and sour cream (optional)

■ Combine broth, salsa, green pepper, onion, garlic, cumin, chili powder and salt in slow cooker. Crumble in ground pork and beef; mix. Cover and cook on HIGH for 6 hours or LOW for 8 hours.

■ Break up meat with a wooden spoon, if necessary. Stir in beans and cilantro. Garnish with sliced scallions, lime and sour cream, if desired.

PER SERVING 306 **CAL**; 18 g **FAT**; 24 g **PRO**; 13 g **CARB**; 3 g **FIBER**

Texas-Style Chili

MAKES 8 servings **PREP** 10 minutes
SLOW COOK 6 hours on HIGH or 9 hours on LOW

- 3 lb beef brisket
- 1 tbsp paprika

1 tsp salt

½ tsp black pepper

1 chopped large onion

1 seeded and chopped sweet green pepper

4 cloves chopped garlic

1 can (14.5 oz) stewed tomatoes

1 can (14.5 oz) reduced-sodium beef broth

¼ cup cider vinegar

3 tbsp chili powder

Sour cream and shredded cheese (optional)

■ Coat slow cooker bowl with nonstick cooking spray. Season brisket with paprika, salt and black pepper. Place in slow cooker.

■ Scatter onion, sweet pepper and garlic over brisket. Combine tomatoes, broth, vinegar and chili powder. Pour over brisket.

■ Cover and cook on HIGH for 6 hours or LOW for 9 hours. Remove meat from slow cooker and cool slightly. Chop into pieces or shred and stir into sauce. If you like, serve with sour cream and shredded cheese.

PER SERVING 405 CAL; 10 g FAT; 44 g PRO; 36 g CARB; 3 g FIBER

Cincinnati Chili

MAKES 8 servings PREP 15 minutes
SLOW COOK 6 hours on HIGH or 8 hours on LOW

2 cups low-sodium beef broth

1 can (8 oz) tomato sauce

¼ cup tomato paste

2 tbsp cider vinegar

2 tbsp chili powder

2 tsp unsweetened cocoa powder

1 tsp ground cumin

1 tsp ground cinnamon

½ tsp ground cloves

¼ tsp ground allspice

1 tsp salt

½ tsp black pepper

3 garlic cloves, chopped

1 large yellow onion, diced

2 lb ground beef

1 lb spaghetti, cooked

Finely shredded cheddar cheese and diced white onions (optional)

■ Whisk broth, tomato sauce, tomato paste, vinegar, chili powder, cocoa powder, cumin, cinnamon, cloves, allspice, salt and pepper in the base of a slow cooker. Add garlic and yellow onion and crumble in beef; mix. Cover and cook on HIGH for 6 hours or LOW for 8 hours.

■ Divide cooked spaghetti among 8 bowls. Top with chili and, if desired, finely shredded cheddar and diced white onions.

PER SERVING 325 CAL; 12 g FAT; 28 g PRO; 24 g CARB; 3 g FIBER

Chicken Chili with Cilantro Pesto

MAKES 6 servings PREP 15 minutes
SLOW COOK 6 hours on HIGH or 8 hours on LOW

1 green sweet pepper, cored, seeded and diced

2 Cubanelle peppers, cored, seeded and diced

1 medium onion, diced

2 lb boneless, skinless chicken thighs

1½ tsp chipotle chile powder

¾ tsp salt

1 tsp cumin seeds

1 can (14.5 oz) low-sodium chicken broth

1 cup cilantro leaves

¼ cup pumpkin seeds

1 large clove garlic

⅛ tsp salt

⅛ tsp black pepper

2 tbsp olive oil

1 tbsp fresh lime juice

1 can (15 oz) hominy, drained and rinsed

1 can (15 oz) cannellini beans, drained, rinsed and mashed

Sour cream or plain yogurt and cilantro pesto

■ Combine peppers and onion in slow cooker. Season chicken thighs with chipotle chile powder and ½ tsp salt. Place on top of peppers and onion. Add cumin seeds and chicken broth.

Cover and cook on HIGH for 6 hours or LOW for 8 hours.

■ Just before chili is done, combine cilantro, pumpkin seeds, garlic, salt, black pepper, olive oil and lime juice in a mini chopper or with a mortar and pestle. Process until fairly smooth, scraping down sides often.

■ Remove chicken from slow cooker and shred with 2 forks. Stir shredded chicken back into slow cooker along with remaining ¼ tsp salt, hominy and cannellini beans. Spoon into bowls and top with sour cream or plain yogurt and cilantro pesto.

PER SERVING 398 CAL; 18 g FAT; 39 g PRO; 26 g CARB; 7 g FIBER

CINCINNATI CHILI

CHICKEN CHILI WITH CILANTRO PESTO

PECAN PIE, PAGE 211

NOVEMBER

255

262

277

TURKEY EVERY WAY

Carve out your Thanksgiving menu options—starting with the bird.

GOLDEN ROAST
TURKEY

Prepping the bird: To thaw, place a frozen 12- to 16-pound (nonbasted) turkey in its packaging on a tray in the refrigerator; it takes 24 hours for every 4 to 5 pounds. When thawed, remove giblets and neck; rinse well with cold water.

Golden Roast Turkey

MAKES 12 servings **PREP** 15 minutes **ROAST** at 425° for 35 minutes, then at 350° for 2 hours **STAND** 20 minutes

- 1 **12- to 16-lb frozen turkey**
- 2 **medium onions**
- 3 **medium carrots, peeled and bias-cut into 2-inch pieces**
- 2 **ribs celery, bias-cut into 2-inch pieces**
- 1 **large onion**
- 2¼ **tsp salt**
- 1¼ **tsp black pepper**
- 2 **tbsp butter**
- 2 **tbsp honey**
- 2 **tsp chopped fresh thyme**
- 2 **tsp chopped fresh rosemary**
- 2 **tsp chopped fresh sage**
   Additional fresh herbs

■ Thaw and prepare the turkey (see "Prepping the bird," above). Pat dry with paper towels. Cut medium onions into wedges and toss with carrots and celery. Place in a large roasting pan. Set turkey on top of vegetables in pan. Cut large onion into wedges and place inside turkey cavity. Tie legs together with cooking twine. Season turkey with 2 tsp of the salt and 1 tsp of the pepper, including under skin and in cavity. Combine butter, honey, thyme, rosemary, sage, and remaining ¼ tsp salt and pepper in a small saucepan. Cook over medium 1 minute. Brush over turkey and under breast skin. Roast at 425° for 35 minutes. Baste with any remaining glaze. Reduce oven temp to 350°. Cover with foil and continue to roast 1½ to 2 hours, until temperature reaches 165° in thickest part of thigh. Transfer turkey to a platter, loosen foil and let stand 20 minutes. Garnish with additional fresh herbs and serve with pan gravy.

Pan Gravy

Strain pan drippings into a fat separator. Pour ½ cup defatted juices into a small saucepan along with 2 tbsp turkey fat. Whisk in 1½ cups turkey stock or water and 2 tbsp all-purpose flour. Bring to a boil over medium-high and cook 3 minutes.

PER SERVING 482 **CAL**; 19 g **FAT**; 65 g **PRO**; 9 g **CARB**; 1 g **FIBER**

HOW TO CARVE

1 Pull leg away from body and slice through skin between breast and thigh. Fold leg until thigh bone pops out of socket. Cut through joint and skin to detach leg completely.

2 Insert knife between center breastbone and one half of breast meat. Cut down, following bones as a guide while gently pulling meat. Repeat on other side.

3 Separate drumstick and thigh by cutting through joint. Slice thigh meat from bone.

4 Transfer one breast half to a cutting board. Slice meat against the grain (crosswise) and fan onto a platter. Repeat with other breast half.

To "spatchcock" a bird simply means to split it down the back and flatten it like a book. It expedites cooking time and creates lots of crispy, golden-brown skin.

Spatchcocked Turkey

MAKES 12 servings **PREP** 10 minutes **ROAST** at 425° for 1 hour 30 minutes **STAND** 15 minutes

■ Thaw turkey and prep vegetables according to recipe for Golden Roast Turkey (page 255). Arrange vegetables on a rimmed baking sheet in a single layer. Fit a wire rack into baking sheet and add ½ cup water. Pat dry 1 spatchcocked 12- to 16-lb turkey (see "How to Spatchcock," below, or ask your butcher to do this). Tuck wings under turkey. Rub with 3 tbsp olive oil and season with 1¼ tsp salt and ½ tsp black pepper. Roast at 425° for 70 to 90 minutes on middle rack, rotating twice during cooking, until golden brown and temperature reaches 165° in thickest part of thigh.

Transfer to a cutting board and loosely cover with foil. Reserve juices from baking sheet, if using for gravy (see page 255). Let stand 15 minutes before carving.

PER SERVING 455 **CAL**; 20 g **FAT**; 64 g **PRO**; 0 g **CARB**; 0 g **FIBER**

HOW TO SPATCHCOCK

1 With the turkey breast side down, use a very sturdy pair of kitchen shears to cut along both sides of backbone, starting at tail end. (Reserve backbone for stock or gravy.) Gently pull apart sides to open turkey.

2 Use the tip of a sharp knife to score the length of the breastbone cartilage down the center—this makes it easier to flatten. Turn the turkey breast side up and press quickly and firmly in center of breast to crack the breastbone and flatten the bird. This may take several tries.

3 Pull thighs outward and flatten bird further. Tuck wings under to secure.

Grilled Turkey

MAKES 12 servings **PREP** 15 minutes **GRILL** 3 hours **STAND** 15 minutes

■ For a charcoal grill, arrange medium-hot coals around a drip pan or foil pan. Test for medium heat above pan. Pat dry 1 brined 12- to 16-lb turkey (see "Brine Instructions," right). Tuck wings under turkey and tie legs together with cooking twine or tuck into flap of skin. Place turkey on grill rack over pan. Cover and grill 2¼ to 3 hours, until temperature in thickest part of thigh reaches 165°. Add coals every 45 to 60 minutes and cut band of skin or twine in last hour of grilling. (For a gas grill, preheat grill, reduce heat to medium and adjust for indirect cooking. Grill as above.) Remove turkey from grill, loosely cover with foil and let stand 15 minutes before carving.

PER SERVING 429 **CAL**; 17 g **FAT**; 64 g **PRO**; 1 g **CARB**; 0 g **FIBER**

Brine Instructions Use to keep fried or grilled turkeys moist or to add tenderness to any bird. In a large stockpot, combine ⅔ cup kosher salt, ⅔ cup firmly packed dark brown sugar, 1 cup hot water, 3 cups cold water, 1 sliced onion, 2 cloves crushed garlic, 1 sliced jalapeño and 12 crushed black peppercorns. Place fresh (not frozen) turkey in pot. Add enough water to cover by 1 inch. Cover and refrigerate overnight, but no longer than 8 hours. Dry turkey inside and out, including cavity, before cooking.

Fried Turkey

MAKES 12 servings **PREP** 15 minutes **FRY** 3 minutes per pound **STAND** 20 minutes

■ Place turkey fryer in an open and level dirt, cement or grassy area (see Note and consult manufacturer's instructions for details). Heat 3 qt peanut oil to 400°. (Oil can take about 40 minutes to heat.) Pat dry one brined 12- to 16-lb turkey (see "Brine Instructions," opposite). When oil reaches 400°, very slowly lower turkey in basket into oil. Oil will rise

and bubble initially. Check temperature; increase or lower as needed to maintain 375°. Fry turkey 3 minutes per pound. Carefully lift from oil to check temperature. It should be 165° in thickest part of thigh. When done, remove from oil and drain on a rack for a few minutes. Loosely cover with foil and let stand 20 minutes before carving.

Note: Certain electric turkey fryers (such as Masterbuilt) can be used indoors. Propane fryers should never be used indoors or in a garage. Do not fry on wood decks.

PER SERVING 549 **CAL**; 31 g **FAT**; 64 g **PRO**; 1 g **CARB**; 0 g **FIBER**

Deconstructed Turkey

MAKES 12 servings **PREP** 15 minutes **ROAST** at 450° for 1 hour 15 minutes **STAND** 10 minutes

■ Thaw turkey and prep vegetables according to recipe for Golden Roast Turkey (see page 255). Arrange vegetables on a rimmed baking sheet in a single layer. Fit a wire rack into baking sheet and add ½ cup water. Pat dry pieces of one 12- to 16-lb turkey (see "Break It Down," below). Rub with 3 tbsp olive oil and season with

1¼ tsp salt and ½ tsp black pepper. Arrange on rack so breast pieces are at outside edges, with tapered parts facing in. Place thighs and legs next to breasts and wings in the middle. Roast at 450° for 55 to 75 minutes, rotating pan twice, until golden brown and temperature reaches 165° in thickest part of thigh. Transfer breasts to a

cutting board and loosely cover with foil. Reserve juices from baking sheet if using for gravy (see page 255). Let rest 10 minutes before slicing. Arrange turkey pieces and breast slices on a platter.

PER SERVING 456 **CAL**; 20 g **FAT**; 64 g **PRO**; 0 g **CARB**; 0 g **FIBER**; 474 mg **SODIUM**

BREAK IT DOWN

1 With the turkey breast side up, pull leg away from body and cut skin between breast and drumstick.

2 Bend leg back until thigh bone pops out of socket. Cut through joint and skin to detach whole leg. Repeat on other side.

3 Turn turkey on its side and pull wing away from body. Cut through joint and remove wing. Repeat.

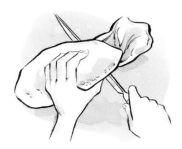  

4 Cut down through rib bones and shoulders, separating breast from back.

5 Turn breast skin side down. Split center bone (this may take a few passes), then slice through meat and skin to make 2 pieces.

6 Turn leg skin side down and cut through joint to separate into drumstick and thigh along fat line.

BEST SIDE STORY

With 50 dishes to choose from, there'll be no fighting over favorites.

RED RICE SALAD

BAKED PENNE WITH
SAUSAGE AND APPLE

CHARRED
CORN FLAN

1. Baked Penne with Sausage and Apple

MAKES 8 servings **PREP** 15 minutes
COOK 11 minutes **BAKE** at 350° for 30 minutes
BROIL 4 minutes

■ Bring a large pot of salted water to a boil. Add 1 lb **penne pasta** and cook 11 minutes. Drain, reserving ¾ cup pasta water. Meanwhile, melt 2 tbsp **butter** over medium-high. Sauté 2 large peeled, cored and sliced **Granny Smith apples**, 12 oz **kielbasa**, cut into coins, and 1 thinly sliced medium **onion** 5 minutes, until softened and lightly golden. Toss cooked pasta with apple mixture, reserved pasta water, 2 tbsp **honey mustard** and ¼ tsp each **salt** and

black pepper. Fold in 1 cup shredded **Gouda cheese** and transfer to a greased 3-qt baking dish. Top with 1 more cup shredded **Gouda** and ⅓ cup **grated Parmesan**. Bake at 350° for 30 minutes. Broil 4 minutes, if desired, to brown top.

PER SERVING 393 **CAL**; 16 g **FAT**; 17 g **PRO**; 44 g **CARB**; 3 g **FIBER**

2. Red Rice Salad

MAKES 10 servings **PREP** 15 minutes
COOK 40 minutes **SOAK** 5 minutes
LET STAND 10 minutes

■ Combine 3 cups **water**, 2 cups **red rice** and ½ tsp **salt** in a lidded pot. Bring to a boil over high, then cover and reduce to medium-low. Cook

40 minutes. Remove from heat and let stand 10 minutes. Meanwhile, bring a small pot of water to a boil. Remove from heat and add ½ cup each **golden raisins** and **sweetened dried cranberries**. Soak 5 minutes, then drain. Whisk ⅓ cup **cider vinegar**, 2 tsp each **grainy mustard** and **honey**, ½ tsp **salt** and ¼ tsp **black pepper**. While whisking, add ⅓ cup **olive oil** in a thin stream. Set aside. Place rice in a large bowl. Stir in plumped raisins and cranberries, ½ cup **parsley leaves**, chopped, ½ cup toasted chopped **pecans** and the dressing.

PER SERVING 287 **CAL**; 11 g **FAT**; 4 g **PRO**; 44 g **CARB**; 2 g **FIBER**

3. Charred Corn Flan

MAKES 8 servings **PREP** 10 minutes
COOK 12 minutes **BAKE** at 350° for 30 minutes

■ Heat a 10-inch cast-iron skillet over medium-high. Add 3 ears shucked **corn on the cob** and cook about 12 minutes, turning frequently, until kernels are lightly charred. Remove and let cool. Cut kernels from cobs; you need 2 cups total. (This can be done up to 2 days ahead.) In a large bowl, lightly beat 5 **large eggs**, then beat in ¾ cup **sour cream**, ½ cup **milk**, 3 tbsp each **cornmeal** and **sugar**, 2 tbsp snipped **fresh chives**, 1 tsp **salt** and ¼ tsp **black pepper**. Stir in charred corn. Melt 2 tbsp **butter** in same skillet. Add corn mixture. Bake at 350° for 30 minutes or until flan is set in middle. Let stand 10 minutes before serving.

PER SERVING 187 **CAL**; 11 g **FAT**; 7 g **PRO**; 15 g **CARB**; 1 g **FIBER**

4. Garlicky Swiss Chard

MAKES 8 servings **PREP** 15 minutes
COOK 11 minutes

■ Remove stems from 2 lb **Swiss chard** and slice into 1-inch pieces; roughly chop leaves. Heat 2 tbsp **extra-virgin olive oil** in a large, lidded pot over medium. Add 6 cloves sliced **garlic**; cook 1 minute. Stir in chard stems and increase heat to medium-high; cook 4 minutes. Add chard leaves and place lid on pot 3 minutes. Remove lid and stir with tongs. Cook 3 more minutes, then stir in ¾ tsp **salt** and ½ tsp **black pepper**.

PER SERVING 55 **CAL**; 4 g **FAT**; 2 g **PRO**; 5 g **CARB**; 2 g **FIBER**

5. Beets and Greens

MAKES 8 servings **PREP** 20 minutes
ROAST at 425° for 40 minutes
COOK 8 minutes

■ Remove stems and leaves from 2 lb **beets**; set aside. Trim beets and cut into 2-inch wedges; toss in 2 tbsp **extra-virgin olive oil** and ½ tsp each **salt** and **black pepper**. Wrap in foil and place on a rimmed baking sheet. Roast at 425° for 40 minutes, until knife-tender. Cool slightly, then peel. Slice beet stems into 2-inch pieces and roughly chop leaves.

Sauté stems in 2 tbsp **extra-virgin olive oil** 3 minutes over medium. Stir in leaves and cook until tender, about 3 to 5 minutes. Stir in peeled beets, 1 tbsp **lemon juice** and ¼ tsp each **salt** and **black pepper**. Transfer to a platter; scatter ½ cup crumbled **soft goat cheese** on top.

PER SERVING 120 **CAL**; 9 g **FAT**; 3 g **PRO**; 7 g **CARB**; 3 g **FIBER**

6. Creamed Spinach

MAKES 8 servings **PREP** 15 minutes
COOK 9 minutes

■ Drain and press liquid from 3 boxes (10 oz each) thawed **frozen spinach leaves**; set aside. In a large skillet, melt 6 tbsp **unsalted butter**. Whisk in 3 tbsp **all-purpose flour**; cook 1 minute. Stir in 1 diced small **yellow onion** and 3 cloves chopped **garlic**; cook 3 minutes. Whisk in 3 cups **milk**; bring to a simmer and cook 5 minutes, until thickened. Whisk in ¼ cup **grated Parmesan**, ¾ tsp **salt**, ½ tsp **freshly cracked black pepper** and ¼ tsp **ground nutmeg**, then stir in spinach until combined and warm.

PER SERVING 190 **CAL**; 12 g **FAT**; 8 g **PRO**; 12 g **CARB**; 3 g **FIBER**

7. Cornmeal Biscuits

MAKES 10 biscuits **PREP** 15 minutes
BAKE at 425° for 20 minutes

■ In a large bowl, blend 2 cups **all-purpose flour**, ¾ cup **cornmeal**, 2 tbsp **sugar**, 2½ tsp **baking powder**, 1 tsp **salt** and ¼ tsp **baking soda**. Pour 1 tbsp **white vinegar** into a measuring cup and add enough **milk** to equal 1 cup. With a pastry cutter, cut ⅔ cup **shortening** into flour mixture until the size of small peas. Add milk mixture and stir until dough comes together. Turn out onto a surface dusted with **cornmeal** and pat to ½-inch thickness. Using a 2¾-inch biscuit cutter, cut out rounds and place on a baking sheet. Reroll scraps and cut as many biscuits as possible. Bake at 425° for 18 to 20 minutes.

PER BISCUIT 275 **CAL**; 14 g **FAT**; 4 g **PRO**; 32 g **CARB**; 1 g **FIBER**

GARLICKY SWISS CHARD

BEETS AND GREENS

CREAMED SPINACH

8. Scallion Mashed Potatoes

MAKES 12 servings **PREP** 15 minutes
COOK 12 minutes

■ Peel 2¾ lb **russet potatoes** and cut into 2-inch pieces. Place in a large pot and add enough cold water to cover. Bring to a boil over high, add 1 tsp **salt** and cook 10 to 12 minutes, until tender. Drain and return to pot. Meanwhile, heat 3 tbsp **salted butter** in a large skillet over medium-high. Add 1 trimmed and sliced bunch of **scallions** (6 to 8) and 3 cloves sliced **garlic**. Cook 4 minutes, stirring. Add 1 cup **milk**, 1 tbsp **salted butter** and ½ tsp each **salt** and **black pepper** to potatoes. Mash to desired consistency; add scallion mixture.

PER SERVING 127 **CAL**; 4 g **FAT**; 3 g **PRO**; 22 g **CARB**; 2 g **FIBER**

9. Cranberry-Orange Chutney

MAKES 12 servings **PREP** 15 minutes **COOK** 15 minutes

■ In a medium saucepan, heat 2 tbsp **vegetable oil** over medium-high. Add ½ chopped **red onion**, 2 cloves chopped **garlic** and 2 tbsp chopped **ginger**; cook 2 minutes. Add 1 pkg (12 oz) **fresh cranberries**, 1 can (15 oz) drained **mandarin oranges**, 1 cup packed **brown sugar**, ⅓ cup **red wine vinegar**, ½ tsp each **salt** and **chipotle chile powder** and 1 **cinnamon stick**. Cook 13 minutes, stirring occasionally, until cranberries are softened.

PER SERVING 133 **CAL**; 2 g **FAT**; 0 g **PRO**; 29 g **CARB**; 1 g **FIBER**

10. Brussels Sprout and Bacon Slaw

MAKES 8 servings **PREP** 10 minutes **COOK** 10 minutes

■ Trim 1¾ lb **Brussels sprouts**. Insert a thin slicing blade into a food processor. With machine running, add Brussels sprouts and shave into thin slices. Alternately, thinly slice sprouts with a sharp knife. Heat a large stainless skillet over medium-high and add 6 oz diced **bacon**. Cook 5 minutes, stirring, until cooked through. Remove to a plate with a slotted spoon. Add shredded sprouts to bacon drippings. Sauté 3 to 5 minutes, seasoning with ½ tsp each **salt** and **black pepper**. Add bacon back to skillet; toss to combine. Sprinkle with 3 tbsp **cider vinegar**.

PER SERVING 128 **CAL**; 8 g **FAT**; 10 g **PRO**; 8 g **CARB**; 3 g **FIBER**

11. Bibb and Arugula Salad with Eggs

MAKES 12 servings **PREP** 15 minutes

■ Whisk 2 tbsp **red wine vinegar**, 1 tbsp **grainy Dijon mustard**, 1 tsp each dried **oregano** and **garlic powder**, ½ tsp **salt** and ¼ tsp **black pepper**. Gradually drizzle in ½ cup **olive oil** while whisking constantly. In a large bowl, combine 1 large head **Bibb lettuce,** torn into bite-size pieces (about 10 cups), 3 cups **baby arugula** and 1 cup cooked **chickpeas**. Toss with ¼ cup dressing. Top with 4 quartered **hard-boiled eggs** and drizzle with 2 tbsp dressing. Serve remaining dressing on the side.

PER SERVING 129 **CAL**; 11 g **FAT**; 3 g **PRO**; 4 g **CARB**; 1 g **FIBER**

12. Tossed Mixed Greens with Buttermilk Dressing

MAKES 12 servings **PREP** 15 minutes

■ Whisk 1 cup **buttermilk**, ¼ cup each **sour cream** and **mayonnaise**, 1 tsp each chopped **shallots**, **cider vinegar** and **sugar**, ½ tsp **salt** and ¼ tsp **garlic powder**. Toss 12 cups mixed **salad greens** with half the dressing. Serve with remaining dressing on the side.

PER SERVING 72 **CAL**; 5 g **FAT**; 3 g **PRO**; 5 g **CARB**; 1 g **FIBER**

13. Spicy Collard Greens

MAKES 6 servings **PREP** 10 minutes **COOK** 18 minutes

■ Remove and discard stems from 2 large bunches **collard greens**; roughly chop leaves. Heat 2 tbsp **extra-virgin olive oil** over medium. Add ½ thinly sliced **red onion**; cook 5 minutes. Stir in 2 cloves chopped **garlic** and ¼ tsp **red pepper flakes**; cook 1 minute. Increase heat to medium-high, stir in collards and cook 12 minutes, until tender. Add 2 tbsp **cider vinegar** and ¾ tsp **salt**.

PER SERVING 70 **CAL**; 5 g **FAT**; 3 g **PRO**; 6 g **CARB**; 4 g **FIBER**

14. Herb-Roasted Parsnips

MAKES 6 servings **PREP** 20 minutes **ROAST** at 425° for 25 minutes

■ Peel 2 lb **parsnips** and slice into 3 x ½-inch pieces. Toss in a large bowl with 2 tbsp **extra-virgin olive oil**, 1 tbsp chopped **fresh thyme**, 2 tsp chopped **fresh rosemary**, ½ tsp **salt** and ¼ tsp **black pepper**. Transfer to a baking sheet and roast at 425° for 25 minutes, tossing halfway through.

PER SERVING 140 **CAL**; 5 g **FAT**; 2 g **PRO**; 23 g **CARB**; 6 g **FIBER**

15. Gingered Cranberry Sauce

MAKES 12 servings **PREP** 5 minutes **COOK** 5 minutes

■ In a saucepan, combine chopped segments from 1 **orange**, 1 pkg (12 oz) **fresh cranberries**, 1 tbsp each grated **ginger** and **lemon juice**, 1¼ cups **sugar** and ½ cup **cranberry juice**. Bring to a boil; reduce heat and simmer 3 to 5 minutes, until most berries have popped. Cool and garnish with 2 tsp **orange zest**.

PER SERVING 53 **CAL**; 0 g **FAT**; 0 g **PRO**; 14 g **CARB**; 1 g **FIBER**

16. Rosemary Roasted Sweet Potatoes

MAKES 12 servings **PREP** 10 minutes **ROAST** at 400° for 40 minutes

■ Cut 3½ lb peeled **sweet potatoes** into 1-inch pieces. Toss with ½ cup **dried cherries**, 2 tbsp **olive oil**, 1 tbsp chopped **fresh rosemary**, ½ tsp **salt** and ¼ tsp **black pepper**. Roast in a shallow pan at 400° for 40 minutes or until tender, turning once. Stir in 1 tbsp **unsalted butter**. Garnish with more **rosemary**.

PER SERVING 147 **CAL**; 3 g **FAT**; 2 g **PRO**; 29 g **CARB**; 4 g **FIBER**

17. Five-Minute Spinach

MAKES 6 servings **PREP** 2 minutes **COOK** 3 minutes

■ In a large pot, heat 3 tbsp **extra-virgin olive oil** over medium-high. Stir in 2 large pkg (1 lb each) **baby spinach**, 3 tbsp fresh **lemon juice**, 1 tbsp **lemon zest**, ½ tsp **salt** and ¼ tsp **black pepper**. Stir until wilted, 2 to 3 minutes. Remove with a slotted spoon.

PER SERVING 120 **CAL**; 7 g **FAT**; 4 g **PRO**; 17 g **CARB**; 7 g **FIBER**

18. Cucumber, Olive and Dill Salad

MAKES 12 servings **PREP** 15 minutes

■ Combine 3 thinly sliced **English cucumbers**, ½ cup each thinly sliced **red onion** and sliced pitted **Kalamata olives**, ¼ cup **lemon juice**, 2 tbsp chopped **fresh dill**, 1 tbsp **canola oil**,

BIBB AND ARUGULA
SALAD WITH EGGS

CUCUMBER, OLIVE
AND DILL SALAD

BAGNA CAUDA–
STYLE SALAD

2 tsp **sugar** and 1 tsp **salt**. Cover and refrigerate at least 2 hours.

PER SERVING 50 CAL; 4 g FAT; 1 g PRO; 4 g CARB; 1 g FIBER

19. Spinach-Apple Salad

MAKES 12 servings PREP 15 minutes

■ Whisk ¼ cup **walnut oil**, 2 tbsp **cider vinegar**, 2 tsp **molasses** and ¼ tsp each **salt** and **black pepper**. In a large bowl, combine 1 pkg (12 oz) **baby spinach**, 16 pitted sliced **dates**, 3 cored and sliced **Gala apples** and ⅓ cup toasted coarsely chopped **walnuts**. Toss with dressing just before serving.

PER SERVING 180 CAL; 8 g FAT; 2 g PRO; 30 g CARB; 5 g FIBER

20. Bagna Cauda-Style Salad

MAKES 10 servings PREP 15 minutes
COOK 5 minutes

■ Heat ¼ cup **unsalted butter** in a small saucepan. Add 6 finely chopped **anchovy fillets** and 4 chopped **cloves garlic**; cook 1 minute over medium-low. Stir in ⅓ cup **olive oil** and cook 4 minutes, stirring occasionally. In a large bowl, combine 8 cups **mixed raw vegetables**, such as cauliflower florets, halved radishes, small white mushrooms, strips of sweet pepper and 1-inch pieces of carrot and celery. Toss with ¼ cup dressing. Serve with thin slices of **baguette** and remaining dressing on the side.

PER SERVING 280 CAL; 16 g FAT; 7 g PRO; 29 g CARB; 3 g FIBER

21. Mushroom Risotto

MAKES 12 servings PREP 10 minutes
COOK 8 minutes SLOW COOK on HIGH for 3 hours

■ Melt 3 tbsp **unsalted butter** in a large skillet. Add 1 diced small onion; sauté 3 minutes. Add 1 pkg (6 oz) **sliced portobello mushrooms**, diced, and 8 oz **sliced white mushrooms**; cook 3 minutes. Stir in 2 cups **Arborio rice**. Add ½ cup **white wine**; cook until most is absorbed, 2 minutes. Season with 1½ tsp **salt** and ½ tsp **black pepper**. Pour into slow cooker along with 4 cups **low-sodium vegetable broth**, 2 cups **water** and 1 tbsp chopped **fresh rosemary**. Cover and cook on HIGH for 3 hours. Uncover and stir in ½ cup **grated Parmesan** and 1 tbsp **unsalted butter**.

PER SERVING 164 CAL; 5 g FAT; 6 g PRO; 28 g CARB; 2 g FIBER

22. Mixed Wild Rice Stuffing with Bacon and Chestnuts

MAKES 12 servings PREP 10 minutes
COOK 30 minutes BAKE at 350° for 30 minutes

■ Cook 4 cups **wild rice blend** 15 minutes, according to pkg instructions, adding 1 tsp **salt** if mix is salt-free. Transfer to a large mixing bowl. In a large skillet, cook ¾ lb **bacon**, cut into ¾-inch pieces, over medium for 4 minutes. When bacon begins to brown, add 1 cup roughly chopped **chestnuts** and cook until browned, about 4 minutes. Use a slotted spoon to transfer mixture to mixing bowl, leaving fat in pan. Return pan to medium-low and add 2 finely diced **yellow onions**, 5 finely diced ribs **celery** and 4 cloves roughly chopped **garlic**. Cook until tender, about 7 minutes, then transfer to mixing bowl. Season with ¼ tsp each **salt** and **black pepper**. Stir in ½ cup chopped **fresh parsley**, 2 tbsp each chopped **fresh thyme** and chopped **fresh rosemary** and ½ tsp each **salt** and **crushed red pepper**. Transfer mixture to a 13 x 9-inch baking dish. Bake at 350° for 30 minutes, until heated through and rice is golden and crispy on top.

PER SERVING 390 CAL; 14 g FAT; 9 g PRO; 61 g CARB; 5 g FIBER

PEAR-CRANBERRY
RELISH

SPICY ITALIAN SAUSAGE
AND MULTIGRAIN BREAD
STUFFING

23. Pear-Cranberry Relish

MAKES 12 servings **PREP** 10 minutes

■ In a food processor, combine 1 pkg (12 oz) **fresh cranberries**, 1 **Bartlett pear**, cored and cut into chunks, ⅓ cup packed **brown sugar**, 3 tbsp chopped **sliced almonds**, 1 tbsp **lemon juice** and a pinch of **salt**. Pulse until combined but still chunky. Garnish with more **almonds** and strips of **lemon peel**.

PER SERVING 59 **CAL**; 1 g **FAT**; 0 g **PRO**; 13 g **CARB**; 2 g **FIBER**

24. Spicy Italian Sausage and Multigrain Bread Stuffing

MAKES 12 servings **PREP** 25 minutes
COOK 12 minutes **MICROWAVE** 45 seconds
STAND 15 minutes
BAKE at 350° for 1 hour 15 minutes

■ Spread 14 cups day-old **multigrain bread**, cut into ¾-inch cubes, on a rimmed baking sheet. Bake at 350° until dry but not toasted, stirring, 30 minutes. Meanwhile, heat 4 tbsp **unsalted butter** in a large skillet over medium-high. Add 1 lb **spicy Italian sausage**, casings removed, and brown, about 5 minutes. Reduce heat to medium-low and add 2 finely diced medium **yellow onions** and 5 finely diced ribs **celery**. Cook until tender, about 7 minutes. Season with ¼ tsp each **salt** and **black pepper**. In a large mixing bowl, combine bread, sausage mixture, ¾ cup chopped lightly toasted **almonds**, ½ cup **dried cranberries or dried tart cherries**, ½ cup chopped **fresh parsley**, 2 tbsp chopped **fresh thyme** and 1½ tsp **orange zest**. In a glass bowl, combine 4 tbsp **unsalted butter** and 2 cups **chicken broth** and microwave until butter melts, about 45 seconds. Whisk in 4 large **eggs** and 1½ tsp **salt**. Pour mixture over bread cubes and gently fold with a spatula until completely coated. Let stand 15 minutes, folding halfway through. Add up to 1 cup **broth**, if needed. Spread mixture evenly in a 13 x 9-inch baking dish. Bake at 350° until bread is golden, 35 to 45 minutes.

PER SERVING 370 **CAL**; 20 g **FAT**; 15 g **PRO**; 33 g **CARB**; 6 g **FIBER**

25. Creamy Wild Mushrooms and Onions

MAKES 8 servings **PREP** 15 minutes
COOK 17 minutes

■ Melt 4 tbsp **unsalted butter** in a large skillet over medium-high. Stir in 2 lb quartered **wild mushrooms** and 1 tbsp chopped **fresh thyme**. Cook 10 minutes, stirring often. Add 1 bag (14 oz) thawed **frozen pearl onions**; cook 2 minutes. Pour in 1 cup **heavy cream**, ¾ tsp **salt** and ½ tsp **black pepper**. Simmer 5 minutes, until liquid is reduced by half and thickened.

PER SERVING 200 **CAL**; 17 g **FAT**; 4 g **PRO**; 10 g **CARB**; 1 g **FIBER**

26. Sicilian Brussels Sprouts

MAKES 8 servings **PREP** 20 minutes
ROAST at 400° for 23 minutes

■ In a small bowl, whisk ¼ cup each **extra-virgin olive oil** and **white balsamic vinegar**, 2 tbsp **honey**, ¾ tsp **salt** and ¼ tsp **black pepper**. Trim and quarter 2 lb **Brussels sprouts**. Toss half the dressing with the Brussels sprouts on a rimmed baking sheet. Roast at 400° for 15 minutes. Stir in ¼ cup **pine nuts** and roast another 6 to 8 minutes. Remove from oven and toss hot Brussels sprouts with remaining dressing, ½ cup **golden raisins** and 2 tbsp **capers**. Serve immediately.

PER SERVING 190 **CAL**; 10 g **FAT**; 4 g **PRO**; 24 g **CARB**; 5 g **FIBER**

27. Rigatoni with Gorgonzola

MAKES 12 servings **PREP** 5 minutes
COOK 17 minutes

■ Bring a large pot of salted water to a boil. Add 1 lb **rigatoni** and cook 12 to 14 minutes. Drain, reserving 1 cup pasta water. Return rigatoni to pot. In a medium saucepan, whisk 1 pkg (8 oz) **cream cheese** with reserved pasta water, ½ tsp **salt**, ¼ tsp **black pepper** and ⅛ tsp **ground nutmeg**. Cook over medium until smooth, about 3 minutes, then stir in 1 cup (4 oz) crumbled **Gorgonzola cheese** and 1 cup thawed **frozen peas**. Heat through. Toss with rigatoni along with

½ cup (2 oz) crumbled **Gorgonzola**. Top with ⅓ cup toasted chopped **walnuts**.

PER SERVING 283 **CAL**; 13 g **FAT**; 10 g **PRO**; 32 g **CARB**; 2 g **FIBER**

28. Spicy Sweet Potatoes

MAKES 12 servings **PREP** 15 minutes
COOK 25 minutes

■ In a large skillet, heat 3 tbsp **vegetable oil** over medium-high. Add 2 thinly sliced medium **onions** and cook 3 minutes. Add 3½ lb **sweet potatoes**, peeled and cut into 1½-inch pieces; cook, stirring occasionally, 10 minutes. Stir in 2 cups **water**, 1 cup **golden raisins**, 2 tbsp packed **light brown sugar**, 1½ tsp **salt**, 1 tsp **ground ginger**, ½ tsp **ground cinnamon** and ¼ tsp **cayenne**. Cook, covered, over medium for 12 minutes, until tender, stirring occasionally.

PER SERVING 235 **CAL**; 4 g **FAT**; 3 g **PRO**; 49 g **CARB**; 5 g **FIBER**

29. Crunchy Mac and Cheese

MAKES 16 servings **PREP** 5 minutes
COOK 8 minutes **BAKE** at 350° for 30 minutes

■ Bring a large pot of salted water to a boil. Add 1 lb **cavatappi pasta** and cook until al dente, about 6 minutes. Drain and return to pot. Meanwhile, melt 4 tbsp **unsalted butter** in a medium saucepan. Whisk in 4 tbsp **all-purpose flour**; cook 2 minutes. While whisking, gradually add 4 cups **2% milk**. Whisk until smooth. Whisk in 2 tbsp **dried minced onion**, 1½ tsp **garlic powder**, ¾ tsp **salt** and ¼ tsp **black pepper**. Bring to a simmer; cook 2 to 3 minutes. Remove from heat and stir in 2 cups each **shredded cheddar** and **shredded Swiss cheese**. Combine with pasta and pour into a greased 13 x 9-inch baking dish. Melt 1 tbsp **unsalted butter** in a medium skillet. Pulse 2 slices **wheat bread** in a food processor until coarse crumbs form. Add to butter; cook 2 to 3 minutes, seasoning with a pinch each of **salt** and **black pepper**. Sprinkle over mac and cheese and bake at 350° for 30 minutes.

PER SERVING 300 **CAL**; 14 g **FAT**; 14 g **PRO**; 30 g **CARB**; 2 g **FIBER**

30. Pumpkin Sage Scones

MAKES 8 scones **PREP** 15 minutes
BAKE at 425° for 20 minutes

■ In a small bowl, blend 1¾ cups **all-purpose flour**, 1 tbsp **baking powder**, ½ tsp **salt** and ⅛ tsp **cayenne**. In a large bowl, blend ¾ cup **canned pumpkin**, ¾ cup **shredded Asiago cheese**, ¼ cup melted **butter**, 1 large **egg** and 1 tbsp chopped **fresh sage**. Fold flour mixture into pumpkin mixture and turn out onto a well-floured piece of parchment paper. Pat into a 7- to 8-inch circle and, with a greased knife, cut into 8 wedges (leave wedges touching). Bake at 425° for 20 minutes, until dry to the touch.

PER SCONE 209 **CAL**; 10 g **FAT**; 6 g **PRO**; 23 g **CARB**; 2 g **FIBER**

31. Citrusy Green Beans and Fennel

MAKES 8 servings **PREP** 20 minutes
COOK 7 minutes

■ Heat 2 tbsp **extra-virgin olive oil** in a large skillet over medium-high. Add 1 lb **green beans**, trimmed and sliced on the bias into 2-inch pieces. Sauté 2 minutes. Add 2 more tbsp **extra-virgin olive oil** and 1 medium **fennel bulb**, cored and thinly sliced (fronds reserved). Sauté 5 minutes, stirring occasionally. Stir in reserved fronds, 2 segmented **navel oranges**, 3 tbsp **tarragon vinegar**, 1 tbsp chopped **fresh tarragon**, 2 tsp **orange zest**, 1 tsp **salt** and ½ tsp **black pepper**.

PER SERVING 100 **CAL**; 7 g **FAT**; 2 g **PRO**; 11 g **CARB**; 3 g **FIBER**

32. Hasselback New Potatoes

MAKES 6 servings **PREP** 30 minutes
ROAST at 400° for 30 minutes

■ Scrub 2 lb assorted **new potatoes**. With a paring knife, cut 5 thin slits into each potato (stopping before reaching bottom). Thinly slice 10 large cloves **garlic** and fit slices into slits in potatoes. (This can be done up to 2 days ahead; store in fridge.) Place on a large baking sheet and drizzle with 3 tbsp **extra-virgin olive oil**. Season with ½ tsp **salt** and ¼ tsp **black pepper**.

Spread out on sheet and roast at 400° for 15 minutes. Gently turn and roast another 15 minutes, until tender. Drizzle with 2 tsp **extra-virgin olive oil** and sprinkle with 1 tsp chopped **fresh thyme**. These can be baked ahead; reheat at 375° for 15 minutes.

PER SERVING 175 **CAL**; 6 g **FAT**; 3 g **PRO**; 28 g **CARB**; 3 g **FIBER**

33. Tropical Sweet Potatoes

MAKES 8 servings PREP 15 minutes
COOK 12 minutes

■ Peel 3½ lb **sweet potatoes** and cut into 2-inch chunks. Place in a large pot and add enough cold water to cover by an inch. Bring to a boil, cook 12 minutes and drain. Mash sweet potatoes, adding ½ cup **coconut milk**, 2 tbsp **coconut oil**, ½ tsp each **salt** and **black pepper** and a pinch of **cayenne pepper**. Transfer to a serving dish and top with ½ cup toasted **sweetened flake coconut**.

PER SERVING 180 **CAL**; 7 g **FAT**; 2 g **PRO**; 28 g **CARB**; 4 g **FIBER**

34. Potato Pancakes

MAKES 15 pancakes PREP 20 minutes
FRY 6 minutes per batch

■ Peel 2¾ lb **russet potatoes**. Shred on the coarse side of a box grater. Add 1 grated medium **onion** and squeeze out excess liquid. Toss with 1 beaten large **egg**, 1 tsp **salt**, ½ tsp **black pepper** and ¼ cup **potato flour or potato starch** (such as Bob's Red Mill potato flour). Heat ¾ cup **vegetable oil** in a large stainless skillet over medium-high. Use a small ice cream scoop to portion pancakes—about ¼ cup for each, 5 per batch. Flatten with a small spatula and fry 3 minutes. Flip over and fry 3 more minutes. Repeat with remaining mixture. Pancakes can be made ahead, cooled on paper towels, wrapped in foil and frozen. To reheat, bake frozen pancakes at 375° for 10 to 15 minutes, turning halfway through.

PER PANCAKE 157 **CAL**; 9 g **FAT**; 2 g **PRO**; 18 g **CARB**; 2 g **FIBER**

35. Green Beans, Hazelnuts and Shallots

MAKES 8 servings PREP 15 minutes
COOK 8 minutes

■ Cook 1½ lb trimmed **green beans** in a large pot of boiling salted water 4 minutes, until crisp-tender. Drain and set aside. In a large skillet, melt 2 tbsp **unsalted butter** over medium. Add 2 large thinly sliced **shallots** and ½ cup roughly chopped **hazelnuts**; cook 4 minutes, until shallots are softened. Stir in cooked beans, ½ tsp **salt** and ¼ tsp **black pepper** until warm.

PER SERVING 125 **CAL**; 8 g **FAT**; 4 g **PRO**; 13 g **CARB**; 4 g **FIBER**

36. Maple-Glazed Acorn Squash

MAKES 8 servings PREP 10 minutes
ROAST at 450° for 40 minutes

■ Halve two 2-lb **acorn squash** through stems. Discard seeds. Cut into ½-inch-thick slices (you will now have half-circles) and place in a large bowl. Toss with 3 tbsp each melted **butter** and **maple syrup**, ½ tsp each chopped **fresh thyme** and **salt** and a few grinds of **freshly cracked black pepper**. Spread onto 2 large baking sheets in a single layer. Roast at 450° for 40 minutes, turning once. Drizzle with additional **maple syrup** and sprinkle with more **fresh thyme**.

PER SERVING 144 **CAL**; 5 g **FAT**; 2 g **PRO**; 28 g **CARB**; 7 g **FIBER**

37. Pretzel Bread Stuffing with Pancetta and Apples

MAKES 12 servings PREP 25 minutes
COOK 15 minutes MICROWAVE 45 seconds
STAND 15 minutes
BAKE at 350° for 1 hour 15 minutes

■ Spread 14 cups (10 to 12 large **pretzel rolls**) day-old pretzel bread, cut into ¾-inch cubes, on a rimmed baking sheet. Bake at 350° until dry but not toasted, stirring, 30 minutes. Meanwhile, heat 4 tbsp **unsalted butter** in a large skillet over medium. Add ¾ lb finely chopped **pancetta** and cook until browned, 5 minutes. Reduce heat to medium-low and add 2 finely diced medium **yellow onions**, 4 finely

diced ribs **celery**, 1 peeled and finely diced large **carrot**, and 4 roughly chopped cloves **garlic**. Cook until tender and onions are translucent, about 7 minutes. Add 1½ cups diced **Gala apples** and cook until apples begin to soften, 3 minutes. Season with ¼ tsp each **salt** and **black pepper**. In a large mixing bowl, combine bread cubes, pancetta mixture, ½ cup roughly chopped **fresh parsley** and 2 tbsp finely chopped **fresh sage**. In a glass measuring cup, combine 4 tbsp **butter** and 2 cups **chicken broth** and microwave until butter melts, 45 seconds. Whisk in 4 large **eggs** and 1½ tsp **salt**. Pour mixture over bread cubes and gently fold with a spatula until completely coated. Let stand 15 minutes, folding halfway through. Add up to ½ cup **broth**, if needed. Spread mixture evenly in a 13 x 9-inch baking dish and bake at 350° until heated through and bread is golden, 35 to 45 minutes.

PER SERVING 430 **CAL**; 23 g **FAT**; 11 g **PRO**; 45 g **CARB**; 3 g **FIBER**

38. Cornbread Stuffing with Golden Raisins and Pecans

MAKES 12 servings PREP 25 minutes
COOK 7 minutes MICROWAVE 45 seconds
LET STAND 15 minutes BAKE at 350° for 1 hour, 30 minutes

■ Spread 14 cups day-old **cornbread**, cut into ¾-inch cubes, on a rimmed baking sheet. Bake at 350° until dry but not toasted, stirring, 30 to 45 minutes. Meanwhile, heat 4 tbsp **unsalted butter** in a large skillet over medium-low. Add 2 finely diced medium **yellow onions** and 5 finely diced ribs **celery**. Cook until tender, 7 minutes. Season with ¼ tsp each **salt** and **black pepper**. In a large mixing bowl, combine bread cubes, onion mixture, 1 cup roughly chopped lightly toasted **pecans**, ½ cup each **golden raisins** and roughly chopped **fresh parsley** and 2 tbsp chopped **fresh sage**. In a glass bowl, combine 2 tbsp **unsalted butter** and 2 cups **chicken broth**. Microwave until butter melts, 45 seconds. Whisk in 3 large **eggs** and

1½ tsp **salt**. Pour mixture over bread cubes and gently fold with spatula until completely coated. Let stand 15 minutes, folding halfway through. Add up to ½ cup **broth**, if needed. Spread evenly in a 13 x 9-inch baking dish and bake at 350° until golden, 35 to 45 minutes.

PER SERVING 320 **CAL**; 20 g **FAT**; 6 g **PRO**; 30 g **CARB**; 4 g **FIBER**

39. Citrus Sweet Potatoes

MAKES 12 servings PREP 15 minutes
COOK 33 minutes

■ Cut rind from 2 **grapefruits** and 2 **navel oranges**. Separate fruit into sections and reserve. In a large skillet over medium, melt 1 stick (½ cup) **unsalted butter** and ¼ cup each **honey** and **sugar**. Cook 5 minutes, until light brown. Add 5 lb peeled **sweet potatoes,** cut into 2-inch pieces, 1 cup **orange juice** and 1 tsp **salt**. Cover and simmer over medium-low for 22 to 25 minutes, until tender. Uncover and cook 3 minutes, until a thick glaze forms. Add fruit sections and 2 tsp **lime zest**.

PER SERVING 208 **CAL**; 6 g **FAT**; 2 g **PRO**; 39 g **CARB**; 5 g **FIBER**

40. Brown-Buttered Carrots

MAKES 8 servings PREP 15 minutes
COOK 23 minutes

■ Cook 6 tbsp **unsalted butter** over medium in a large skillet until browned, about 8 minutes. (Watch carefully so it does not burn.) Stir in ¾ tsp **kosher salt**, ½ tsp **smoked paprika** and ¼ tsp each **ground cinnamon** and **black pepper**. Add 2 lb **peeled carrots**, sliced on the bias into 1-inch pieces. Cook 15 minutes or until tender, stirring occasionally.

PER SERVING 120 **CAL**; 9 g **FAT**; 1 g **PRO**; 10 g **CARB**; 3 g **FIBER**

41. Balsamic Squash with Feta

MAKES 8 servings PREP 15 minutes
ROAST at 400° for 35 minutes

■ In a large bowl, whisk 3 tbsp **extra-virgin olive oil**, 2 tbsp **balsamic vinegar**, 1 tbsp **honey** and ½ tsp each **kosher salt** and **black pepper**. Halve 3 lbs **delicata squash** lengthwise; scoop out pulp and seeds and discard. Quarter each half. Toss squash with dressing in bowl. Place on a baking sheet in a single layer. Roast at 400° for 20 minutes. Carefully turn pieces with tongs; roast 15 minutes more. Transfer to a platter, brush with 2 tbsp **balsamic vinegar**, season with ¼ tsp **kosher salt** and scatter ⅓ cup crumbled **feta** on top.

PER SERVING 140 **CAL**; 7 g **FAT**; 2 g **PRO**; 20 g **CARB**; 5 g **FIBER**

42. Pineapple-Cranberry Sauce

MAKES 12 servings PREP 10 minutes
COOK 10 minutes

■ In a food processor, combine 1 pkg (12 oz) **fresh cranberries**, 1 can (8 oz) **crushed pineapple** in juice, ¾ cup **sugar** and ¼ cup **orange juice**. Pulse until coarsely chopped. Add to a saucepan and bring to a boil. Reduce heat and simmer 10 minutes or until thickened, stirring occasionally. Add ¼ cup **sugar**, 1 tsp **orange zest** and 2 tsp **vanilla extract**. Cool and refrigerate to chill.

PER SERVING 65 **CAL**; 0 g **FAT**; 0 g **PRO**; 19 g **CARB**; 1 g **FIBER**

POTATO PANCAKES

HASSELBACK NEW POTATOES, PAGE 263

TROPICAL SWEET POTATOES

SHAVED BUTTERNUT
SQUASH WITH ASIAGO
DRESSING

ROASTED
CAULIFLOWER

WARM RADISHES AND
BUTTER LETTUCE

43. Twice-Baked Potatoes

MAKES 12 servings **PREP** 5 minutes
BAKE at 400° for 1 hour, 15 minutes
BROIL 2 minutes

■ Scrub 6 small **russet potatoes**; pierce with a fork. Place directly on oven rack and bake at 400° for 55 minutes, until tender. Cool slightly and halve lengthwise. Scoop flesh into a large bowl and place skins on a large baking sheet. Mash flesh with 4 oz **⅓-less-fat cream cheese**, 3 slices crumbled cooked **bacon**, ½ cup **milk**, 2 sliced **scallions** and ½ tsp each **salt** and **black pepper**. Divide filling among potato skins and sprinkle with **grated Parmesan**. (These can be made up to this step the day before serving; finish baking and broiling day of.) Bake filled potatoes at 400° for 20 minutes. Broil 2 minutes to brown.

PER POTATO HALF 96 **CAL**; 3 g **FAT**; 3 g **PRO**; 14 g **CARB**; 1 g **FIBER**

44. Roasted Cauliflower

MAKES 8 servings **PREP** 15 minutes
ROAST at 450° for 30 minutes

■ On 1 or 2 large baking sheets, toss 12 cups **cauliflower florets** with 3 tbsp **olive oil** and ½ tsp each **salt** and **black pepper**. Spread in a single layer on baking sheet(s); roast at 450° for 15 minutes. Stir florets and roast an additional 15 minutes, until browned. Meanwhile, make tahini dressing: Whisk 2 tbsp each **tahini** and **lemon juice**, 1 tbsp each **olive oil** and **honey** and ¼ tsp **salt** and **black pepper** until smooth. In a serving dish, toss florets with ½ cup **pomegranate seeds** and ⅓ cup chopped toasted **walnuts**. Serve cauliflower with tahini dressing.

PER SERVING 172 **CAL**; 12 g **FAT**; 5 g **PRO**; 14 g **CARB**; 4 g **FIBER**

45. Warm Radishes and Butter Lettuce

MAKES 8 servings **PREP** 15 minutes
COOK 7 minutes

■ Trim tops from 2 large bunches **radishes**; quarter. Remove leaves from 2 small heads **butter lettuce** and roughly chop. Heat 2 tbsp **unsalted** butter in a large skillet over medium-high. Add radishes and sauté 5 minutes. Add lettuce, ¼ cup finely chopped **chives**, 1 tbsp **white wine vinegar**, 1 tsp **Dijon mustard** and ½ tsp each **salt** and **black pepper**. Stir in leaves and cook until wilted, about 2 minutes. Garnish with more **chives** and **black pepper**.

PER SERVING 35 CAL; 3 g FAT; 1 g PRO; 2 g CARB; 1 g FIBER

46. Shaved Butternut Squash with Asiago Dressing

MAKES 8 servings PREP 25 minutes

■ In a small bowl, whisk ½ cup **Fage Total Greek yogurt**, ¼ cup **buttermilk**, 2 tbsp **white wine vinegar** and ¼ tsp each **salt** and **black pepper**. Stir in ½ cup shredded **Asiago cheese**. Peel a medium **butternut squash** and trim both ends. Using a vegetable peeler, shave long pieces of squash into a large bowl until you reach the core. Discard seeds and pulp. Toss squash with ⅓ cup each thinly sliced **shallots**, **sunflower seeds** and chopped **fresh parsley**, ½ tsp **salt** and ¼ tsp **black pepper**. Drizzle dressing on top. Toss just before serving. Serve with more Asiago, if desired.

PER SERVING 110 CAL; 5 g FAT; 5 g PRO; 14 g CARB; 4 g FIBER

47. Sourdough Stuffing with Mushrooms and Walnuts

MAKES 12 servings PREP 25 minutes
COOK 12 minutes MICROWAVE 45 seconds
LET STAND 15 minutes BAKE at 350° for 1 hour 15 minutes

■ Spread 14 cups day-old **sourdough bread** (cut into ¾-inch cubes) on a rimmed baking sheet. Bake at 350° until dry but not toasted, stirring, 30 minutes. Meanwhile, heat 4 tbsp **unsalted butter** in a large skillet over medium-high. Add 1 lb sliced **mixed mushrooms** and cook until browned, about 5 minutes. Add ⅓ cup **sherry** and cook until liquid evaporates. Reduce heat to medium-low and add 2 medium finely diced **yellow onions**,

5 ribs finely diced **celery** and 4 cloves roughly chopped **garlic**. Cook until tender and onions are translucent, about 7 minutes. Season with ¼ tsp each **salt** and **black pepper**. In a large mixing bowl, combine bread cubes, mushroom mixture, 1 cup roughly chopped lightly toasted **walnuts**, 6 oz grated **Swiss cheese**, ½ cup roughly chopped **fresh parsley** and 2 tbsp each chopped **fresh thyme** and chopped **fresh rosemary**. In a glass measuring cup, combine 4 tbsp **unsalted butter** and 2 cups **chicken broth** and microwave until butter melts, 45 seconds. Whisk in 4 large **eggs** and 1½ tsp **salt**. Pour mixture over bread and gently fold with a spatula until completely coated. Let stand 15 minutes, folding halfway through. Add up to 1 cup **broth**, if needed. Spread mixture evenly in a 13 x 9-inch baking dish and bake at 350° until bread is golden, 35 to 45 minutes.

PER SERVING 390 CAL; 22 g FAT; 13 g PRO; 35 g CARB; 3 g FIBER

48. Au Gratin Potatoes

MAKES 10 servings PREP 15 minutes
COOK 5 minutes SLOW COOK 5 hours on LOW

■ Coat a 4-qt slow cooker with **nonstick cooking spray**. In a saucepan, melt 3 tbsp **unsalted butter** over medium. Whisk in 3 tbsp **all-purpose flour**; cook 2 minutes. Whisk in 3 cups **milk**. Bring to a simmer; cook, whisking, 3 minutes. Stir in ½ tsp each **salt** and **chipotle chile powder**, ¼ tsp **black pepper** and 2 cups shredded **Gruyère cheese**. Peel 3 lb **Yukon gold potatoes** and cut into ¼-inch-thick slices. Layer half in slow cooker and season with **salt** and **black pepper**. Top with 1 thinly sliced **medium onion** and half the cheese sauce. Layer remaining potatoes, season with **salt** and **pepper** and top with remaining sauce. Sprinkle with 1 cup shredded **Gruyère**. Drape a towel over slow cooker and cover with lid. Cook on LOW for 5 hours.

PER SERVING 319 CAL; 16 g FAT; 15 g PRO; 31 g CARB; 3 g FIBER

49. Potatoes, Carrots and Onions

MAKES 6 servings PREP 5 minutes
ROAST 1 hour at 425°

■ Toss 2 lbs **tricolor new potatoes**, 3 large **carrots**, peeled and cut into 1-inch pieces, and 2 quartered **small onions** with 2 tbsp **olive oil**, 1 tbsp chopped **fresh rosemary**, ¾ tsp **salt** and ¼ tsp **black pepper**. Spread over 1 or 2 large rimmed baking sheets. Roast at 425°, stirring occasionally, for 45 minutes to 1 hour, until potatoes are browned and pierced easily with a knife.

PER SERVING 208 CAL; 5 g FAT; 5 g PRO; 37 g CARB; 5 g FIBER

50. Glazed Sweet Potatoes and Pecans

MAKES 12 servings PREP 15 minutes
COOK 19 minutes

■ Heat 2 tbsp **vegetable oil** in a large nonstick skillet over medium-high. Add 3 lbs peeled **sweet potatoes**, cut into 1-inch chunks, and sauté 10 minutes. Add ¾ cup **water** and ¼ tsp **salt**; reduce heat to medium and cook, covered, 8 minutes, stirring occasionally. In a small skillet, melt 6 tbsp **unsalted butter** over medium. Stir in ⅔ cup packed **dark brown sugar**, ½ tsp **pumpkin pie spice** and ½ tsp **salt**. Cook 1 minute. Spoon glaze over potatoes and sprinkle with ½ cup **toasted pecans**.

PER SERVING 266 CAL; 11 g FAT; 2 g PRO; 40 g CARB; 4 g FIBER

SUPER-SIZE PIES

Nine-inch rounds are so last year. This holiday, think big! Like, 15x10-inch baking pan big.

CRANBERRY PIE

Slab pies—those baked in a 15 x 10-inch pan—are easy to assemble and serve a big crowd.

Cranberry Pie

MAKES 16 servings **PREP** 30 minutes
BAKE 40 minutes at 400°

- **4** refrigerated piecrusts (2 boxes), at room temperature
- **2** pkg (16 oz each) frozen cranberries (about 8 cups), thawed
- **2** cups plus 1 tbsp sugar
- **⅓** cup all-purpose flour
- **¼** cup lemon juice
- **½** tsp almond extract
- **¼** tsp salt
- **1** large egg, beaten

■ Heat oven to 400°. Lightly flour a surface. Unroll 2 piecrusts and stack on top of each other. Use a rolling pin to combine crusts into a 17 x 12-inch rectangle. Place in bottom of a rimmed 15 x 10-inch sheet pan. Repeat with the last 2 piecrusts, but instead of fitting into pan, gently lay on top. Refrigerate 30 minutes.

■ In a large bowl, toss cranberries, 2 cups sugar and next 4 ingredients. Remove crusts from refrigerator and set top crust aside. Fill bottom crust with cranberry mixture. Place top crust over pie and crimp edges. Using a paring knife, cut slits into crust. Brush top and sides with egg and sprinkle with 1 tbsp sugar.

■ Bake 35 to 40 minutes, until browned and bubbling. Cool 45 minutes before slicing.

PER SERVING 340 **CAL**; 13 g **FAT**; 3 g **PRO**; 57 g **CARB**; 3 g **FIBER**

CHOCOLATE-ESPRESSO PIE

Chocolate-Espresso Pie

MAKES 16 servings **PREP** 30 minutes **BAKE** 15 minutes at 350° **COOK** 8 minutes **CHILL** overnight

- **1½** boxes (9 oz each) Nabisco Famous Chocolate Wafers
- **1½** sticks (¾ cup) unsalted butter, melted
- **⅔** cup sugar
- **½** cup cornstarch
- **⅓** cup unsweetened cocoa powder
- **2** tbsp instant espresso powder
- **¼** tsp salt
- **6** cups 2% or whole milk
- **½** cup semisweet chocolate chips
- **1** tsp vanilla extract
  Whipped cream and chocolate-covered espresso beans (optional)

■ Heat oven to 350°. In a food processor, pulse cookies until fine crumbs form. Pour in melted butter and combine until well blended.

Transfer to a rimmed 15 x 10-inch sheet pan. Using the bottom of a measuring cup, press firmly into bottom and up sides of pan. Bake 15 minutes. Cool while preparing filling.

■ In a medium pot, whisk sugar and next 4 ingredients until combined. Whisk in milk, then bring to a boil, stirring occasionally. Reduce to a simmer and cook 6 to 8 minutes, stirring often, until thickened. Remove from heat and stir in chocolate chips and vanilla extract until smooth.

■ Pour filling into crust. Gently cover with plastic wrap and refrigerate overnight. Serve with whipped cream and chopped chocolate-covered espresso beans, if desired.

PER SERVING 320 **CAL**; 16 g **FAT**; 6 g **PRO**; 40 g **CARB**; 2 g **FIBER**

GINGERED PEAR CRUMB PIE

Gingered Pear Crumb Pie

MAKES 16 servings PREP 30 minutes BAKE 1 hour at 350° COOL 1 hour

- 1 box (14.4 oz) graham crackers
- ⅔ cup plus 3 tbsp granulated sugar
- 1¾ sticks (14 tbsp) unsalted butter, melted
- 1 cup all-purpose flour
- ¾ cup rolled oats
- ¾ cup packed light brown sugar
- ⅓ cup chopped crystallized ginger
- ½ tsp salt
- 1¼ sticks (10 tbsp) unsalted butter, cut into cubes and chilled
- 3 lb pears, peeled, cored and sliced ⅛ inch thick
- ⅓ cup peeled and thinly sliced fresh ginger
- 2 tbsp lemon juice

  Butter pecan or vanilla ice cream (optional)

■ Heat oven to 350°. In a food processor, pulse graham crackers and 3 tbsp sugar until fine crumbs form. Pour in melted butter and combine until well blended. Transfer to a rimmed 15 x 10-inch sheet pan. Using the bottom of a measuring cup, press firmly into bottom and up sides of pan. Bake 15 minutes. Remove from oven and cool 15 minutes.

■ In a bowl, combine ⅔ cup flour, the oats, brown sugar, crystallized ginger and ¼ tsp salt. Mix in cubed butter with your hands, breaking up into pea-size pieces. Set aside.

■ In a separate bowl, gently toss pears, ⅔ cup granulated sugar, fresh ginger, ⅓ cup flour, lemon juice and ¼ tsp salt. Spread into crust. Scatter on crumb topping.

■ Bake 40 to 45 minutes, until topping is browned and pie is bubbling. Cool at least 1 hour before slicing. Serve with ice cream, if desired.

PER SERVING 413 CAL; 18 g FAT 3 g PRO; 61 g CARB; 4 g FIBER

Pecan Pie

MAKES 16 servings PREP 15 minutes
BAKE 40 minutes at 350°

- 2 refrigerated piecrusts (1 box), at room temperature
- 1½ cups packed light brown sugar
- 1 cup light corn syrup
- 1¼ sticks (10 tbsp) unsalted butter
- 5 large eggs, beaten
- 1 tsp vanilla extract
- ¾ tsp salt
- 3 cups shelled pecan halves

■ Heat oven to 350°. Lightly flour a surface. Unroll piecrusts and stack on top of each other. Use a rolling pin to combine crusts into a 17 x 12-inch rectangle. Place in bottom of a rimmed 15 x 10-inch sheet pan; fold over any edges. Refrigerate while preparing filling.

■ In a medium pot over medium, combine brown sugar, corn syrup and butter, whisking until smooth and barely bubbling. Remove from heat and slowly stir in next 3 ingredients.

■ Scatter pecans over crust in an even layer. Slowly pour filling over pecans. Bake 40 minutes, until crust is browned and filling is set. Cool completely before slicing into squares.

PER SERVING 450 CAL; 28 g FAT; 5 g PRO; 50 g CARB; 2 g FIBER

PECAN PIE

Because they're generously sized and easy to make, slab pies are perfect for taking to holiday potlucks.

Pumpkin Pie

MAKES 16 servings **PREP** 30 minutes
BAKE 45 minutes at 400°

- 3 **refrigerated piecrusts (from 2 boxes), at room temperature**
- 3 **cans (15 oz each) pure pumpkin puree**
- 3 **large eggs**
- 1 **can (14 oz) sweetened condensed milk**
- ¼ **cup packed light brown sugar**
- 2 **tsp pumpkin pie spice**
- ¾ **tsp salt**

■ Heat oven to 400°. Lightly flour a surface. Unroll 2 piecrusts and stack on top of each other. Use a rolling pin to combine crusts into a 17 x 12-inch rectangle. Place in bottom of a rimmed 15 x 10-inch sheet pan. Slightly roll out third piecrust. Using a 2-inch pumpkin cookie cutter, remove 16 shapes and place on a separate baking sheet. (Save leftover crust for another use.) Refrigerate while preparing filling.

■ In a large bowl, beat all remaining ingredients until smooth. Spread into pie shell and place pumpkin cutouts on top.

■ Bake 40 to 45 minutes, until crust is browned and filling is set. Cool completely before slicing into squares.

PER SERVING 260 **CAL**; 11 g **FAT**; 6 g **PRO**; 38 g **CARB**; 3 g **FIBER**

PUMPKIN PIE

HEALTHY FAMILY DINNERS

10 easy meals for crazy-busy weeknights.

**THAI RICE
NOODLE BOWL**

Thai Rice Noodle Bowl

MAKES 4 servings **PREP** 16 minutes
COOK 2 minutes **GRILL OR BROIL** 6 minutes

7	oz (½ a 14-oz box) thin stir-fry rice noodles
⅓	cup rice vinegar
3	tbsp low-sodium soy sauce
3	tbsp creamy peanut butter
2	tbsp fish sauce
2	tbsp warm water
1	tbsp plus 1 tsp sugar
¼	tsp red pepper flakes
½	seedless cucumber
¾	lb small chicken breast halves, boneless pork chops or steak
¾	tsp cornstarch
1	cup sweet pepper strips
½	cup shredded carrot
3	scallions, trimmed and sliced
⅓	cup cilantro leaves, sliced, plus more for serving
½	cup chopped peanuts
	Lime wedges

■ Bring a large saucepan of water to a boil. Add noodles, turn off heat and let soak 6 to 8 minutes.

■ Meanwhile, in a small bowl, whisk vinegar, soy sauce, peanut butter, fish sauce, the warm water, sugar and red pepper flakes until smooth. Peel, halve and slice cucumber into half-moons.

■ Heat grill pan or broiler. Place chicken in a resealable plastic bag or a glass dish. Add 3 tbsp of the dressing, turning to coat.

■ Place remaining dressing in a small saucepan with cornstarch. Bring to a boil; boil 2 minutes. Remove from heat.

■ Grill or broil chicken 6 minutes, turning once, until cooked through.

■ Drain and rinse noodles and transfer to a large bowl. Add sweet pepper, shredded carrot, cucumber, scallions and sliced cilantro. Drizzle dressing into bowl and toss to combine. Divide among 4 bowls. Slice chicken and divide among bowls. Sprinkle with cilantro leaves and chopped peanuts. Serve each bowl with a lime wedge.

PER SERVING 468 **CAL**; 16 g **FAT**; 32 g **PRO**; 51 g **CARB**; 4 g **FIBER**

PORK TENDERLOIN WITH CREAMY APPLE CIDER SAUCE

Pork Tenderloin with Creamy Apple Cider Sauce

MAKES 6 servings **PREP** 15 minutes **BAKE** 12 minutes at 425° **COOK** 13 minutes **STAND** 5 minutes

2	small pork tenderloins, about ¾ lb each
1	tsp salt
½	tsp black pepper
1	tbsp olive oil
2	tbsp all-purpose flour
2	cups reduced-sodium chicken broth
1	cup apple cider
½	cup heavy cream
2	tbsp Dijon mustard
2	tbsp chopped parsley
1½	cups couscous
	Cooked snow peas

■ Heat oven to 425°. Season pork with ½ tsp of the salt and ¼ tsp of the pepper. Heat oil in a large ovenproof nonstick skillet over medium-high heat. Brown pork on all sides, about 7 minutes total. Place skillet in oven and bake 12 minutes or until internal temperature registers 145°. Carefully remove from oven (handle will be hot), place meat on a serving platter and cover.

■ Stir flour into 1 cup of the broth until flour is dissolved; add to skillet. Add apple cider and simmer 5 minutes, stirring occasionally. Stir in cream and ¼ tsp each of the salt and pepper; add mustard and simmer 1 minute. Add parsley.

■ Meanwhile, place the remaining 1 cup broth, ½ cup water and the remaining ¼ tsp salt in a medium saucepan and bring to a simmer. Turn off heat and stir in couscous. Cover; let stand 5 minutes. Fluff with a fork.

■ Slice pork and serve with sauce, couscous and cooked snow peas.

PER SERVING 464 **CAL**; 14 g **FAT**; 32 g **PRO**; 51 g **CARB**; 3 g **FIBER**

CURRIED
CHICKEN AND
CAULIFLOWER

Curried Chicken and Cauliflower

MAKES 6 servings **PREP** 15 minutes **COOK** 19 minutes

- 1 **can (14 oz) light coconut milk**
- 1 **cup low-sodium chicken broth**
- 2 **tbsp sugar**
- 1 **to 2 tbsp yellow curry paste**
- 2 **tbsp olive oil**
- 1 **lb boneless, skinless chicken breast halves, cut into 1-inch pieces**
- 1 **head cauliflower, trimmed and cut into florets**
- 4 **scallions, trimmed and sliced**
- 1 **tbsp cornstarch**
- 1 **can (15 oz) chickpeas, rinsed and drained**
- ¾ **tsp salt**
  Cooked basmati rice (optional)

■ In a small bowl whisk coconut milk, ¾ cup of the chicken broth, sugar, and curry paste. Heat olive oil in a stockpot over medium-high. Add chicken and brown on all sides, about 4 minutes. Remove to a bowl with a slotted spoon. Add cauliflower to pot and cook 1 minute. Reduce heat to medium. Stir in coconut milk mixture and bring to a simmer. Cover and simmer 6 minutes. Uncover and add chicken, with accumulated juices, and scallions. Simmer, uncovered, 5 minutes.

■ Meanwhile, whisk remaining ¼ cup chicken broth and cornstarch. Stir chickpeas, cornstarch mixture and salt into pot. Raise heat to medium-high and cook 3 minutes. Serve with basmati rice, if desired.

PER SERVING 461 **CAL**; 15 g **FAT**; 28 g **PRO**; 54 g **CARB**; 7 g **FIBER**

Tomato and Eggplant Fusilli

MAKES 6 servings **PREP** 15 minutes
COOK 30 minutes

- ¼ **cup olive oil**
- 4 **cups cherry tomatoes**
- 1 **large eggplant (about 1¼ lb), cut into ½-inch cubes**
- 3 **large cloves garlic, sliced**
- ¾ **tsp salt**
- 1 **lb whole wheat fusilli**
- 1 **cup fresh basil, hand torn**
- 1 **cup heaping (4 oz) shredded ricotta salata**

■ In a large lidded skillet, heat 2 tbsp of the oil over medium. Stir in tomatoes and eggplant. Cook, covered, 15 minutes. (If skillet does not have a lid, try covering tightly with aluminum foil or a baking sheet.) Stir in garlic and ¼ tsp of the salt; cover and cook another 10 to 15 minutes, until tomatoes are slightly wilted.

■ Meanwhile, bring a pot of lightly salted water to a boil. Cook fusilli according to package directions, reserving ¾ cup of the pasta water. Using a slotted spoon, transfer fusilli to skillet with tomato eggplant mixture. Stir in ½ cup of the pasta water, ¾ cup of the basil, ¾ cup of the ricotta salata, the remaining 2 tbsp oil and remaining ½ tsp salt. (If pasta seems dry, stir in ¼ cup pasta water.) Garnish with remaining ¼ cup basil and ¼ cup ricotta salata.

PER SERVING 434 **CAL**; 13 g **FAT**; 13 g **PRO**; 67 g **CARB**; 11 g **FIBER**

BEEF AND BROCCOLI LO MEIN

SALMON TACOS
WITH GUACAMOLE

Beef and Broccoli Lo Mein

MAKES 4 servings **PREP** 20 minutes
COOK 15 minutes

- 1   **cup reduced-sodium beef broth**
- 3   **tbsp reduced-sodium soy sauce**
- 3   **tbsp ketchup**
- 1   **tbsp rice vinegar**
- 1   **tbsp cornstarch**
- ¼   **tsp red pepper flakes**
- 1   **large head broccoli, cut into florets**
- ½   **lb whole-grain linguine**
- 2   **tbsp canola oil**
- ½   **lb flank steak, cut into ¼-inch-thick slices**
- 1   **large green sweet pepper, cored, seeded and thinly sliced**
- 1   **can (8 oz) chopped water chestnuts, drained**

■ In a small bowl, whisk broth, soy sauce, ketchup, rice vinegar, cornstarch and red pepper. Set aside. Bring a large pot of lightly salted water to a boil. Add broccoli. Return to a boil and cook 3 minutes. Scoop out with a slotted spoon and reserve. In the same pot, cook linguine 6 minutes; drain and set aside.

■ In a large nonstick skillet, heat canola oil over medium-high. Add steak and green pepper. Stir-fry 3 minutes. Stir in sauce and simmer 1 minute, until thickened. Add broccoli and water chestnuts; cook 2 minutes. Toss with pasta and serve.

PER SERVING 453 **CAL**; 12 g **FAT**; 26 g **PRO**; 63 g **CARB**; 7 g **FIBER**

Salmon Tacos with Guacamole

MAKES 4 servings **PREP** 15 minutes **COOK** 15 minutes **STAND** 5 minutes **BAKE** 15 minutes at 400°

- 1   **cup RiceSelect Texmati Royal Blend (red, white, brown and wild rice)**
- 1   **tbsp plus 2 tsp olive oil**
- ¾   **tsp salt**
- ¼   **tsp black pepper**
- 1   **ripe avocado**
- 1   **tsp lime juice**
- 1   **clove garlic, grated**
- 1   **tbsp chopped cilantro, plus more for garnish (optional)**
- 1   **lb salmon (four 4-oz fillets)**
- ½   **tsp ground coriander**
- ½   **tsp sweet paprika**
- 8   **small corn tortillas**
- ½   **cup Cilantro-Lime Yogurt**
      Lime wedges (optional)

■ Heat oven to 400°. In a small, lidded pot, combine 1½ cups water, rice and 1 tbsp of the oil. Bring to a boil, then reduce heat to low and cook, covered, 15 minutes. Remove from heat and let stand 5 minutes. Fluff with a fork and stir in ¼ tsp of the salt and ⅛ tsp of the pepper. Cover and set aside.

■ Meanwhile, make guacamole. Mash avocado in a bowl. Stir in lime juice, garlic, cilantro and ¼ tsp of the salt. Set aside.

■ Pat salmon dry. Place on a foil-lined baking sheet and rub with remaining 2 tsp olive oil. In a small bowl, combine coriander, paprika, remaining ¼ tsp salt and remaining ⅛ tsp pepper. Rub onto salmon. Bake at 400° for 15 minutes or until fish flakes easily with a fork.

■ Wrap tortillas in foil; place in oven a few minutes, until warmed through. To assemble, flake salmon into large pieces, leaving skin on foil, and place on warm tortillas with guacamole, Cilantro-Lime Yogurt and, if desired, cilantro and lime wedges. Serve rice on side.

Cilantro-Lime Yogurt Combine 1 container (6 oz) Chobani 0% plain Greek yogurt with 1 tsp lime juice, 1 tsp lime zest, 1 tbsp chopped cilantro and ⅛ tsp salt.

PER SERVING 446 **CAL**; 18 g **FAT**; 30 g **PRO**; 41 g **CARB**; 8 g **FIBER**

MOROCCAN SHRIMP AND COUSCOUS

BEEF AND BARLEY SOUP

Moroccan Shrimp and Couscous

MAKES 4 servings PREP 20 minutes COOK 12 minutes BAKE 12 minutes at 400°

- 1 tsp ground cumin
- ½ tsp salt
- ½ tsp ground cinnamon
- ½ tsp ground turmeric
- ¼ tsp ground ginger
- ⅛ tsp ground cayenne
- 1 tbsp olive oil
- ¼ cup minced shallots
- 2 cloves garlic, minced
- 1 cup whole wheat Israeli couscous, halved
- 1¼ lb peeled and deveined shrimp (tails left on)
- 1 cup dried apricots
- 1 cup pitted dates
- 8 Italian- or Spanish-style green olives with pits
- 2 tbsp lemon juice plus 1 tsp zest
- 2 tbsp white wine, chicken broth or water
- ½ cup fresh parsley, chopped
- ½ cup fresh cilantro, chopped
- ¼ cup chopped almonds

■ Heat oven to 400°. In a small bowl, combine cumin, salt, cinnamon, turmeric, ginger and cayenne.

■ Heat olive oil in a medium pot over medium. Add half each of the shallots, garlic and spice mixture. Cook 2 minutes, until soft. Stir in couscous and 1¼ cups water; cover and bring to a boil. Reduce to a simmer and cook 8 to 10 minutes. Set aside, covered.

■ In a large bowl, toss shrimp with apricots, dates, olives, lemon juice and zest, wine and remaining shallots, garlic and spice mixture. Transfer to 2 large parchment cooking bags and seal per package directions. Place bags on a rimmed baking sheet. Bake at 400° for 10 to 12 minutes. Carefully open to release steam; toss in a bowl with parsley, cilantro and almonds. Serve shrimp over couscous.

PER SERVING 550 CAL; 10 g FAT; 30 g PRO; 88 g CARB; 10 g FIBER

Beef and Barley Soup

MAKES 6 servings START TO FINISH 30 minutes

- 2 tbsp vegetable oil
- 1 lb sirloin steak, trimmed and cut into ¾-inch chunks
- 3 carrots, peeled and sliced
- 2 ribs celery, trimmed and sliced
- 3 parsnips, peeled and sliced
- 1 medium onion, chopped
- 2 cans (14.5 oz each) low-sodium beef broth
- ½ tsp dried thyme
- 1 cup quick-cook barley
- ½ tsp salt
- ¼ tsp pepper

■ Heat oil in a large pot over high. Add beef and brown 1 minute. Turn and brown another minute. Remove to a bowl with a slotted spoon.

■ Reduce heat under pot to medium. Add carrots, celery, parsnips and onion. Cook, stirring, 5 minutes. Add broth, 2 cups water and the dried thyme. Increase heat to high and bring to a boil.

■ Add barley and reduce heat to medium. Cook 12 minutes or as per package instructions. Stir in beef and any accumulated juices, salt and pepper. Cook 2 minutes and serve.

PER SERVING 310 CAL; 8 g FAT; 21 g PRO; 39 g CARB; 7 g FIBER

Lentil-Chickpea Chili

MAKES 8 servings **PREP** 15 minutes
SLOW COOK 8 hours on LOW

- 6 cups vegetable stock or broth
- 2 tbsp tomato paste
- 1 tbsp Dijon mustard
- 2 tsp ground cumin
- ½ tsp turmeric
- ¼ tsp cayenne
- 1 tsp salt
- 1 16-oz bag red lentils
- 1 can (14.5-oz) diced tomatoes
- 1 sweet onion, diced
- 1 carrot, diced
- 2 celery stalks, diced
- 3 garlic cloves, diced
- 2 bay leaves
- 2 cans (15-oz each) chickpeas, drained and rinsed
- ¼ cup chopped fresh cilantro
- Flatbread (optional)

■ Whisk together stock, tomato paste, mustard, cumin, turmeric, cayenne and salt in a slow cooker. Stir in lentils, diced tomatoes, onion, carrot, celery, garlic and bay leaves. Cover and cook on LOW for 8 hours.

■ Stir in chickpeas and cilantro. Serve with flatbread, if desired.

PER SERVING 341 **CAL**; 3 g **FAT**; 22 g **PRO**; 57 g **CARB**; 15 g **FIBER**

LENTIL-CHICKPEA CHILI

BEEF SOUVLAKI

Beef Souvlaki

MAKES 4 servings **PREP** 20 minutes **BROIL** 7 minutes

- 1 lb ground beef
- 1½ tsp Greek seasoning
- 2 cloves garlic, chopped
- 2 tbsp lemon juice
- ⅛ tsp each salt and black pepper
- ½ cucumber, grated
- 7 oz Greek 2% yogurt
- 3 tbsp chopped mint
- 2 tbsp lemon juice
- ⅛ tsp each salt and black pepper
- 4 whole wheat pitas
- 2 cups leaf lettuce, shredded
- ½ cup crumbled feta cheese

■ Heat broiler. In a large bowl, combine ground beef, Greek seasoning, garlic, lemon juice and salt and pepper.

Divide into 16 pieces, shaping into balls, and thread onto 2 or 3 metal skewers. Coat broiler pan with nonstick cooking spray; place skewers on pan. Set aside.

■ Squeeze excess water from cucumber in paper towels. In a small bowl, stir cucumber, yogurt, mint, lemon juice, salt and pepper. Set aside.

■ Wrap pitas in foil and place in bottom of oven. Broil skewers 4 minutes. Carefully flip over and broil an additional 3 minutes. Top each with some sauce, shredded lettuce, 4 pieces meat and 2 tbsp feta.

PER SERVING 446 **CAL**; 16 g **FAT**; 36 g **PRO**; 42 g **CARB**; 6 g **FIBER**

PRIME RIB ROAST,
PAGE 281

DECEMBER

281

287

297

CELEBRATE!

Simple but special menu ideas for Christmas Eve, morning and day. Relax, you've got this.

CREAMED CAULIFLOWER

THREE GREENS, BEETS AND PORTOBELLOS

Christmas Eve

Three Greens, Beets and Portobellos

MAKES 8 servings **PREP** 25 minutes
COOK 10 minutes

¼	cup extra-virgin olive oil
3	tbsp balsamic vinegar
1	tbsp honey
1	tsp Dijon mustard
¾	tsp salt
¼	tsp black pepper
1	tbsp unsalted butter
12	oz portobello mushrooms, cleaned and thinly sliced
4	mixed beets (purple and golden), 2 inches wide, sliced very thin on a handheld mandoline
12	cups mixed greens (4 cups each baby kale, spinach and arugula)
¼	cup chopped roasted pistachios
¼	cup chopped walnuts

■ In a large bowl, whisk 3 tbsp each oil and vinegar, the honey, mustard, ¼ tsp salt and ⅛ tsp pepper. Set aside.

■ In a large skillet, heat 1 tbsp each oil and butter. Carefully stir in sliced mushrooms. Cook, stirring every few minutes, until mushrooms soften and begin to brown, about 10 minutes. Season with ¼ tsp salt and ⅛ tsp pepper.

■ Toss mushrooms, remaining 4 ingredients and ¼ tsp salt in bowl with dressing.

PER SERVING 220 **CAL**; 17 g **FAT**; 6 g **PRO**; 16 g **CARB**; 4 g **FIBER**

Creamed Cauliflower

MAKES 8 servings **PREP** 15 minutes
COOK 12 minutes

- 1 **large head cauliflower, cut into florets (about 8 cups)**
- ⅓ **cup heavy cream**
- 2 **tbsp unsalted butter**
- 1 **tsp salt**
- ½ **tsp black pepper**
- ¼ **tsp ground nutmeg**

■ Place cauliflower in a large pot, adding 2 inches of water. Bring to a boil, covered. Reduce to a simmer and cook 10 to 12 minutes, until fork-tender.

■ Drain cauliflower and transfer to a food processor. Add all remaining ingredients and process until semismooth.

PER SERVING 80 **CAL**; 7 g **FAT**; 2 g **PRO**; 4 g **CARB**; 2 g **FIBER**

Prime Rib Roast

MAKES 12 servings **PREP** 15 minutes
ROAST at 450° for 30 minutes and at 350° for 1 hour **LET REST** 30 minutes

- 1 **(3-rib) standing beef rib roast (about 6 lb)**
- 3 **cloves garlic, minced**
- 1 **small shallot, minced**
- 3 **tbsp chopped fresh parsley**
- 2 **tbsp extra-virgin olive oil**
- 1 **tbsp chopped fresh thyme**
- 2 **tsp chopped fresh rosemary**
- 2 **tsp kosher salt**
- ½ **tsp black pepper**

■ Place beef in a baking pan fitted with a flat wire rack. Pat dry. Allow to sit at room temperature 1 hour.

■ Heat oven to 450°. In a small bowl, combine garlic and all remaining ingredients. Rub all over beef. Roast at 450° for 30 minutes. Reduce oven to 350° and roast 1 hour or until temperature reaches 130° for medium-rare. (Test roast at its thickest spot.)

■ Let rest 30 minutes before slicing. Serve with Blender Béarnaise Sauce (recipe follows).

PER SERVING 530 **CAL**; 43 g **FAT**; 31 g **PRO**; 2 g **CARB**; 0 g **FIBER**

LINGUINE WITH CLAMS

Blender Béarnaise Sauce

MAKES 12 servings **PREP** 10 minutes
COOK 5 minutes **COOL** 2 minutes

- 1 **small shallot, minced**
- ¼ **cup champagne or white wine vinegar**
- ¼ **cup dry white wine**
- 3 **tbsp chopped fresh tarragon**
- ½ **tsp salt**
- ¼ **tsp black pepper**
- 1½ **sticks unsalted butter**
- 3 **pasteurized egg yolks**

■ In a small pot, combine shallot, vinegar, wine, 1 tbsp tarragon, the salt and pepper. Bring to a simmer and cook until reduced by half, about 5 minutes. Melt butter in a separate small pot until steaming. Let both cool 2 minutes.

■ Transfer liquid to a blender. While running on low, drop in yolks one at a time. Slowly pour in warm butter. Increase speed, blending until well combined.

■ Pour into a bowl and stir in 2 tbsp tarragon. Serve warm with roast.

PER SERVING 130 **CAL**; 13 g **FAT**; 1 g **PRO**; 2 g **CARB**; 0 g **FIBER**

Linguine with Clams

MAKES 8 servings **PREP** 15 minutes
COOK 16 minutes

- 1 **lb linguine**
- ¼ **cup extra-virgin olive oil, plus more for drizzling (optional)**
- 4 **cloves garlic, sliced**
- 4 **lb littleneck clams, scrubbed and rinsed in cold water**
- ½ **cup clam juice**
- ¼ **cup dry white wine**
- 1 **cup fresh parsley, chopped, plus more for serving (optional)**
- ¼ **tsp salt**

■ Bring a large pot of salted water to a boil. Add linguine and cook 9 minutes, until al dente. Drain, reserving ½ cup pasta water. Place pasta in a large bowl.

■ Meanwhile, heat 2 tbsp oil in a second large pot. Stir in garlic; cook 1 minute. Add clams, clam juice and wine. Bring to a boil, then reduce to a simmer and cover. Cook 4 to 6 minutes, until clams just open.

■ Pour clams and juice, 2 tbsp oil, the parsley and salt into bowl with linguine. Gently toss. If desired, drizzle with more oil and top with additional parsley.

PER SERVING 330 **CAL**; 8 g **FAT**; 16 g **PRO**; 45 g **CARB**; 2 g **FIBER**

Christmas Morning

Jumbo Nutella Cinnamon Rolls

MAKES 9 rolls **PREP** 20 minutes
LET REST 5 minutes **LET RISE** overnight plus
2 hours **BAKE** at 350° for 40 minutes
COOL 10 minutes

- **1** envelope (¼ oz) active dry yeast
- **¼** cup warm water (100° to 110°)
- **3** tbsp granulated sugar
- **4** oz cream cheese (from an 8-oz pkg), at room temperature
- **½** cup plus 4 tsp whole milk
- **2** large eggs
- **4** cups all-purpose flour, plus more as needed
- **½** tsp salt
- **¾** cup Nutella chocolate-hazelnut spread
- **¾** cup miniature chocolate chips
- **½** cup toasted chopped hazelnuts
- **2** tsp ground cinnamon
- **1** cup confectioners' sugar

■ Sprinkle yeast over the warm water in a cup. Add 1 tbsp sugar and let stand until foamy, 5 minutes.

■ Meanwhile, beat cream cheese until smooth. Gradually beat in 2 tbsp sugar and ½ cup milk. On low, beat in eggs, 1½ cups flour and the salt, followed by yeast mixture. With a wooden spoon, stir in 2½ cups flour until soft dough begins to form. Transfer to a floured surface and knead 5 minutes, adding more flour as needed. Let rest 5 minutes.

■ Roll out dough on a lightly floured surface to a 16 x 12-inch rectangle. Spread Nutella on dough, leaving a ½-inch border. Top with chocolate chips, nuts and cinnamon. Starting on one long side, roll up jelly-roll style and pinch seam to close, wetting edge with water to help seal.

■ Cut crosswise into 9 pieces. Place in a greased 13 x 9 x 2-inch pan (rolls will not fill pan). Cover with plastic and refrigerate until the next morning.

■ Remove pan from refrigerator and let rolls rise on countertop 2 hours.

JUMBO NUTELLA CINNAMON ROLLS

Heat oven to 350°. Uncover and bake rolls until golden, 35 to 40 minutes. Cool 10 minutes on a wire rack.

■ Mix confectioners' sugar and 4 tsp milk to make smooth glaze. Drizzle over rolls. Serve warm.

PER ROLL 610 **CAL**; 23 g **FAT**; 12 g **PRO**; 90 g **CARB**; 5 g **FIBER**

Dutch Baby with Berries

MAKES 4 servings **PREP** 10 minutes
COOK 2 minutes **BAKE** at 400° for 18 minutes

- **1** cup strawberries, hulled and sliced
- **1** cup blueberries
- **2** tbsp plus 2 tsp granulated sugar
- **2** tbsp unsalted butter
- **2** large eggs
- **½** cup milk
- **½** cup all-purpose flour
- **⅛** tsp salt
- Confectioners' sugar, for dusting

■ Heat oven to 400°. In a medium bowl, combine berries and 2 tsp sugar. Set aside.

■ Melt butter in a 10-inch castiron skillet over medium, 2 minutes. Brush butter up sides of pan.

■ Combine eggs, milk, flour, 2 tbsp sugar and the salt in a blender. Blend 1 minute, until mixture is well combined and foamy. Pour into skillet and carefully transfer hot pan to oven.

■ Bake 18 minutes, until puffy and lightly browned on top. Remove from oven and dust with confectioners' sugar. Top slices with berry mixture and serve.

PER SERVING 227 **CAL**; 10 g **FAT**; 6 g **PRO**; 30 g **CARB**; 2 g **FIBER**

DUTCH BABY WITH BERRIES

SAVORY BREAD PUDDING

Christmas Day

Savory Bread Pudding

MAKES 10 servings **PREP** 20 minutes
COOK 14 minutes **REFRIGERATE** 2 hours or
overnight **BAKE** at 350° for 1 hour

- 1 pkg (12 oz) fresh maple-flavor breakfast sausage links
- 1 Gala apple, cored, thinly sliced
- 1 loaf (1 lb) Italian bread, cut into 1-inch cubes
- 2 tbsp fresh sage, chopped
- 10 large eggs
- 2 cups milk
- ⅓ cup maple syrup
- 1 tsp salt
- ½ tsp freshly ground black pepper
- 2 cups shredded white cheddar

■ Place sausage in a large skillet and add 1 cup water. Cook 6 minutes over medium-high, until water cooks off. Cook 6 more minutes, browning on all sides. Remove to a board and add apple to same pan. Cook 2 minutes. Cut sausage into ½-inch pieces; place in a very large bowl along with apples. Toss with bread and sage.

■ Whisk eggs with next 4 ingredients. Pour over bread mixture and toss to coat. Transfer half to a greased 3-qt shallow baking dish (13 x 9 x 2-inch or similar) and top with 1 cup cheddar. Add remaining bread mixture and cover with plastic wrap. Refrigerate at least 2 hours or overnight.

■ Heat oven to 350°. Replace plastic with foil. Bake 30 minutes. Uncover; top with 1 cup cheddar. Bake 30 minutes.

PER SERVING 486 **CAL**; 27 g **FAT**; 23 g **PRO**; 36 g **CARB**; 2 g **FIBER**

Broccoli and Snap Pea Salad

MAKES 12 servings **PREP** 10 minutes

- ½ cup buttermilk
- ⅓ cup mayonnaise
- 2 tbsp cider vinegar
- 4 tsp sugar
- 1 tsp salt
- ½ tsp black pepper
- 8 cups broccoli slaw
- 1 cup thinly sliced snap peas
- 1 cup matchstick-cut carrots
- ½ cup crumbled cooked bacon

■ Combine buttermilk and next 5 ingredients; whisk until smooth.

■ In a large salad bowl, combine slaw, snap peas and carrots. Toss with dressing; stir in bacon.

PER SERVING 121 **CAL**; 8 g **FAT**; 5 g **PRO**; 7 g **CARB**; 2 g **FIBER**

Cherry-Glazed Ham

MAKES 20 servings **PREP** 15 minutes
COOK 6½ minutes **BAKE** at 375° for 2 hours

- 1 **tbsp olive oil**
- ½ **medium red onion, chopped**
- 1 **tsp chili powder**
- 1½ **cups red cherry preserves**
- 2 **tsp Dijon mustard**
- 1 **tbsp cider vinegar**
- 8 **lb fully cooked reduced-sodium ham, bone-in shank portion**

■ Heat oven to 375°.

■ Make cherry sauce: In a medium pot, heat oil over medium-high; add onion and cook 3 minutes. Stir in chili powder and cook 30 seconds. Add preserves and mustard; simmer 3 minutes, until smooth. Stir in vinegar.

■ Place ham on a rack in a large roasting pan; add 2 cups water. Cover with foil and bake 1½ hours. Uncover and brush with ¾ cup sauce, reserving the balance. Bake 30 minutes.

■ Serve ham with remaining sauce.

PER SERVING 243 **CAL**; 9 g **FAT**; 25 g **PRO**; 16 g **CARB**; 0 g **FIBER**

Lemon Farro with Peas

MAKES 8 servings **PREP** 15 minutes
COOK 28 minutes

- 1 **tbsp olive oil**
- 3 **scallions, thinly sliced**
- 3 **cloves garlic, chopped**
- 1½ **cups uncooked farro**
- 3½ **cups chicken broth**
- ½ **tsp fresh thyme**
- 1 **cup frozen peas, thawed**
- 3 **scallions, cut diagonally into ½-inch pieces**
- ½ **cup plain Greek yogurt**
- 2 **tbsp lemon juice**
- ¼ **tsp salt**
- ¼ **tsp black pepper**
- ½ **cup dried cherries**

■ In a saucepan, heat oil over medium. Add sliced scallions and garlic; cook 3 minutes. Add farro, broth and thyme. Simmer with lid slightly ajar 25 minutes, until tender.

■ Stir in peas and diagonally cut scallions during last 2 minutes. Drain; let cool.

■ Whisk yogurt, lemon juice, salt and pepper; stir into farro and add cherries.

PER SERVING 250 **CAL**; 4 g **FAT**; 9 g **PRO**; 47 g **CARB**; 7 g **FIBER**

Cheddar and Thyme Scones

MAKES 12 scones **PREP** 15 minutes
BAKE at 400° for 25 minutes

- 3 **cups all-purpose flour**
- ⅓ **cup sugar**
- 4 **tsp baking powder**
- 1 **tsp baking soda**
- ½ **tsp salt**
- ¼ **tsp ground nutmeg**
- ⅛ **tsp cayenne pepper**

CHERRY-GLAZED HAM

BROCCOLI AND SNAP PEA SALAD, 283

1 stick (½ cup) cold unsalted butter, cut into small pieces
1 cup buttermilk
1 cup shredded white cheddar
1 tsp fresh thyme
1 egg white, lightly beaten

■ Heat oven to 400°. Coat a baking sheet with nonstick cooking spray.

■ In a large bowl, blend flour and next 6 ingredients. Cut in butter with a pastry cutter until mixture resembles coarse crumbs.

■ Add buttermilk, cheddar and thyme and stir until dough forms. Knead a few times in bowl. Divide dough in half and form into 2 balls.

■ Place dough balls on baking sheet and flatten into 7-inch circles. Cut each into 6 wedges; brush with egg white.

■ Bake 20 to 25 minutes, until golden. Recut wedges and serve.

PER SCONE 254 CAL; 11 g FAT; 7 g PRO; 31 g CARB; 1 g FIBER

Mushroom and Squash Lasagna

MAKES 12 servings PREP 30 minutes
COOK 10 minutes BAKE at 375° for 55 minutes
COOL 20 minutes

2 tbsp olive oil
1 lb summer squash, cut into ½-inch dice
1¼ lb cremini mushrooms, sliced
½ red onion, sliced
6 cloves garlic, chopped
3 cups marinara sauce
1 tsp salt
½ tsp black pepper
1 tsp dried oregano
1 container (15 oz) ricotta
1 pkg (10 oz) frozen chopped spinach, thawed and squeezed dry
2 eggs, lightly beaten
¼ tsp ground nutmeg
12 lasagna noodles
4 cups shredded 4-cheese pizza blend
¼ cup grated Parmesan

■ Heat oven to 375°.

■ Heat oil in a large skillet over medium-high; add squash and next 3 ingredients. Cook 10 minutes, stirring often. Stir in 2 cups sauce, the salt, pepper and oregano; bring to a simmer.

■ Combine ricotta and next 3 ingredients.

■ Cook lasagna noodles following package directions. Drain.

■ Spread ½ cup sauce in bottom of a 13 x 9 x 2-inch baking dish. Layer 3 noodles, ⅓ of ricotta mixture, ⅓ of vegetables and 1 cup pizza cheese. Repeat layering twice. Top with ½ cup sauce and 1 cup pizza cheese.

■ Cover with foil and bake 30 minutes. Remove foil and bake 25 minutes. Sprinkle Parmesan over top during last 10 minutes. Cool 20 minutes before serving.

PER SERVING 376 CAL; 17 g FAT; 22 g PRO; 34 g CARB; 4 g FIBER

CHEDDAR AND THYME SCONES
LEMON FARRO WITH PEAS
MUSHROOM AND SQUASH LASAGNA

25 DAYS OF COOKIES

A festive assortment of classics to make the season that much sweeter.

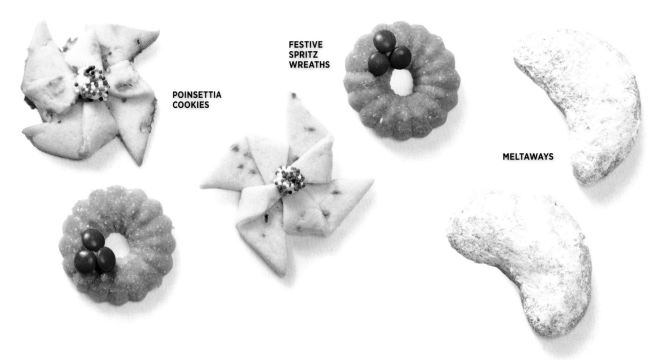

POINSETTIA COOKIES

FESTIVE SPRITZ WREATHS

MELTAWAYS

Poinsettia Cookies

MAKES 5 dozen **PREP** 1 hour
REFRIGERATE 2 hours
BAKE at 350° for 8 minutes

■ Mix 2⅓ cups **all-purpose flour** and 1 tsp **salt** in a bowl. Beat 2 sticks (1 cup) softened **unsalted butter** in another bowl until creamy, 3 minutes. Beat in 1 cup sifted **confectioners' sugar** until light and fluffy, about 3 minutes. Beat in 1 **large egg**. Using a wooden spoon, stir in flour mixture. Crush 9 **cinnamon starlight mints** (about ¼ cup crushed candies). Stir into dough. Divide in half; shape each half into a 4 x 4-inch square and wrap each in plastic. Refrigerate until firm, about 2 hours. Line 2 baking sheets with parchment paper. Roll out dough, half at a time, between 2 sheets of wax paper into a 12 x 10-inch rectangle to ⅛-inch thickness. If dough is too soft, refrigerate until firm. Cut each half into 2-inch squares. Cut each square diagonally about ¾ inch from each corner toward center. Turn down alternate corners of each cookie,

placing tips in center to create a pinwheel effect. Place cookies 1 inch apart on prepped baking sheets. Bake at 350° for 6 to 8 minutes, until firm; watch carefully so edges of cookies do not overbrown. Remove cookies to wire racks to cool completely. Fill a pastry bag fitted with ¼-inch writing or star tip with **canned frosting**. Pipe a medium dot in center of each cooled poinsettia. Dip frosting into **colored nonpareil sprinkles** to cover dot. Let stand until set.

PER COOKIE 77 **CAL**; 4 g **FAT**; 1 g **PRO**; 9 g **CARB**; 0 g **FIBER**

Festive Spritz Wreaths

MAKES 6½ dozen **PREP** 10 minutes
BAKE at 350° for 10 minutes

■ In a large bowl, beat 2 sticks (1 cup) softened **unsalted butter**, ⅔ cup **granulated sugar**, 1 **large egg** and ¼ tsp **salt** until fluffy, 3 minutes. On low speed, beat in 2¼ cups **all-purpose flour** until smooth. Tint pale green with **green food coloring**. Spoon dough into a cookie press fitted

with standard wreath disk, following manufacturer's directions. Press out wreaths onto large baking sheets, spacing cookies about ¾ inch apart. Before baking, press in **Red Hots candies or M&M's minis** as "holly berries," if desired. Bake at 350° for 8 to 10 minutes, until slightly puffed and set. Transfer cookies directly to racks to cool. Make glaze: In a bowl, whisk ½ cup **confectioners' sugar** and 4 tsp **water**. Brush over cookies; if desired, sprinkle on green decorator's **sugar**. Let dry 15 minutes before stacking.

PER COOKIE 57 **CAL**; 3 g **FAT**; 1 g **PRO**; 8 g **CARB**; 0 g **FIBER**

Meltaways

MAKES 4½ dozen **PREP** 15 minutes
REFRIGERATE 1 to 2 hours **BAKE** at 325° for 20 minutes

■ In a bowl, beat 2 sticks (1 cup) softened **unsalted butter** and 1 cup **confectioners' sugar** until smooth and creamy. Add 2 tsp **vanilla extract**. On low speed, beat in 2 cups **all-purpose** flour and 1 cup finely ground **pecans**. Wrap dough in plastic and refrigerate 1 to 2 hours, until firm. Pinch off pieces of dough in rounded teaspoonfuls. Roll into logs, taper ends and bend into crescents. Place on 2 ungreased baking sheets. Bake at 325° for 19 to 20 minutes, until lightly browned. Remove cookies to a wire rack. Sprinkle on a heavy layer of **confectioners' sugar**. Cool completely. Sprinkle again with **confectioners' sugar**.

PER COOKIE 73 **CAL**; 5 g **FAT**; 1 g **PRO**; 7 g **CARB**; 0 g **FIBER**

Spiced Crackle Cookies

MAKES 4 dozen **PREP** 20 minutes
REFRIGERATE 1 hour
BAKE at 350° for 12 minutes

■ In a large bowl, beat 1 stick (½ cup) softened **unsalted butter**, 1 cup **granulated sugar** and ¼ cup **molasses** on medium speed until blended. Beat in 1 **large egg** until blended, scraping down sides of bowl. Sift 2 cups **all-purpose flour**, 1 tbsp **ground ginger**, ¾ tsp **baking soda**, ½ tsp **ground cinnamon** and ¼ tsp each **salt** and **white pepper** into another bowl. Add to butter mixture; beat on low speed until blended. Stir in 1 tbsp finely chopped **crystallized ginger**. Cover and refrigerate 1 hour. Line 2 large baking sheets with parchment paper. Place ¾ cup **confectioners' sugar** in a small bowl. Dust hands lightly with **flour**. Roll pieces of dough into 1-inch balls, using about 2 tsp per ball. Roll dough in confectioners' sugar to coat completely. Transfer to prepped baking sheets, spacing at least

SPICED
CRACKLE
COOKIES

2 inches apart. Bake at 350° for 12 minutes, until cookies have expanded and flattened—they'll have cracks. Let cool on baking sheets on wire racks 2 minutes. Transfer cookies directly to racks; let cool completely.

PER COOKIE 67 **CAL**; 2 g **FAT**; 1 g **PRO**; 12 g **CARB**; 0 g **FIBER**

German Chocolate Bars

MAKES 36 bar cookies **PREP** 10 minutes
BAKE at 350° for 25 minutes
REFRIGERATE 2 hours

■ Line a 13 x 9-inch baking pan with nonstick aluminum foil. Pulse 1½ boxes **Nabisco Famous chocolate wafer cookies** in a food processor until very fine crumbs. Transfer to a bowl and stir in 1 stick (½ cup) melted **unsalted butter** until well combined. Press mixture firmly and evenly into prepped pan (the flat side of a measuring cup works well). Pour 1 can (14 oz) **sweetened condensed milk** evenly over crust. Sprinkle with 1 bag (12 oz) **semisweet chocolate chips**, followed by 1½ cups **sweetened flake coconut** and 1 cup coarsely chopped **pecans**. Bake at 350° for 25 minutes. Cool completely. Refrigerate 2 hours. Remove from pan by lifting foil and place on a cutting board. Slice into 36 bars.

PER BAR 177 **CAL**; 10 g **FAT**; 3 g **PRO**; 21 g **CARB**; 1 g **FIBER**

Peanut Blossoms

MAKES 5 dozen **PREP** 15 minutes
BAKE at 375° for 12 minutes

■ In a large bowl, combine 1¾ cups **all-purpose flour**, ½ cup each **granulated sugar** and packed **brown sugar**, ½ cup

GERMAN
CHOCOLATE
BARS

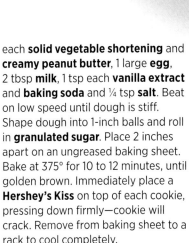

PEANUT
BLOSSOMS

each **solid vegetable shortening** and **creamy peanut butter**, 1 large **egg**, 2 tbsp **milk**, 1 tsp each **vanilla extract** and **baking soda** and ¼ tsp **salt**. Beat on low speed until dough is stiff. Shape dough into 1-inch balls and roll in **granulated sugar**. Place 2 inches apart on an ungreased baking sheet. Bake at 375° for 10 to 12 minutes, until golden brown. Immediately place a **Hershey's Kiss** on top of each cookie, pressing down firmly—cookie will crack. Remove from baking sheet to a rack to cool completely.

PER COOKIE 81 **CAL**; 4 g **FAT**; 1 g **PRO**; 10 g **CARB**; 0 g **FIBER**

[S]ugar Cookie Dough

MAKES 3 dozen **PREP** 15 minutes
REFRIGERATE 4 hours or overnight
BAKE at 350° for 12 minutes per batch

■ In a medium bowl, whisk 1½ cups **all-purpose flour**, ½ tsp **baking powder** and ⅛ tsp **salt**. Set aside. In a large bowl, beat 1 stick (½ cup) softened **unsalted butter** and ¾ cup **granulated sugar** until smooth, about 2 minutes. Beat in 1 **large egg** and ¾ tsp **vanilla extract**. On low speed, beat in flour mixture until just combined. Divide dough in half and form each half into a disk. Wrap each in plastic and refrigerate 4 hours or overnight. On a lightly floured surface, roll out one disk to ¼-inch thickness. Using a 2½-inch cookie cutter, cut out stars or snowflakes. Brush cookies with 1 lightly beaten **egg white** and cover with **clear or white sparkling sugar**. Place on a large parchment-paper-lined baking sheet. Bake at 350° for 10 to 12 minutes, until lightly golden around edges. Remove cookies to wire racks to cool completely. Repeat with remaining dough. Gather scraps and refrigerate. Reroll and cut into additional shapes. Bake and cool as above.

PER COOKIE 79 **CAL**; 3 g **FAT**; 1 g **PRO**; 13 g **CARB**; 0 g **FIBER**

Lemon Bars

MAKES 4 dozen **PREP** 15 minutes
BAKE at 350° for 43 minutes

■ Line a 13 x 9 x 2-inch baking pan with foil. Make Basic Sugar Cookie Dough; do not refrigerate. Knead ½ cup **confectioners' sugar** into dough and press in a single layer into prepped pan. Bake at 350° for 17 minutes. Meanwhile, in a large bowl, blend 2 cups **granulated sugar** and ⅓ cup **all-purpose flour**. Whisk in 6 **large eggs** until smooth. Stir in 2 tsp fresh **lemon zest** and ½ cup **fresh lemon juice**. Pour filling over crust. Bake at 350° for 23 to 26 minutes, until set. Let cool in pan on a wire rack. Dust with ¼ cup **confectioners' sugar**. Refrigerate to set. Cut into 24 squares, then in half diagonally to form triangles. Sift additional **confectioners' sugar** over bars, if desired.

PER BAR 98 **CAL**; 3 g **FAT**; 1 g **PRO**; 17 g **CARB**; 0 g **FIBER**

Peppermint Drops

MAKES 3 dozen **PREP** 15 minutes **BAKE** at 375° for 12 minutes per batch **MICROWAVE** 1 minute

■ Make Basic Sugar Cookie Dough; do not refrigerate. Beat in ½ cup **all-purpose flour** and ⅓ cup crushed **candy canes** (4) **or starlight mints** (9). Roll into 1-inch balls and place on a parchment-paper-lined baking sheet. Bake at 375° for 12 minutes per batch. Cool completely. Once cool, microwave 1 cup **bright white candy melting discs** at 50% power 1 minute. Stir. Continue to microwave in 30-second increments and stir until smooth. Dip half of each cooled cookie in melted candy. Cool to harden candy.

PER COOKIE 99 **CAL**; 4 g **FAT**; 1 g **PRO**; 14 g **CARB**; 0 g **FIBER**

Linzer Sandwiches

MAKES 3 dozen filled cookies **PREP** 25 minutes
REFRIGERATE 2 hours or overnight
BAKE at 375° for 10 minutes per batch

■ Make Basic Sugar Cookie Dough; do not refrigerate. Beat in ¾ cup **pistachios, finely ground,** and ¼ cup **all-purpose flour**. Divide in half, wrap each half in plastic and refrigerate 2 hours or overnight. On a well-floured surface, roll half the dough to ⅛-inch thickness. Cut into 2-inch squares. Transfer to 2 large parchment-paper-lined baking sheets. With a ¾-inch cutter, cut out centers of half the cookies. Bake at 375° for 8 to 10 minutes. Repeat with remaining dough. Cool completely. Spread each solid cookie with ½ to 1 tsp **seedless raspberry jam**. Dust cutout cookies with **confectioners' sugar**. Place on top of jam-covered cookies.

PER COOKIE 132 **CAL**; 6 g **FAT**; 2 g **PRO**; 18 g **CARB**; 1 g **FIBER**

Cutouts

MAKES 3 dozen **PREP** 15 minutes
REFRIGERATE 4 hours or overnight
BAKE at 350° for 15 minutes per batch

■ Make Basic Sugar Cookie Dough; do not refrigerate. Knead in 1 tbsp grated **fresh orange zest**. Divide dough into thirds. Tint one third green with **food coloring**. Blend 2 tbsp **cocoa powder** into second piece of dough. Leave third piece as is. Wrap each in plastic wrap and refrigerate 4 hours or overnight. Roll on a floured sheet of wax or parchment paper to ¼-inch thickness. Cut out 2½-inch trees and transfer to 2 large parchment-paper-lined baking sheets. Snip a 3-inch piece from a **drinking straw**. Using straw, cut holes in each tree to resemble ornaments (save cut pieces). Poke cutouts from straw with a wooden skewer or chopstick. Fit

LEMON BARS

contrasting-color "ornaments" into holes in trees. Bake at 350° for 12 to 15 minutes per batch. Cool on a wire rack.

PER COOKIE 61 CAL; 3 g FAT; 1 g PRO; 8 g CARB; 0 g FIBER

Chocolate Brownie Cookies

MAKES 3½ dozen PREP 15 minutes
MICROWAVE 2 minutes
BAKE at 350° for 10 minutes

■ Make Basic Sugar Cookie Dough; do not refrigerate. In a glass bowl, combine 6 oz chopped **bittersweet chocolate** and 2 tbsp **unsalted butter**. Microwave until melted, about 1 minute. Stir until smooth. Beat 1 **large egg** with a hand mixer until pale and thick, about 2 minutes. Beat in melted chocolate mixture. Add to dough and beat until smooth. Drop teaspoonfuls onto 2 large parchment-paper-lined baking sheets. Bake at 350° for 10 minutes. Cool slightly. Chop 2 oz **bittersweet chocolate** and place in a small glass bowl. Microwave 1 minute, stirring halfway through. Place in a small plastic bag and snip off a small corner. Drizzle over cookies. Let dry completely.

PER COOKIE 85 CAL; 5 g FAT; 1 g PRO; 10 g CARB; 1 g FIBER

Thumbprints

MAKES 3 dozen PREP 15 minutes
REFRIGERATE 4 hours or overnight
BAKE at 350° for 17 minutes per batch

■ Make Basic Sugar Cookie Dough; do not refrigerate. Beat in 4 oz (½ pkg) softened **cream cheese**, ½ cup **almond flour**, ¼ cup **all-purpose flour** and ½ tsp **almond extract**. Wrap in plastic; refrigerate 4 hours or overnight. Roll into 1-inch balls and roll balls in ⅓ cup **granulated sugar** to coat. Place on a baking sheet. With your thumb, make a large indent in top of each piece of dough. Fill each indent with ¼ tsp **strawberry jam**. Bake at 350° for 17 minutes.

PER COOKIE 71 CAL; 3 g FAT; 1 g PRO; 9 g CARB; 0 g FIBER

Pinwheels

MAKES 3 dozen PREP 15 minutes
REFRIGERATE 4 hours or overnight
BAKE at 350° for 15 minutes

■ Make Basic Sugar Cookie Dough; do not refrigerate. Divide dough in half and mix ½ tsp **coconut extract** into one half. Roll on a floured sheet of wax or parchment paper into a 10½ x 7½-inch rectangle. To second half, add 2 tsp **lime zest** and enough **green food coloring** to evenly color dough. Roll on a floured sheet of wax or parchment paper into a 10½ x 7½-inch rectangle.

Stack green dough over white dough, offsetting by ½ inch on a long side. Fold exposed white dough over green dough and tightly roll up to form a pinwheel. Cut roll in half. Roll each half in **green sparkling sugar** to coat, wrap in plastic and refrigerate 4 hours or overnight. Unwrap dough and slice into ¼-inch-thick rounds (18 slices per roll). Place on 2 large baking sheets. Bake at 350° for 15 minutes, until set. Cool on a wire rack.

PER COOKIE 66 CAL; 3 g FAT; 1 g PRO; 10 g CARB; 0 g FIBER

WHITE CHOCOLATE AND HAZELNUT BISCOTTI

BOURBON BALLS

WALNUT-RAISIN RUGELACH

White Chocolate and Hazelnut Biscotti

MAKES 3 to 4 dozen **PREP** 15 minutes
BAKE at 350° for 40 minutes **COOL** 10 minutes

■ Grease a baking sheet. In a bowl, beat 1 stick (½ cup) softened **unsalted butter** and ¾ cup **sugar** until light and fluffy. Beat in 2 **large eggs**, one at a time. Stir in 1 tsp **vanilla extract**. In a medium bowl, whisk 2 cups **all-purpose flour**, 1½ tsp **baking powder** and ¼ tsp **salt**. Add to butter mixture along with 1 cup toasted chopped **hazelnuts** and ⅔ cup **white chocolate chips**; mix well. Divide dough in half. Place one half on prepped baking sheet. Pat into a 12 x 2-inch loaf. Repeat with second half, placing on baking sheet 2 inches from first. Bake at 350° until lightly browned, about 25 minutes. Remove from oven. Let cool 10 minutes. On a cutting board, cut logs diagonally into ½-inch-thick slices. Place slices, cut sides down, on baking sheet. Bake 12 to 15 minutes. Transfer to a rack to cool.

PER COOKIE 90 **CAL**; 5 g **FAT**; 2 g **PRO**; 10 g **CARB**; 0 g **FIBER**

Bourbon Balls

MAKES about 2 dozen **PREP** 20 minutes
REFRIGERATE 24 hours

■ In a medium bowl, mix 2½ cups **Nilla wafers** cookie crumbs, 1¼ cups **confectioners' sugar**, 2 tbsp finely ground **hazelnuts**, ¼ cup **bourbon**, 2 tbsp **unsweetened cocoa powder**

and 3 tbsp **light corn syrup.** Press together all ingredients in bowl to form a large ball. Using 1 tbsp mixture for each, form into small balls; place on wax paper. Place ⅓ cup **granulated sugar** in a small shallow dish. Roll balls in sugar to coat. Store in a tightly covered container for at least 24 hours to let flavors develop.

PER BALL 76 **CAL**; 1 g **FAT**; 0 g **PRO**; 15 g **CARB**; 0 g **FIBER**

Walnut-Raisin Rugelach

MAKES 32 cookies **PREP** 30 minutes
REFRIGERATE 4 hours or overnight
BAKE at 350° for 30 minutes

■ Position rack in top third of oven. Beat 2 sticks (1 cup) softened **unsalted butter**, 1 pkg (8 oz) softened **cream cheese** and ¼ cup **sugar** in a bowl until smooth and creamy, 2 minutes. Stir in 2 large **egg yolks**, 1 tsp **vanilla extract** and ½ tsp **salt**. Stir in 2 cups **all-purpose flour** until smooth dough forms. Divide into fourths; shape into disks. Wrap each disk in plastic and refrigerate 4 hours or overnight. Line 2 baking sheets with nonstick aluminum foil. Roll out a disk into an 8-inch round. Spread with 2 tbsp **apricot jam**. Sprinkle with ¼ cup **raisins** and 3 tbsp finely chopped **walnuts**. Cut round into 8 wedges. Starting at outside edge, roll up each wedge. Place on baking sheet, 1 inch apart. Repeat with remaining disks. Lightly brush each cookie with milk and sprinkle with **sugar**. Bake at 350°

in top third of oven until lightly browned, 25 to 30 minutes. Remove to a wire rack to cool.

PER COOKIE 162 **CAL**; 10 g **FAT**; 2 g **PRO**; 16 g **CARB**; 1 g **FIBER**

Mint Meringues

MAKES about 4½ dozen **PREP** 15 minutes
BAKE at 200° for 2 hours **STAND** 30 minutes

■ Line 2 large baking sheets with nonstick foil. In a bowl, combine 4 **large egg whites** and ½ tsp **cream of tartar**. Beat on high speed with whip attachment until whites become foamy. Gradually add ¾ cup **sugar**, until thick, then add ¼ tsp **mint extract**. Divide batter in half. Tint one half pink with **red food coloring**, the other green with **green food coloring**.

Transfer to 2 large resealable bags (or pastry bags fitted with large round tips). Snip a ½-inch corner off bags. Squeeze meringue batter onto baking sheets, about 26 per sheet. Crush 2 **candy canes** and sprinkle a little over each meringue. Bake at 200° for 2 hours, then turn off oven and let cookies sit in oven for 30 minutes. Remove from pans and transfer to a wire rack. Cool completely.

PER COOKIE 14 **CAL**; 0 g **FAT**; 0 g **PRO**; 3 g **CARB**; 0 g **FIBER**

Venetians

MAKES 6 dozen **PREP** 30 minutes
BAKE at 350° for 15 minutes
ASSEMBLY 20 minutes **REFRIGERATE** overnight

■ Grease three 13 x 9 x 2-inch baking pans, line with wax paper and grease paper. In a bowl, break up 1 can (8 oz) **almond paste** with a fork. Add 3 sticks (1½ cups) softened **unsalted butter**, 1 cup **sugar**, 4 **large egg yolks** (reserve whites) and 1 tsp **almond extract**. Beat with a mixer until fluffy, 5 minutes. Beat in 2 cups sifted **all-purpose flour** and ¼ tsp **salt**. Beat reserved **egg whites** in a bowl until stiff peaks form. Stir into almond mixture with a wooden spoon, using turning motion similar to folding. Spread 1½ cups batter evenly into one pan. Add 1½ cups batter to a small bowl, tint with **green food coloring** and spread into second pan. Tint remaining batter pink using **red food coloring** and spread into third pan. Bake at 350° for 15 minutes, until edges are lightly golden; cake layers will be ¼ inch thick. Immediately remove cakes from pans and place on large wire racks. Carefully peel off wax paper. Cool. Place pink layer upside down on a jelly-roll pan. Heat 1 jar (12 oz) **apricot preserves** and strain (leftovers can be saved). Spread half of strained preserves over pink layer. Top with yellow layer and spread on remaining preserves. Add green layer, top side up, and cover with plastic wrap. Press down with a large wooden cutting board, heavy flat tray or large book (this will help layers stay together). Refrigerate overnight. Melt 5 oz chopped **semisweet chocolate** in top of a double boiler over hot water. Trim cake edges even. Cut cake crosswise into 1-inch-wide strips. Frost pink layer of one strip with chocolate. Turn strip on side and frost green layer. Let dry. Cut into 1-inch pieces. Repeat with remaining strips.

PER COOKIE 98 **CAL**; 6 g **FAT**; 1 g **PRO**; 11 g **CARB**; 0 g **FIBER**

VENETIANS

MINT MERINGUES

FLORENTINES

FRUITED PALMIERS

ALMOND SHORTBREAD

Florentines

MAKES 2 dozen filled cookies
PREP 20 minutes **BAKE** at 350° for 8 minutes

■ Grease a 12-cup 3-inch muffin or muffin-top tin. (For free-form cookies, line a baking sheet with aluminum foil and grease foil.) In a medium saucepan, combine ⅔ cup **sugar**, 1 stick (½ cup) **salted butter** and 2 tbsp each **light corn syrup** and **milk**. Cook over medium until mixture registers 235° (soft-ball stage) on a candy thermometer. Remove pan from heat. Stir in 1 cup **sliced almonds**, ½ cup **all-purpose flour**, 2 tbsp each finely chopped **glacé cherries** and **citron** and ½ tsp **vanilla extract**. Drop teaspoonfuls into muffin cups (or 4 inches apart on foil). Bake at 350° until edges brown, 7 to 8 minutes. (If free-form, shape into circles while warm.) Loosen cookies with a small spatula; remove from cups to a wire rack to cool. If cookies stick in cups, return to oven 30 seconds. Repeat with remaining batter. In a bowl over hot (not boiling) water, melt 1 cup **semisweet chocolate chips**. Spread smooth sides of cookies with chocolate; sandwich 2 cookies, chocolate sides together. Chill to set chocolate.

PER COOKIE 142 **CAL**; 8 g **FAT**; 2 g **PRO**; 16 g **CARB**; 1 g **FIBER**

Almond Shortbread

MAKES 2 dozen **PREP** 15 minutes
BAKE at 350° for 14 minutes

■ Lightly grease a large baking sheet. In a small bowl, stir 1¼ cups **all-purpose flour**, ½ cup finely chopped

natural almonds and ¼ tsp **salt.** In a medium bowl, beat 1 stick (½ cup) **unsalted butter**, ⅓ cup **granulated sugar** and 1 tsp each **vanilla** and **almond extract** until creamy and smooth, about 2 minutes. Stir in flour mixture. Divide dough into 4 equal balls. On prepped baking sheet, pat or roll out each ball of dough into a 4½-inch round. Smooth edges; if desired, press with tines of fork all around edges. Cut each round into 6 equal wedges, but do not pull wedges apart. Bake at 350° for 12 to 14 minutes, until lightly browned at edges. While still hot, recut rounds into wedges and remove to a wire rack to cool completely. In a small bowl over a pan of hot water or in a microwave, melt ½ cup **semisweet chocolate morsels**. Drizzle over wedges. Sprinkle evenly with **confectioners' sugar**. You can redust cookies with **confectioners' sugar** just before serving.

PER COOKIE 112 **CAL**; 7 g **FAT**; 2 g **PRO**; 12 g **CARB**; 1 g **FIBER**

Fruited Palmiers

MAKES 30 palmiers **PREP** 10 minutes
BAKE at 425° for 15 minutes per batch

■ Place 1½ cups **fruit-nut crunch cereal (such as Post Selects Blueberry Morning or Great Grains Banana-Nut Crunch)** in a resealable plastic food bag; crush with a rolling pin. Unfold 1 sheet thawed frozen **puff pastry** (from a 17.3-oz pkg) on work surface. Spread with 2 tbsp **seedless red raspberry jam**. Sprinkle with half the crushed cereal. Roll in from two opposite sides until sides meet in center. With a serrated knife, cut crosswise into ½-inch-thick slices. Place, cut sides down, on an ungreased baking sheet. Sprinkle with 1 tbsp **sugar**. Bake at 425° until golden, about 15 minutes. With a spatula, remove to a wire rack to cool. Repeat with remaining **puff pastry sheet**, 2 more tbsp **seedless red raspberry jam**, remaining cereal and 1 tbsp **sugar.** Serve warm or at room temperature.

PER PALMIER 101 **CAL**; 5 g **FAT**; 2 g **PRO**; 13 g **CARB**; 1 g **FIBER**

Gingerbread Men

MAKES about 3½ dozen **PREP** 15 minutes
REFRIGERATE 2 hours
BAKE at 350° for 11 minutes

■ In a large bowl, beat 1 stick (½ cup) **unsalted butter** and ½ cup **sugar**. Beat in 1 **large egg** and ¼ cup **light molasses**. In another bowl, combine 2⅓ cups **all-purpose flour**, 1 tbsp **unsweetened cocoa powder**, ¾ tsp **baking soda**, 1 tbsp **ground ginger**, 1 tsp **white pepper** and ½ tsp **ground cinnamon**. Stir into butter mixture. Divide dough in half. Wrap each piece in plastic wrap and refrigerate 2 hours. Roll one piece on a floured surface to ⅛ inch thick. Cut shapes with a 3-inch cutter; transfer to 2 ungreased baking sheets. Reroll scraps and cut more shapes. Repeat with remaining dough. Bake at 350° for 11 minutes. Transfer cookies to racks to cool. To prepare icing, in a bowl, beat 2 cups **confectioners' sugar**, 2 tbsp **powdered egg whites** and 3 tbsp **water** until thick and shiny, about 5 minutes. Tint some of the icing with food coloring, if desired; transfer to pastry bags with writing tips and decorate cooled cookies.

PER COOKIE 110 **CAL**; 3 g **FAT**; 2 g **PRO**; 18 g **CARB**; 1 g **FIBER**

Pfeffernüsse Crescents

MAKES 5 dozen **PREP** 20 minutes
REFRIGERATE overnight
BAKE at 350° for 8 minutes

■ In a large bowl, whisk 2½ cups **all-purpose flour** with ½ tsp each **baking soda**, **baking powder** and **ground cinnamon** and ¼ tsp each **salt**, **black pepper**, **ground nutmeg** and **ground cloves**. Set aside. In another large bowl, beat ½ stick (¼ cup) softened **unsalted butter**, 2 **large eggs** and 1 tbsp **grated orange zest** until smooth, about 3 minutes. Beat in 1 cup **honey** until combined. On low speed, beat in dry ingredients until just combined. Cover and refrigerate dough overnight. With well-floured hands, form 1 level tsp dough into a ball. On a well-floured work surface, form each ball into a 2½-inch-long log. Bend into a crescent shape and place on an ungreased baking sheet. Repeat with remaining dough. Bake at 350° for 8 minutes, until slightly golden. Remove from oven; cool on baking sheet on a wire rack 1 minute. Roll warm cookies in **confectioners' sugar**. Place on a wire rack to cool completely.

PER COOKIE 48 **CAL**; 1 g **FAT**; 1 g **PRO**; 9 g **CARB**; 0 g **FIBER**

PFEFFERNÜSSE CRESCENTS

HOLIDAY NUT DROPS

Holiday Nut Drops

MAKES 2 dozen **PREP** 10 minutes
BAKE at 350° for 12 minutes

■ Lightly coat 2 baking sheets with nonstick cooking spray. In a bowl, mix 1½ cups **all-purpose flour** and ½ tsp each **baking soda** and **salt**. In a medium bowl, beat ¾ cup packed **brown sugar** and 1 stick (½ cup) softened **unsalted butter** until creamy and smooth, 2 minutes. Beat in 1 **large egg** and 1 tsp **vanilla extract**. Stir in flour mixture. Fold in 1 cup chopped **unsalted mixed nuts** and ½ cup **red and green M&M's**. Drop by rounded measuring tablespoonfuls, 2 inches apart, onto baking sheets. Bake at 350° for 10 to 12 minutes, until lightly browned at edges. Let cool slightly on baking sheets. Transfer cookies to a rack to cool.

PER COOKIE 142 **CAL**; 8 g **FAT**; 2 g **PRO**; 17 g **CARB**; 1 g **FIBER**

GINGERBREAD MEN

HEALTHY FAMILY DINNERS

10 easy meals for crazy-busy weeknights.

POTATO-TOPPED
BEEF STEW

Potato-Topped Beef Stew

MAKES 5 servings **PREP** 15 minutes
COOK 5 minutes **SLOW COOK** on HIGH for
5 hours or LOW for 7 hours

- 2 tbsp vegetable oil
- 1½ lb beef chuck for stew
- 3 tbsp all-purpose flour
- ¼ tsp salt
- ¼ tsp black pepper
- 1 pkg (8 oz) cremini mushrooms, cleaned and quartered
- 1 medium onion, diced
- 2 carrots, peeled and cut into ½-inch slices
- 2 cloves garlic, chopped
- ½ cup reduced-sodium beef broth
- ½ cup red wine
- 1 cup thawed frozen peas
- 3 tbsp snipped chives
- 1 pkg (24 oz) prepared mashed potatoes

■ Heat oil in a large skillet over medium-high. Toss beef with 2 tbsp of the flour, ¼ tsp of the salt and the pepper. Add beef to skillet and brown on all sides, 5 minutes. Remove from heat.

■ Meanwhile, coat a 4-qt slow cooker with nonstick cooking spray. Add mushrooms, onion, carrots and garlic. Season with remaining ¼ tsp salt. Stir in broth and wine, then browned beef. Cover and cook on HIGH for 5 hours or LOW for 7 hours.

■ Scoop ½ cup liquid from slow cooker and whisk in remaining 1 tbsp flour. Stir back into slow cooker along with thawed peas and 1 tbsp of the chives. Cover slow cooker and keep warm.

■ Heat potatoes per package directions. Stir in remaining 2 tbsp chives and ¼ cup warm water. Spread potatoes over filling and serve.

PER SERVING 503 CAL; 10 g **FAT**; 35 g **PRO**; 38 g **CARB**; 6 g **FIBER**

BUTTERNUT SQUASH
AND BLACK BEAN CHILI

Butternut Squash and Black Bean Chili

MAKES 8 servings **PREP** 20 minutes **SLOW COOK** on HIGH for 6 hours or LOW for 8 hours

- 2 large onions, chopped
- 4 cloves garlic, chopped
- 1 butternut squash (2 lb), seeded, peeled and cut into 1 ½-inch pieces (5 cups)
- 1 large green sweet pepper, seeded and chopped
- 1 large jalapeño pepper, seeded and chopped
- 2 cans (14.5 oz each) stewed tomatoes
- 4 tsp ancho chili powder
- 2 tsp ground cumin
- ½ tsp salt
- 2 cans (15 oz each) black beans, drained and rinsed
- ½ red sweet pepper, seeded and cut into 1-inch dice
- ½ yellow sweet pepper, seeded and cut into 1-inch dice
- ½ orange sweet pepper, seeded and cut into 1-inch dice
- 2 tbsp cilantro, chopped
- 1 cup shredded taco cheese
- 2 scallions, thinly sliced

■ Coat slow cooker with nonstick cooking spray.

■ Add onions, garlic, squash, green pepper and jalapeño. Combine tomatoes, chili powder, cumin and salt. Pour over mixture in cooker.

■ Cover and cook on HIGH for 6 hours or LOW for 8 hours. Add beans and sweet peppers during last 30 minutes.

■ To serve, stir in cilantro. Top with cheese and scallions.

PER SERVING 209 CAL; 5 g **FAT**; 10 g **PRO**; 38 g **CARB**; 11 g **FIBER**

CREOLE SAUSAGE AND SHRIMP

Creole Sausage and Shrimp

MAKES 6 servings **PREP** 15 minutes **SLOW COOK** on HIGH for 6 hours or LOW for 8 hours, plus 7 minutes

- 1 large onion, chopped
- 1 green sweet pepper, cored, seeded and chopped
- 2 ribs celery, sliced
- 2 large carrots, peeled and diced
- 4 cloves garlic, chopped
- 1 can (14.5 oz) no-salt-added diced tomatoes
- ¾ cup reduced-sodium chicken broth
- 2 tsp Creole seasoning
- 3 jalapeño-flavor fully cooked chicken sausages from a 12-oz pkg (such as Aidells), sliced into ½-inch-thick coins
- 1 pkg (10 oz) frozen corn, thawed
- 1 tbsp tomato paste
- 1 lb raw, cleaned and deveined large shrimp
- 3 cups cooked brown rice

■ Coat slow cooker with nonstick cooking spray. Place onion, green pepper, celery, carrots, garlic, tomatoes, broth and Creole seasoning in bowl; stir to combine. Mix in sausage and corn.

■ Cover and cook on HIGH for 6 hours or LOW for 8 hours. Stir in tomato paste and shrimp; cook until shrimp is just cooked through, about 5 to 7 minutes.

■ Serve over cooked brown rice.

PER SERVING 345 CAL; 7 g FAT; 28 g PRO; 42 g CARB; 5 g FIBER

Seafood Veggie Chowder

MAKES 5 servings **PREP** 25 minutes
SLOW COOK on HIGH for 4 hours or LOW for 7 hours

- 2 leeks, cleaned and sliced
- 2 carrots, peeled and sliced
- 1 celery rib, diced
- 1 lb russet potatoes, peeled and diced
- 2 cups milk
- 2 cups ⅓-less-sodium vegetable broth
- 1 tsp ⅓-less-sodium Old Bay seasoning
- ½ tsp garlic powder
- Pinch ground nutmeg
- ½ lb green beans, trimmed and cut into ½-inch pieces
- ½ lb peeled and deveined shrimp, cut in half
- ½ lb bay scallops
- ½ lb lump crabmeat or imitation crab, torn in small pieces
- 3 tbsp instant potato flakes
- Salt and black pepper

■ Coat slow cooker with nonstick cooking spray. Place leeks, carrots, celery, and potatoes in bowl. Stir in milk, broth, and seasonings. Cover and cook on HIGH for 4 hours or LOW for 7 hours.

■ Uncover and stir in green beans, shrimp, scallops, crab and potato flakes. Cover and cook 15 minutes. Season to taste with salt and pepper.

PER SERVING 330 CAL; 5g FAT; 29 g PRO; 44 g CARB; 5 g FIBER

SEAFOOD VEGGIE CHOWDER

CHICKEN AND
RICE SOUP

Chicken and Rice Soup

MAKES 6 servings **PREP** 25 minutes
SLOW COOK on LOW for 6 hours

- 1 cup peeled and sliced carrots
- 1 cup sliced celery
- 1 cup diced onion
- 2 sprigs fresh thyme
- 4 whole cloves
- 1 tsp whole black peppercorns
- 1 whole chicken (4 lb), quartered
- 4 cups unsalted chicken stock
- ½ cup fresh dill, chopped
- 1½ tsp salt
- 1 pkg (8.8 oz) Uncle Ben's whole grain brown Ready Rice

  Freshly cracked black pepper

■ Place carrots, celery, onion, thyme, cloves and peppercorns in slow cooker. Arrange chicken, including back and wings, on top. Pour in chicken stock and 1 cup water. Cook on LOW for 6 hours.

■ Remove chicken from slow cooker. Shred, discarding bones and skin. Return meat to slow cooker and stir in dill, salt and rice. Serve with freshly cracked pepper.

PER SERVING 372 **CAL**; 7 g **FAT**; 55 g **PRO**; 17 g **CARB**; 2 g **FIBER**

BBQ BEEF BRISKET

BBQ Beef Brisket

MAKES 8 servings **PREP** 10 minutes **SLOW COOK** on HIGH for 6 hours or LOW for 8 hours **COOK** 3 minutes **STAND** 15 minutes

- 2 tbsp packed dark brown sugar
- 1 tbsp Italian seasoning
- 1 tsp onion powder
- ¼ tsp salt
- ¼ tsp black pepper
- 3 lb natural beef brisket
- 2½ cups beef broth
- 3 tbsp molasses
- 2 tbsp Worcestershire sauce
- 3 dashes liquid smoke (optional)
- 2 tbsp cornstarch
- 1 tbsp white vinegar
- 8 onion rolls
- 2 cups prepared creamy coleslaw

■ In small bowl, combine brown sugar, Italian seasoning, onion powder, salt and pepper. Rub onto brisket and place in slow cooker.

■ In a bowl, whisk broth, molasses, Worcestershire and, if desired, liquid smoke. Add to slow cooker. Slow cook on HIGH for 6 hours or LOW for 8 hours.

■ Carefully remove brisket from slow cooker and shred with 2 forks. In a small bowl, combine ¼ cup water, cornstarch and vinegar. Strain liquid in slow cooker into a saucepan and add cornstarch mixture. Bring to a boil over medium-high heat and cook 3 minutes, until thickened and clear. Combine 5 cups of the sauce with brisket in a large bowl. Let stand, covered, 15 minutes.

■ Split onion rolls and fill with brisket and coleslaw. Serve immediately.

PER SERVING 427 **CAL**; 11 g **FAT**; 43 g **PRO**; 37 g **CARB**; 2 g **FIBER**

ASIAN PORK WRAPS

TUSCAN CHICKEN AND BEANS

Asian Pork Wraps

MAKES 8 servings **PREP** 15 minutes **COOK** 12 minutes **SLOW COOK** on HIGH for 4½ hours or LOW for 6 hours **MICROWAVE** 30 seconds

- 1 tsp onion powder
- 1 tsp ground ginger
- 1 tsp sugar
- ½ tsp ground cumin
- ½ tsp ground allspice
- ¼ tsp cayenne pepper
- ¼ tsp salt
- 2½ lb boneless pork loin roast
- 1 tsp toasted sesame oil
- 1 tbsp canola oil
- ¾ cup hoisin sauce, plus more for serving (optional)
- 8 large flour tortillas
- 2 tbsp rice vinegar
- 1 tsp sugar
- ½ tsp salt
- ½ tsp black pepper
- 3 tbsp canola oil
- 1 tsp toasted sesame oil
- 1 bag (14 oz) coleslaw mix

■ In a small bowl, combine onion powder, ginger, sugar, cumin, allspice, cayenne pepper and salt. Rub pork with sesame oil, then rub spice mixture into pork.

■ Heat canola oil in a large skillet over medium-high heat. Brown pork on all sides, about 3 minutes per side. Transfer to slow cooker. Whisk ¼ cup of the hoisin sauce with 1 cup water. Pour around pork in slow cooker. Cover and cook on HIGH for 4½ hours or LOW for 6 hours.

■ Remove pork to a large bowl. Shred with 2 forks into large pieces and toss with remaining ½ cup hoisin sauce.

■ In a large bowl, combine vinegar, sugar, salt and black pepper. Whisk in canola oil and sesame oil. Toss with coleslaw mix.

■ To serve, microwave tortillas 30 seconds or until heated through. Spread each tortilla with a little additional hoisin sauce, if desired. Top with slaw and shredded pork. Fold up and serve.

PER SERVING 443 **CAL**; 20 g **FAT**; 31 g **PRO**; 39 g **CARB**; 4 g **FIBER**

Tuscan Chicken and Beans

MAKES 6 servings **PREP** 15 minutes **SLOW COOK** on HIGH for 6 hours or LOW for 8 hours

- 1 large onion, chopped
- 2 cloves garlic, chopped
- 3 lbs bone-in chicken thighs
- 1½ tsp dried Greek seasoning
- ½ tsp dried thyme
- ¼ tsp black pepper
- 2 tbsp lemon juice
- 1 can (15 oz) fire-roasted diced tomatoes
- ½ cup pitted Kalamata olives, halved
- 1 can (15 oz) Great Northern beans, drained and rinsed
- ¼ cup fresh oregano leaves
- 3 cups cooked orzo
  Lemon wedges, for garnish

■ Coat slow cooker with nonstick cooking spray. Place onion and garlic in slow cooker. Season chicken on both sides with Greek seasoning, thyme and pepper; arrange in slow cooker. Drizzle lemon juice over chicken and evenly spoon tomatoes and olives on top.

■ Cover and cook on HIGH for 6 hours or LOW for 8 hours. During last 30 minutes of cooking time, stir in beans.

■ To serve, stir in oregano and spoon over cooked orzo. Garnish with lemon wedges.

PER SERVING 502 **CAL**; 16 g **FAT**; 41 g **PRO**; 46 g **CARB**; 6 g **FIBER**

Vegetable Curry

MAKES 6 servings PREP 20 minutes
SLOW COOK on HIGH for 5½ hours or LOW for 7½ hours

- 1 head cauliflower, cut into florets
- 1 lb diced potatoes
- 1 bunch red Swiss chard, stems trimmed and chopped (reserve leaves)
- 1 medium onion, diced
- 1 can (15.5 oz) chickpeas, rinsed and drained
- 2 tbsp olive oil
- ¼ tsp salt
- ¼ tsp black pepper
- ⅓ cup mild curry paste (such as Patak)
- ½ cup warm water
- 3 tbsp packed light brown sugar
- 1 can (14.5 oz) diced tomatoes
- ¾ cup golden raisins
- 3 cups cooked basmati rice
- Cashews (optional)
- Yogurt (optional)

■ Combine cauliflower, potatoes, chard stems, onion and chickpeas in slow cooker. Stir in olive oil, salt and pepper. In a small bowl combine curry paste, the water and brown sugar. Add to slow cooker along with tomatoes and raisins; stir to combine. Cover and cook on HIGH for 5 hours or LOW for 7 hours. Chop chard leaves and add to slow cooker. Cover and cook 30 minutes. Gently stir. Serve curry over basmati rice. Top with cashews and yogurt, if desired.

PER SERVING 542 CAL; 13 g FAT; 14 g PRO; 97 g CARB; 12 g FIBER

PORK CARNITAS TACOS

Pork Carnitas Tacos

MAKES 6 servings PREP 15 minutes SLOW COOK on HIGH for 3 hours or LOW for 5 hours

- 2 lb thick-cut boneless loin pork chops
- 1 tsp dried oregano
- 1 tsp ground cumin
- ½ tsp salt
- ¼ tsp black pepper
- 2 cups tomatillo salsa
- 1 sweet red pepper, cored, seeded and diced
- ½ cup cilantro leaves
- 3 scallions, trimmed and sliced
- 4 cloves garlic, chopped
- 12 hard taco shells
- Chopped tomato, shredded lettuce, chopped onion, lime wedges, sour cream and sliced radishes (optional)

■ Coat slow cooker with nonstick cooking spray.

■ Place pork chops in slow cooker; season both sides with oregano, cumin, salt and black pepper. Add 1½ cups of the salsa, the red pepper, cilantro, scallions and garlic.

■ Cover and cook on HIGH for 3 hours or LOW for 5 hours.

■ Remove pork and shred with 2 forks. Return meat to slow cooker. Stir in remaining ½ cup salsa.

■ Serve pork in taco shells topped with garnishes, if using.

PER SERVING 361 CAL; 15 g FAT; 32 g PRO; 21 g CARB; 1 g FIBER

VEGETABLE CURRY